New Roles and Relevance

NEW ROLES AND RELEVANCE

Development NGOs and the Challenge of Change

David Lewis and Tina Wallace, editors

KUMARIAN
PRESS

New Roles and Relevance: Development NGOs and the Challenge of Change

Published 2000 in the United States of America by Kumarian Press, Inc.,
1294 Blue Hills Avenue, Bloomfield, Connecticut 06002 USA.

Production and design by Nick Kosar.
The text of this book is set in New Baskerville 10/13.5.
Proofread by Jody El-Assadi. Index by Barbara J. DeGennaro.

Printed in Canada on acid-free paper by
Transcontinental Printing and Graphics, Inc.
Text printed with vegetable oil-based ink.

∞ The paper used in this publication meets the minimum requirements
of the American National Standard for Information Sciences—Permanence of
Paper for Printed Library Materials, ANSI Z39.48–1984.

Library of Congress Cataloging-in-Publication Data
New roles and relevance : development NGOs and the challenge of change / David
Lewis, Tina Wallace, editors.
    p.   cm.
    Includes bibliographical references and index.
    ISBN 1–56549–121–1 (cloth : alk. paper). — ISBN 1–56549–120–3
(pbk. : alk. paper)
    1. Non-governmental organizations. I. Lewis, David. II. Wallace, Tina.
HC60 .N4744 2000
338.9—dc21   00–060740

09 08 07 06 05 04 03 02   10 9 8 7 6 5 4 3 2

First Printing 2000

Contents

Acknowledgments

We would like to thank all the contributors, who labored long and hard and often at short notice to meet our deadlines and tight word limits. We would also like to thank all those who participated in the conference "NGOs in a Global Future" and challenged many fondly held beliefs and so contributed to the development of the thinking that is reflected in this volume. We would like to acknowledge the richness of these debates around the future roles of NGOs; these have moved understanding and analysis forward.

The authors would like to thank the donors who supported the preparation of this volume and the conference from which many of the papers are drawn. The donors were the Joint Funding Scheme and the Social Development Department at the Department for International Development (DfID) in UK; the Swedish International Development Cooperation Agency (SIDA); and the NGO Service in the Swiss Agency for Development and Co-operation.

Finally we would like to thank Linda Curry for her tireless work as administrator of the conference and congratulate her on successfully bringing together 400 people from all over the globe, many of whom had never travelled internationally before; and Sarah Lister for her invaluable help with preparing the book for publication.

David Lewis and Tina Wallace

Introduction

David Lewis and Tina Wallace

Nongovernmental organizations (NGOs) have a relatively long history, but their numbers and profile rose significantly during the past decade (Edwards and Hulme 1995). The rise of NGOs in development work and humanitarian intervention throughout the late 1980s and 1990s was associated both with the increasing incidence of violent conflict and with the renewed dominance of neoliberal economic ideas. The promotion of the liberal democratic "good governance" agenda by multilateral and bilateral development donors became known as the "new policy agenda" within the development studies field and more widely as the "Washington Consensus," because of its strong association with the Bretton Woods institutions and the United States government. The basic principles of this agenda were an assertion of the inherent superiority of economic liberalism and the need to design an international economic order based on free markets, private property, individual incentives, and a minimal "enabling" role for the state (Gore 2000). NGOs in both North and South either participated in these processes of structural change as service delivery agents or raised their voices (as actors within a wider "civil society") against the increasing dominance of these policy frameworks and principles.

However, the latter years of the twentieth century witnessed rising challenges and dissent from many sources against what had previously appeared as virtually ubiquitous orthodoxy in the development mainstream. The first and most striking was the financial disorder that spread through Southeast Asia during 1997. Many of the affected countries had scrupulously followed International Monetary Fund prescriptions during the 1990s, and the inadequacy of these policy prescriptions became painfully apparent; soon even the World Bank was joining the critique of the International Monetary Fund (MacKewan 1999). A second set of challenges has been the recent call for the "renewal of social democracy" and the development of new approaches to political change, such as the "democratization of democracy" (Giddens 1998). While various ideas and approaches have been lumped together under the general banner of the "third way," a key theme has been that diverse organizations within "civil society" potentially have roles to play in building more democratic political institutions, enlarging political space for grassroots change, and generating alternative thinking and approaches to poverty reduction.

There are signs that the period of economic dogma and inflexible political ideology is slowly being superceded by processes of rethinking and reflection—with some international donors talking about "bringing the state back in" and with the European political debates about the "third way." In 1997 the World Bank in the World Development Report wrote about "the folly of choosing between the state and the market" (1997a:38). What might be termed "market fundamentalism" may, according to Giddens (1998), be on the retreat at some local and national levels, although it remains, even in its revisionist form, the dominant ideology at the global level. The emerging challenge to neoliberal orthodoxy lies in the generation of alternatives which refuse to engage with the terms of a debate that was, until recently, starkly framed as a simple choice between the inefficiency of the overdeveloped state or the radical dynamism of the market.

The new attention being given to NGOs as actors in "civil society" unleashes a new set of difficult conceptual and terminological problems, partly because "nongovernmental organization" is in many ways a virtually meaningless label. For some analysts the term is synonymous with the "aid industry," in which NGOs are viewed as effective tools or channels for donors to provide international development funds to low-income countries. Conversely, they are seen as vehicles for privatizing foreign assistance, making it less accountable to either government authorities or local people because of a lack of clear governance structures for NGOs. Some see *NGO* as a term strongly associated with grassroots action and community organizing, which may exist outside the domain of the formal development world. Others see NGOs primarily as service contractors, able to work more efficiently and more effectively than government agencies, but with comparatively little legitimacy with which to challenge policy or represent people. There is now a growing interest in NGOs as international policy actors in the environmental and human rights fields.

The concept of the "third sector" has also recently emerged and has been used by some to describe and analyze the broader group of organizations that are not formally part of the state or the for-profit business world and that may provide services, represent people's interests, or offer a structure for self-help initiatives.[1] The concept is potentially useful because it removes some of the problems of the current, commonly used terminologies, which are culture bound and ill defined—such as *voluntary, not-for-profit, non-governmental, citizen's organizations*. The term *third sector* appears to be gaining usage in both North and South. However, the term is itself arguably culture bound and has been criticized in some quarters because it is unable to take account of the private character of NGOs (Uphoff 1995). We have not defined *NGO* in this book, but rather have worked within a broad conceptual framework that uses the term as useful shorthand for a wide variety of different kinds of nongovernmental development organization and work. These include large or small organizations, formal or informal, international or local, self-help or public interest, internally aided or locally resourced, and service delivery or advocacy—all of which are working in the general field of poverty reduction.

NGOs have long been seen to play a wide variety of roles in development. This book focuses on one broad area of NGO activity—that of innovation in the broadest sense. Innovation has become one of the assumed areas of comparative advantage that NGOs have over governments. In his influential study at the start of the last decade, Clark (1991) argued that NGOs may be less constrained by orthodox thinking and by inflexible bureaucratic structures that could allow staff to engage in experimentation and adaptation in tackling development problems. Some NGOs have become bureaucratic and increasingly bogged down in concerns about their ability to raise funds, profile, and market share, and others have become subcontractors of donors or governments. We argue that for NGOs to maintain and increase their relevance in addressing the complex causes and manifestations of poverty, innovation and change based on learning are essential. Innovation is difficult to define, but the sense in which we wish to engage with it in this book goes beyond the definition in Fyvie and Ager (1999:1384), which stresses the "creation, development and application of new ways of working." We would include the exploration and demonstration of potentially useful alternatives to mainstream thought and action as integral to an understanding of innovation. For example, NGOs have been at the forefront in recent years of development in microfinance provision for the poor; the evolution of more inclusive, participatory planning, and evaluation techniques; and in raising public awareness about environment, poverty, and human rights issues. In many parts of the world, NGOs have been involved in developing innovative solutions to practical development problems, such as new technological responses to the challenges faced by low-income, marginal farmers, whose needs are often excluded from mainstream agricultural extension policy and practice (Farrington and Bebbington 1993). NGOs are also regarded as important actors within changing conceptual frameworks that emphasize the importance of "social capital" in addition to material deprivation, as a way of understanding and addressing problems of livelihoods and linking policy responses at local, national, and regional levels (Bebbington 1999). Although their practice sometimes belies their advocacy, some NGOs have been pioneers of work on gender and the need to address women"s subordination as a central development issue, as well as one of human rights. Their work has been important on the ground and at policy levels.

NGOs have participated in the new policy agenda with varying levels of enthusiasm, ranging from the new crop of northern humanitarian organizations that emerged in the wake of increased official emergency relief funding for Eastern Europe following the end of the Cold War, to radical environmental or human rights NGOs, which have stood firmly outside the mainstream, campaigned for fundamental transformation, and aligned with social movements. Some NGOs have tempered their involvement in "official processes" with negotiation and dialogue over policy issues, whereas others have raised their voices in opposition and refused to engage in these processes. The current policy climate arguably requires NGOs to play the role of the innovator more than ever in order to find real relevance in addressing poverty, inequality, and issues of social change. The new pragmatic climate provides opportunities in which new ideas have the potential to be influential as old orthodoxies come under strain. It also presents challenges as other institutions take up the rhetoric—and sometimes the practice—previously the domain of development NGOs, on participation, gender, and the renewed focus on poverty and rights. These (and other) areas of NGO work, thinking, and practice may be badly in need of an injection of fresh analysis and new approaches if they are to remain vibrant and effective. However, there are some worrying signs: the increased levels of "standardization" within some northern development policy and practice between donors and NGOs is a real cause for concern (Wallace et al. 1997). The growing and rather comfortable orthodoxy surrounding the win/win logic of NGO microfinance provision is another area of conformity and even complacency (Morduch 2000). Many NGOs are allowing the rhetoric of gender to lull them into a sense of achievement while their own practices—both within their organizations and in their development work—fall far short of achieving real changes in the status and condition of women.

There is of course another reason why NGOs need to think more carefully about changing the status quo, one that is more linked to their own survival. Voices are increasingly being raised that question the levels of performance and accountability that NGOs have long taken for granted (Edwards and Hulme 1996). NGOs will need to work hard if they are to justify the attention they have drawn to themselves and avoid the backlash that could easily follow. This is especially the case around their continuing lack of structures and procedures for accountability to the very people they claim to work for and represent—poor women and men themselves—and their real difficulties with being open about their mistakes and trying to learn from them.

NGOs are operating in a context of rapid change, including economic and cultural globalization, the growth of intrastate violence and the complexity of humanitarian responses, and the ongoing reform of the international development industry, each of which are discussed by Edwards et al. (Chapter 1). As actors in development, NGOs are strongly shaped by the wider changes taking place in their environment, yet they must find ways to contribute to the ultimate direction and form that such changes take as they engage in acts of resistance and negotiation. The main premise of this book is that against this backdrop of change, the questioning of deep-rooted beliefs and ideologies, and the signs of a new pragmatism in development policy, NGOs need to find new roles and relevance. One part of this search for relevance is to be found in the ability of NGOs to innovate at all levels: in theory, in policy, and in their development practice. Subsequent chapters present different perspectives on these global changes, taking NGOs as the entry point for developing new understandings, and exploring how NGOs themselves are adapting, changing, and rising to the challenge of working and finding a voice within increasingly complex and unpredictable environments.

At a more theoretical level, the current preoccupations with the idea of "civil society" and the concept of social capital raise important questions about the changing roles and activities of NGOs within wider political and social processes. In particular, many of the authors draw attention in their work to tensions between the global and the local. It may be that currently many northern NGOs and commentators pay too much attention to global changes and the need to engage with global institutions and issues without giving due weight to the ways in which local conditions either remain unchanged or are conditioned and constrained by global forces. Several chapters in this volume challenge the growing trend for working globally and help to bring local realities into focus (for example, Johnson et al. on microfinance, Chapter 11) and highlight the importance of working at all levels in order to effect real change with lasting impacts on the poor (for example, Chapman on advocacy, Chapter 13).

At the organizational level, a key theme that emerges from the chapters that follow is the problem of learning. The concept of organizational learning has become a mantra in the NGO world from Korten (1980) to Britton (1998), and this is clearly a vital area for improving the performance and effectiveness of NGO work. It is essential if NGOs are to innovate in ways that are relevant to communities and southern partners, and are to address the roots of poverty—NGOs can only know how useful or appropriate their work is if they learn from their experiences. What becomes clear from the work of authors such as Smillie (Chapter 2) are the myriad ways in which NGOs still do *not* learn: Learning continues to be severely constrained by the structures of development institutions and project funding; it is constrained by time and the race "to do" rather than to "reflect"; and as Hailey (Chapter 6) shows, it may only take place under very specific and controlled conditions. Finding ways of becoming learning organizations—as well as finding ways to increase accountability at all levels—largely continue to evade NGOs, yet the successful search lies at the heart of NGOs' ability to respond in ways that are truly relevant.

This book presents nineteen chapters, which have their origins in a set of critical papers presented by researchers and practitioners at the Third International NGO conference held at Birmingham University in 1999. Some chapters are theoretical, whereas others offer very practical views; we have tried to represent as many different views and writing styles as possible. Broadly, the chapters that follow explore the contributions of NGOs as organizational actors to three main development themes: (1) NGOs as contributors to alternative thinking about development concepts and ideas; (2) the experience of NGOs in developing new approaches to influencing policy; and (3) the role of NGOs in bringing innovations to development practice. In a chapter prepared originally as the conference background paper (Edwards, Hulme, and Wallace, Chapter 1), a number of relevant global themes are set out for discussion and debate. The first is the phenomenon of "globalization," in which economic activity is becoming interlinked and cultures are becoming homogenized, but with concomitant processes of reform and resistance at the local level. The second is the rise of the "complex political emergency" and the growth of interstate conflicts characterized by a strong ethnic dimension. The third is the reality that international development cooperation is increasingly under pressure to reform its institutions and its practices. One example of this is the U.K. Overseas Development Administration becoming the Department for International Development and beginning to speak of aid to strengthen people's rights and the institutions of civil society, rather than the strengthening of infrastructure and the delivery of food aid.

However, the priorities reflected in this agenda were challenged by some of the participants at the original conference, in particular by many people speaking from a southern perspective. The focus on globalization was criticized by some who saw it as a particularly "northern" agenda that ran the danger of overgeneralization (globalization has been highly selective as to the areas of the world in which it has incorporated local structures and processes) and emphasized macro-level issues to the detriment of micro-level manifestations of power at household and community levels. Although the intention was to find ways to link the global to the local, some felt the complexities and diversity at the local level—including issues of gender, ethnicity, and culture—had been insufficiently taken into account. There was also criticism of the blandness of some discussions of a "third way," which was regarded as a path toward unacceptable compromise at the expense of the need for deep-rooted structural change and realignment of power relations.

Some of these concerns are reflected here; others are not. This is a reflection of the wide gap that still exists between activists and researchers in this field. In putting together a volume such as this, the differences in priority and incentive become clear. Whereas academics are happy to edit their contributions to fit the requirements of scholarly conventions and commercial publishing guidelines, practitioners channel their energies into taking home their learning and moving on quickly to the challenges of applying knowledge rather than documenting and formalizing it. Similarly, the lack of contributions from authors from the South in this volume reflects these different realities and priorities, which continue to silence certain voices.

Many of the authors in this book are concerned with challenging some of the fondly held concepts and beliefs of the NGO sector, whereas others are seeking to push forward new understandings of what NGOs do and how they work. Part 1 examines the evolution of alternative thinking and ideas about development challenges. Hailey (Chapter 6) outlines the idea of the NGO as a learning organization and draws upon positive and negative lessons from the South Asian NGO experience. Kaplan (Chapter 3) explores the ways in which learning and drawing lessons are inhibited within current paradigms of development. He proposes a new paradigm for NGOs that understands development as a living process and values humility, reflection, and facilitation over the macho tendencies of many NGOs to claim that they have the solutions to complex problems. The changing arena of NGO relationships with the corporate sector is discussed by Zadek (Chapter 4), who questions how far levels of corporate responsibility are being raised by NGO action and what other forces are at work. Smillie (Chapter 2) tackles the thorny question of shifting from relief to development and shows that developmental approaches to humanitarian work still elude much of the NGO work that is undertaken. Discontinuities and problems continue because relief and development efforts remain separated at the levels of staffing, funding, and intervention practice, preventing both learning from experience and the development of new practice. Cameron (Chapter 5) shifts the focus to "understanding" and the need to make the understanding of NGOs more rigorous; he discusses the advantages of a using a conceptual framework informed by new institutional economics for achieving this.

Part 2 examines aspects of the challenge for NGOs of influencing development policy. Karim (Chapter 9), using case studies, describes the role of some NGOs in Bangladesh, which is shifting from emphasizing service delivery to becoming "civil society organizations" in the activist sense. Blair (Chapter 10) addresses the need to link local and national agendas in strengthening civil society and democracy, and questions the rush to decentralization as necessarily increasing democracy and participation. Howell and Pearce (Chapter 7) explore the ways in which donors have instrumentalized the concept of civil society and outline the dangers this poses for coopting its radical potential. Hudson (Chapter 8) examines the relationships between northern and southern NGOs within advocacy networks, and the claims to legitimacy made in the North in relation to advocacy work in the South. Freres (Chapter 12) addresses the subject of where northern NGOs should focus their advocacy work in his chapter on the European Union, in which he suggests that key development issues such as trade, the arms business, and conflict resolution are critical for addressing poverty, yet are currently poorly understood by NGOs. In order to influence global policy on these issues, NGOs will need to form new networks and alliances and much more sophisticated ways of working. Johnson et al. (Chapter 11) in their paper examine the policy implications of the realities of uncertainties, shocks, and crises that characterize the lives of the poor, while most micro-credit programs are based on concepts of stability and predictability. They explore the implications of these global and recurrent crises for the provision of micro-finance intended to benefit poor women and men.

Part 3 examines innovations in development practice and focuses on local contexts and actions. Chapman (Chapter 13) researches international advocacy work by NGOs and shows how changes in formal policy may have only a limited impact on the everyday lives of poor people. In the rush to undertake high-level advocacy, NGOs must focus on the need to link this with detailed work at the level of the household and community and develop close links with local NGOs in this process. Crowther (Chapter 15) continues this theme in her analysis of the lack of understanding among some NGOs of the ways in which their ideas and intervention styles mesh with ongoing local organizing processes. NGOs need to be both open to and guard against the different ways in which their activities can be captured by and incorporated into the agendas of local people. Biggs and Matsaert (Chapter 19) show the importance for NGOs to build local networks for sustaining small and micro enterprise, and Richardson and Langdon (Chapter 16) explore some of the possibly difficult issues facing development NGOs working in the field of promoting local for-profit enterprises. Simbi and Thom (Chapter 18) offer an informed critique of the discourse of "NGO capacity building" currently popular within the northern NGO community, and show how this discourse can be rethought so that it is less dependent on the "aid chain" and more responsive to NGO partners' skills, contexts, and needs. The role of NGO efforts in postconflict and peace building is the theme of Mbabazi and Shaw (Chapter 17), which focuses on a case study from Uganda.

Many of these themes have not been addressed in much detail in the NGO literature, whereas others are presented from new perspectives. These are complex and diverse issues, that cannot be covered comprehensively. Rather, this book centers on an important element of NGO activity often overlooked in the preoccupation with the concerns of the "new policy agenda," which claims that NGOs are "innovative" organizations with a special ability to develop alternative ideas, approaches, and technologies with which to challenge mainstream development policy and practice. The abilities of NGOs to live up to these claims will help to determine whether the development NGO community can make an effective and productive transition into the new roles and purpose that will be required in international development in the coming years. We argue that it is only through effective engagement with the local as well as the global, with learning, reflection, and informed change in development policy and practice, that NGOs will find ways to address poverty reduction and social justice agendas that are relevant to poor women and men, local institutions, and partners, as well as pertinent to international and more influential global development actors.

Notes

1. The precise origins of the term *third sector* are not very clear. Some writers, such as Levitt (1975), first began using the term in the context of campaigning groups, whereas others have taken the term as referring to a third sector of service delivery (Uphoff 1995).

Increasing Leverage for Development: Challenges for NGOs in a Global Future

Michael Edwards, David Hulme, and Tina Wallace

At the start of the new millennium, nongovernmental organizations (NGOs), along with others, share a sense of excitement about new possibilities, tempered by widespread anxiety about the future. The excitement stems from the quickly expanding opportunities for civic action that global trends are creating; the anxiety arises from the increasingly critical questions being asked about the role development NGOs will play in this future.[1] In this chapter, we explore three key trends: globalization and the reshaping of global poverty, inequality, and insecurity; "complex political emergencies" in the "post–Cold War disorder"; and the reform of international cooperation to address these changes, moving from foreign aid to a focus on rules, standards, and interventions to protect the most vulnerable.

These three interrelated trends require new forms of action—new "social contracts"—between citizens of different polities and new structures of authority at different levels of the world system. These new relationships, partnerships, alliances, and other forms of collaboration will shape NGO innovations in economics, politics, and social policy in future. However, responding effectively to these challenges requires NGOs to develop different roles, relationships, and capacities.

The Changing Global Context

Globalization

Although defining "globalization" is problematic, there is a basic reality that cannot be ignored. Globalization as instant electronic communication; declining transport costs; flexible, mobile forms of economic organization in which assets (finance, knowledge) move freely across national borders;

integrated global markets; and international decisions about jobs and investment are all part of that reality. The consequences, in a world of unequal
producers and consumers, are spectacular rewards for those able to take advantage of these opportunities around the world and increasing pressures on
those less well endowed to sell their labor, family life, or environment cheaply
in order to survive. In 1998, the combined income of three billion people in
the South was less than the collective assets of 358 multibillionaires (United
Nations Development Program 1998a). NGOs in the twenty-first century will
confront a rapidly changing patchwork of poverty and exclusion that requires
new international responses. As recent events have demonstrated, the "new
rich" (those in East and Southeast Asia) and those previously under social
protection (the former Soviet Union) can quickly become the "new poor"
on an epic scale. Inequality, exclusion, and insecurity look set to drive global
politics for the next generation and beyond.

Accompanying these trends is "globalization as culture": the homogeniz-
ing of values and aspirations to western norms of individualism and consum-
erism (Hobsbawm 1994). The media, now a global institution controlled by
a small number of multinational corporations, play a key role in these cultural processes. Some commentators see culture as pivotal in the coming
"clash of civilizations," in which those who are threatened and disempowered
by cultural recolonization turn to ethnic or religious identity, often violently
expressed.

However, there is room for maneuver, and nothing is predetermined,
raising the question about the role for NGOs in reshaping the processes of
evolving global capitalism so that all can enjoy the fruits of economic progress
without losing their culture and identity. Here there is no consensus. Some
NGOs advocate delinking from the world economy to promote self-reliance
and protect local cultures; others opt for various forms of constructive engagement; the most optimistic embrace globalization as a progressive social
revolution in the making (Edwards 1999a). Although there are no easy answers, especially because so much analysis has been abandoned in the post–
Cold War retreat from grand theory, there are some common threads. One
is that civil society can act as a countervailing force to the expanding influence of markets and the declining authority of states. Although the erosion
of national sovereignty does leave some more vulnerable to the abuse of unaccountable power, it does open up possibilities for civic organizations to
link across national boundaries in new, flexible structures of governance,
especially using information technology.

The true extent and potential of civil society is a controversial subject,
especially at the global level. Some perceive a fundamental "power shift" as
state-based authority recedes, whereas others question the ability of nonstate

groups to fill the political vacuum. These doubts apply especially to development NGOs because of their dependence on foreign aid and their nonrepresentative character. Nevertheless, some NGOs are diversifying their funding sources and generating their own income, especially in South Asia and Latin America. They are sinking roots into their own societies and assuming the characteristics of genuine civic actors, rather than service delivery contractors. The rise of civil society in the South is uneven and often slow, but even where there are few civil society organizations, individual agencies are developing research and policy-lobbying capacity with important implications for northern NGOs and the broader global civic alliances that are developing around the world.

Globalization has often exacerbated the skewed distribution of productive resources, skills, and capacities that lie at the heart of poverty. Underlying these inequalities are power structures that discriminate against certain groups of people. NGOs have a vital role in advocating for redistribution and addressing these inequalities. NGOs believe that human rights standards and other social values can be mainstreamed, whether in markets, politics, or social policy. Translating these principles into practice at different levels of the world economy is difficult and complex, but the case for doing so is clear.

Confronting globalization begins and ends at the grassroots level, where NGOs are developing strategies to help poor people address their position in global markets and play a creative role in reshaping economic forces. They are improving the endowments of the poor, enabling them to compete more effectively and achieve a basic level of security, voice, and equality of rights. This continues the traditional NGO role of developing skills, confidence, and forms of association and improving access to credit, services, and economic opportunities, but also involves a systematic attempt to link different levels and sectors of the economy. NGOs are attempting to turn market forces to the advantage of poorer groups by reclaiming benefits normally siphoned off by intermediaries—using, for example, joint marketing associations in Latin America (Bebbington 1996) or work with community associations in South Africa. Civic groups are exploring alternative modes of production and exchange less costly in social and environmental terms, building more "social capital" (trust, cooperation, and honesty) for use in market settings, and supporting men and women to combine their market and nonmarket roles to distribute profits with a social purpose. These deeper changes are crucial in addressing the "Achilles heel" of most empowerment strategies: a failure to think through what happens when people with less power obtain more of it. This challenge—the regulation of all exclusionary systems of power—is one that most NGOs have tended to ignore, but it is the key to an agenda for transforming capitalism rather than "humanizing" it. At the opposite extreme, NGOs continue their role as carers of last resort, operating safety nets and providing welfare to the casualties of globalization.

At the national level, grassroots innovations need support from pro-poor macroeconomic and social policies. Although globalization does erode state authority, the redistributive and protective functions of states remain paramount. There is a tendency among some NGOs to focus on global advocacy to the exclusion of the national-level processes of state-society relations that are essential for any country to pursue progressive goals in an integrated economy. Few NGOs have given enough thought to their roles in the national arena because of a lingering suspicion of states in any form, and because of the temptation to "leap-frog" the national arena and go directly to Washington or Brussels. In sustainable development terms, this is a serious mistake.

At the global level, successful strategies must be connected to actions in other parts of the international system. Globalization means not only that NGOs must engage strategically with market forces on a bigger scale, but they must do so in ways that link micro- to macro-forces in a coherent way. With their international presence and connections, NGOs have a natural strength in this field, and in some areas this has begun, especially around ethical consumption, investment, and trading. NGOs have been key players in attempts to reform corporate accountability, test out multinational codes of conduct, reshape consumer demand, and alter patterns of global trade. Inevitably, enthusiasm tends to run ahead of actual achievements, but the principles involved have now been identified.

NGOs are becoming more strategic in their lobbying of the International Financial Institutions, the monitoring of international commitments, and the democratization of global economic and other regimes. Although there has been little concrete progress in opening these regimes to civil society participation, they are likely to be central to the global system and demand a response. There is an unusual global consensus around the inadequacy of the International Financial Institutions; their focus on ensuring that public sector finances are not overextended has led them to neglect the regulation of private financial transactions. The consequences—financial panic and massive overexposure—are fueling a global recession that has already cost the world ten million formal sector jobs.[2] Talk by the G7 leaders about "a new global financial architecture" has not hidden the fact that they have little idea what this might look like, or how new solutions might be negotiated; are NGOs better prepared? Critiquing the World Bank and the International Monetary Fund was relatively easy; redesigning the international system will require far more complex analysis.

The Reform of International Cooperation

Development NGOs face another set of changes. The overall decline of foreign aid is now well entrenched, caused by failures in arguing the case for aid, continued political disinterest, and the emergence of new forms of international cooperation better suited to the global economy in which private capital flows (outside sub-Saharan Africa) and economic integration are perceived as the best motor for change. The international system is now based more around rules and standards than subsidized resource transfers. This poses a threat to aid-funded NGOs, although there is a positive side to these changes. Although NGOs are divided about the interventions they advocate in the global economy, they can all be committed to a more democratic process of setting the "rules of the game." Already, municipalities in Latin America and elsewhere are experimenting with "dialogic politics," in which civil society and business representatives share with local government in decision making. If these experiments can be connected to more democratic structures at higher levels of the world system, the results could be revolutionary.

How can NGOs help to ensure that the regimes of the future work to the benefit of poor people and deliver concrete benefits on the ground? Who decides the relative importance of economic growth, political equality, and social benefit? These questions take NGOs way beyond their traditional roles as project implementers, providers of funds, and advocates on the margins of world affairs. For the first time in history, NGOs have the opportunity to become vehicles for international cooperation in the mainstream of politics and economics, if they put their own house in order.

It is unlikely that foreign aid will disappear completely, especially in the world's poorest countries. Rather, it will play a supporting role in future global regimes, used selectively to help countries meet their obligations under international agreements or structural change. There is consensus now on the need to change the way this aid is provided, moving from a "supply" to a "demand-led" framework, in which consolidated resources are given to local institutions that "own" the uses to which they are put—ideally through dialogues between government, business, and civil society. These proposed changes have important implications for NGOs, especially those based in the North.

Current trends are confused. The evidence suggests high levels of funding through northern NGOs despite declining aid budgets, a slowly rising proportion sent directly to NGOs in the South, and a small redistribution of resources among different NGOs in the North. So far there is little evidence of a major break with the patterns of the past for northern NGOs, and donor agencies continue to value them as reliable delivery systems for their funds, whereas southern counterparts are seen to be weak. There are few southern NGOs with the capacity to deliver large-scale humanitarian relief, so there is little sense of a crisis for northern NGOs yet, and the absence of such a crisis is one of the reasons that they are proving so slow to make changes.

However, the new trends pose challenges for all NGOs. They imply a gradual shift in roles, away from the direct implementation of aid-funded projects and services, toward capacity building, "learning-for-leverage," support for local institutions to set development priorities, and operation as motors for change in economic systems, governance, and social policy (Fowler 1997). Although fashionable, the record of capacity building in practice is not impressive. Concerns about quality led to the formation of the International Forum on Southern NGO Capacity Building in 1998, to share experience of "good practice" and foster innovation. The record of northern agencies is particularly poor in the area of sustainability: Micro-credit is seen as a panacea for financial sustainability rather than one of many possibilities; project planning procedures are emphasized to the detriment of research and media skills; internal organization takes precedence over external linkages; and the ability of southern NGOs to participate as equals in international alliances is handicapped by the exclusive focus of most donors on their domestic role.

Traditional NGO work will play a smaller part in a broader menu of options, administered in a different framework of power dynamics and South-North relationships. Northern NGOs should relinquish work on the ground as southern NGO sectors mature in their research and policy capacity as well as project implementation and support. A similar process may start in the South as other groups in civil society and business take on the roles traditionally ascribed to intermediary NGOs.

Another challenge concerns the role of NGOs in building constituencies for international cooperation as a prerequisite for the success of global regimes. Codes of conduct for multinational corporations are of little use unless they are supported by large-scale consumer pressure and viable alternatives on the ground. NGOs talk of the need to build constituencies but have focused on problems in the South instead of changes at home; mass-based public protest against western indifference to genocide, for example, is given little attention in NGO strategy. It is too expensive or too "political." Most northern NGOs are disinvesting in development education, claiming that past efforts have been disappointing. It is unlikely that this situation will be reversed without changes in current NGO communications strategies, which fail to engage the public beyond an emotional outpouring of concern when starvation hits the headlines. "Development" has proved too abstract a concept, and aid is both dull and complex. Reversing this situation requires a massive investment of imagination and resources to help people connect complex global trends with simple individual responsibilities. It is here that ethical consumption and alliances with movements could provide a vital link for development NGOs. Constituency building means creating an agenda for concern over the long term, not just narrow policy lobbying within the international aid system.

The gradual replacement of foreign aid by a wider agenda of international cooperation makes it easier for NGOs and other civil society organizations to work together without the distorting effects of contracts, conditions, and unequal access to funding. The most interesting and potentially powerful cases of transnational civic organizing are those in which funding is a secondary consideration, leaving participants to focus on exchanging complementary roles and resources that are equally valued in support of broad but common goals. In a world of "complex multilateralism," these alliances are certain to grow: More than 15,000 transnational civic networks are already active on the global stage (O'Brien et al. 1998). One should not romanticize these experiences, because they continue to raise difficult questions of:

- Legitimacy: Who speaks for whom, and how differences of opinion are resolved when individual participants vary in strength and resources

- Accountability: Who enjoys the benefits and suffers the costs of what the alliance achieves, especially at the grassroots level

- Structure: How to deal with the challenges of genuinely international governance, decision making, and communication

- Strategy: The need to develop more rigorous arguments and more credible alternatives as a contribution to policy debates

However, all of these problems can be managed, given courage and imagination.

Humanitarian Assistance, Conflict, and Peace Building[3]

In areas of conflict and complex political emergencies, choices are hard, and the dilemmas for NGOs are drawn starkly. NGO involvement in efforts to provide humanitarian assistance and resolve violent conflict has changed profoundly during the 1990s, as understanding of the dynamics of insecurity has evolved. Initial optimism at the end of the Cold War with talk of a "peace dividend" soon foundered as "small wars" spread and nationalist conflicts reappeared, often fueled by interests bent on exploiting the political legacy of sectarian history and the financial benefits of a war economy (Keen 1994). Contemporary conflicts are largely internal struggles in which clear interests are difficult to disentangle; death and disablement are concentrated on civilians; and population movements take place within as well as across national borders (Goodhand and Hulme 1999; Duffield 1999b). In 1995, approximately 14 million people were refugees, and 23 million were internally displaced (Overseas Development Institute 1998). Globalization has been associated with increased intrastate tensions; far from the "end of history" predicted by liberal commentators after the collapse of communism, "history" (or at least historical forces) has returned with a vengeance as ethnic, nationalist, religious, and cultural groups have proclaimed their identities in aggressive and exclusive forms. These events serve to remind us that civil society (like states and businesses) has a dark side too.

When the Cold War ended, the response of the international humanitarian system was to increase the use of direct military action to end civil wars and coordinate relief efforts more effectively (ODI 1998). However, the debacle of United Nations and U.S. forces in Somalia in 1993 led to a rapid reversal of policy, with disastrous consequences in Rwanda, where the U.N. peacekeeping force was reduced and only 470 U.N. troops were stationed in Rwanda when the (predicted) violence killing 800,000 people erupted. These shifts in policy have presented NGOs with complex dilemmas. Caught between the scale of human suffering on the ground and the international community's unwillingness to tackle the politics of intervention, NGOs have been sucked, ill prepared, into a vortex of conflicting needs and demands (Duffield 1994). Relief budgets expanded rapidly and accounted for a steadily increasing share of development aid. The numbers of NGOs involved rose, with more than 200 in the Great Lakes by 1994, and northern NGOs "prospered" as the number of southern NGOs able to deliver relief on a large scale remained small. Despite the fact that "something had to be done," many NGO staff returned home from the Great Lakes, the Horn of Africa, West Africa, Angola, Central Asia, Sri Lanka, and Cambodia, harboring grave doubts about the effectiveness of humanitarian assistance. Had they provided additional resources for "conflict entrepreneurs" to prosecute "small wars?" Is relief a function of western strategic interests—a Band-aid that allows the international system to claim it is involved when in truth it has disengaged (Prendergast 1997)? How should NGOs react when the principle of voluntary repatriation is overridden on a vast scale (ODI 1998)? Relief agencies now have to relate to local militia groups and foreign armies, raising difficult questions about mandates, competencies, and coordination.

All this led to a period of intense questioning for the northern NGOs involved. The picture in the South is less clear because NGOs have fewer forums to reflect on their experiences and articulate an independent voice. Inevitably, the questions that confront NGOs vary with context and circumstance, but some common issues can be discerned. A traditional relief focus (on which many NGOs were founded) is increasingly rare, apart from the International Committee of the Red Cross. From the late 1980s, researchers and donors have encouraged NGOs to conceptualize their interventions along a relief-development continuum so that relief activities contribute to development programs as peace returns. Recently, NGOs have engaged directly in the processes of peace building and conflict resolution. Such activities may concentrate on the micro-level building of "social capital" through inclusive forums or the training of local conflict-resolution activists; macro-level support to diplomatic negotiations; or creating opportunities for the leaders of opposing groups to meet informally. They can be either neutral and impartial, helping all parties to have an open discussion, or informed by political analysis that identifies victims and only provides support to them.

There are voices in favor of all these strategies. The dictum of "do no harm" has been developed (Anderson 1999), saying NGOs should adopt an analytical approach that ensures that humanitarian aid is not captured by warring factions; others counter that claiming support to armed groups has probably been slight (ODI 1998). The codes of practice and evaluations that are being promoted now may foster increased effectiveness in NGO relief activities, although few NGOs have the analytical skills and detailed local knowledge that are needed to conduct the strategic analyses necessary for success in peace building and conflict resolution in the complex environments in which they operate.

Analysis of the role of NGOs in humanitarian and conflict resolution work reveals that networking and influencing strategies are essential for achieving a significant impact in reducing the suffering that occurs in complex political emergencies. A number of options are emerging that a few NGOs have begun to explore: influencing national governments to operate in ways that go beyond "realist" foreign policy considerations; monitoring the effectiveness of regional forces in peacemaking to assess their potential; examining how the U.N. might regain its credibility and engage effectively in peacemaking and coordination; exploring strategies to enable national and global civil societies to move beyond charitable donations to mobilize governments to react early to emerging conflicts; and overseeing the private sector to monitor and sanction businesses that gain from war economies.

To implement these strategies, NGOs need to reduce dysfunctional competition in relief funding and operations; work more closely with southern groups to develop their relief and peace-building capacity; widen the current North-centric humanitarian policy dialogue; and make a reality of codes of conduct by institutionalizing accountability and developing "peace audits" (Goodhand and Hulme 1998). NGOs have an important role to play (Edwards 1999a), however, to play it well they will need to invest in their own credibility and legitimacy by becoming more knowledgeable and transparent about their existing humanitarian and peace-building work.

Organizational Implications

The changing global context sketched out previously suggests four challenges for NGOs in the future:

- Mobilizing a genuinely inclusive civil society at every level of the world system

- Holding other institutions accountable for their actions and ensuring they respond to social and environmental needs

- Ensuring that international regimes are implemented effectively and work to the benefit of poor people and poor countries

- Ensuring that gains at the global level are translated into concrete benefits at the grassroots

These challenges raise major questions about how NGOs organize themselves to work in more global and strategic ways in the future. Four areas of organizational change seem especially important: roles, relationships, capacities, and—underlying all these things—the thorny issues of legitimacy and accountability.

Nongovernmental Organization Roles

NGOs operate in so many contexts and at so many levels that generalization is hazardous. However, some requirements can be identified for thinking and acting globally. NGOs cannot succeed through stand-alone projects at the local level. They must build from concrete innovations at the grassroots level to connect with the forces that influence patterns of poverty, prejudice, and violence. Some NGOs are doing this by integrating micro- and macrolevel action in their project and advocacy activities, but the changing global context challenges them to make this their natural way of working, not an optional extra. Moving from *development as delivery* to *development as leverage* characterizes this shift and has major implications for NGO organization, fundraising, and relations to others.

Despite the changing context, many NGOs appear reluctant to shed their traditional roles. Some northern NGOs continue to be operational on the ground, and even when they work through "partners," they dictate the scope and pace of work through their control over funding and procedures (Fowler 1998; Wallace et al. 1997). There is little evidence that they are handing over activities to southern groups and limiting their roles to those most appropriately played in the North. Building constituencies for international cooperation has been relegated to the margins of NGO activity. Development education is largely out of fashion, and few agencies try to communicate complex development messages through the media, which are used for fundraising through advertisements for emergencies and child sponsorship.

In the South, some NGOs have a strong, independent funding base, but most remain dependent on external resources; donor demands as well as local needs determine their roles. Although some do pioneering work in confronting inequalities at every level, many remain deliverers of development designed or imported from outside. In the future, they will need to find ways of building constituencies for their work and working in strategic partnerships to link local and global processes. By sinking roots into their own societies, NGOs can generate the potential to influence things through mobilizing a concerned citizenry to work for change.

Relationships

Competition for resources in tight funding environments is characteristic of NGOs in all countries. Much NGO advertising, media work, and lobbying is driven by the need to gain a higher profile in the marketplace to ensure a continued flow of resources from public and official donors. Donor requirements drive changes to systems and procedures that are passed down the aid chain from northern to southern NGOs. Participatory approaches should be a countervailing force, but they are often used as a tool to involve communities in NGO-driven agendas: few NGOs have developed structures that genuinely respond to grassroots demands. Although NGOs talk of "partnership," control over funds and decision making remains highly unequal.

This picture is familiar but partial, and the changing global context opens up new possibilities for NGOs to relate in healthier ways: Alliances among equals and genuine partnerships can replace the asymmetries of power and voice that have characterized North-South relationships for so long. Information technology can help by enabling less hierarchical modes of organization and communication. Rather than trying to impose order on a chaotic world, the most successful organizations will try to generate order *out of* chaos through nonauthoritarian relationships between people who are genuinely developing new learning capacities.

These structural innovations are especially important for NGO activities that stretch across national borders—like lobbying—but thus far conflicts of interest and the need for profile have slowed their development. Friction continues over who speaks for whom and on what basis: Northern NGOs still prefer to present the case for change "on behalf of" others; southern NGOs may "speak for" communities who are unaware of the campaign or unsure of its benefits. The new global agenda requires that NGOs link with each other in different ways and forge relationships with other groups in civil society that can reach deeper into the mainstream of politics and economics—such as trade unions, consumer groups, the women's and environmental movements, and universities. NGOs need new ways of relating to the public, and they must manage their relationship with official donors so that the pipers do not call an inappropriate tune for organizations that claim to respond to the voices of the people they serve.

Capacities

To support these roles and relationships, NGOs need to develop new skills in learning, bridging, mediation, dialogue, and influencing. NGOs' current focus on narrow management issues (often borrowed uncritically from the corporate sector), the acquiring of skills valued by donors, and traditional concepts of lobbying need to be replaced by a broader base of capacities that include the ability to listen, learn, and work with others at both local and global levels. NGOs need a more strategic understanding of how and where global issues "bite" and how organizations need to change in order to respond to new demands. NGOs need to develop ways of working that are concerned with building alliances and dividing roles and responsibilities in a collaborative way. Openness to new ideas and a greater willingness to learn will be essential in the context of new actors and problems.

Fast-changing contexts challenge NGOs to develop deeper analysis and recognize the implications for their practice. Finely nuanced judgments in complex political emergencies require improved information gathering and analytical skills. NGOs will need help from the research community, demanding an expansion of academic-practitioner collaboration and new forms of working across institutional boundaries. Engaging with others over the long term in a process of mutual learning and innovation becomes more important than claiming that NGOs have the answers and trying to convert others to their point of view. This will be a major challenge to organizations that have grown used to occupying the moral high ground.

Legitimacy and Accountability

Underlying these changes are fundamental questions about NGO legiti-macy and accountability; it is this area—the right of NGOs to do what they do and say what they say—that is being challenged by world events and the chang-ing climate of ideas. The legitimacy of NGOs (especially those based in the North) is now an accepted topic of public debate. Much of the criticism is motivated more by ideology than intellectual rigor and is in danger of "throw-ing the baby out with the bathwater." However, it will continue, especially around the key issue of representation. Claiming the right to speak simply because an NGO has projects on the ground is unlikely to be acceptable to a skeptical media or a critical local population. Southern NGOs are question-ing the right of northern NGOs to speak for them; women are questioning the right of male-dominated NGOs to represent them; As access to technol-ogy grows, communities can speak for themselves through video and the Internet as well as via the more traditional marches and demonstrations. An internet conference on women in Africa (1999) found that more than 40 percent of contributors were women from Africa,[4] even though they are the group most excluded from resources and technology. As poor people find ways to access information and gain a voice in global debates, the legitimacy of northern-based, male-dominated organizations to appropriate the voices of others will collapse. They will have to learn to share their financial and technological resources through more democratic networks.

To counter the growing criticism, NGOs must become good civic actors; however, few NGOs have democratic systems of governance or accountability. As service providers, they do not need them; as social actors, they certainly do. NGOs will have to become more open and transparent once institutional accountability becomes a condition for a seat at the negotiating table. The tradition of hiding controversial issues behind closed doors, and a persistent failure to convert NGO rhetoric about equity and participatory management into institutional practice, is no basis for persuading others of the need for reform. For NGOs to become social actors in a global world, pushing for justice, equity, democracy, and accountability, these characteristics need to be reflected in their own structures.

Conclusion

Against such a complex canvas it is unrealistic to expect a consensus to emerge in NGO positions or reactions, nor is such a consensus necessarily desirable. However, a theme that does unite different voices is the crucial importance of civic values as a motor for change. Although NGOs are unlikely to agree on the details of how to confront globalization and issues of conflict and humanitarian action—or their implications for NGOs as organizations—they would probably all agree that certain (nonmarket) values are crucial to our common future: cooperation, nonviolence, respect for human rights, and democratic process. Whether these are understood as "civic" or "social" values, or just as values that all sectors of society can support and represent, is less important than working together to make them the bottom line in decisions over economics, the environment, social policy, and politics. NGOs must be leaders in cultivating a global moral order that finds poverty and violence unacceptable. They must be exemplars of the societies they want to create and work much harder to mainstream civic values into the arenas of economic, social, and political power. This is clearly an agenda for radical change.

The fundamental question facing all NGOs is how to move from their current position—as unhappy agents of a foreign-aid system in decline—to being vehicles for international cooperation in the emerging global arena. Global trends challenge all NGOs to rethink their mandate, mission, and strategies; this requires major organizational changes and a degree of self-sacrifice in the short term, but it will be a force for liberation in the longer term.

Notes

1. Throughout the chapter, the term *civil society* is used to cover the broad grouping of nonstate, nonmarket organizations that include NGOs, community groups, churches, social movements, trade unions, business associations, political parties, and think tanks. NGOs form a subgroup of civil society, although a very heterogeneous one.
2. BBC News, September 22nd, 1998.
3. The focus of this section is on complex political emergencies. This is not to infer that natural hazards are insignificant. However, NGOs have made great strides in their capabilities to respond to these natural hazards.
4. This was an e-mail discussion group preceding the U.N. Economic Commission for Africa meeting on women in Addis Ababa, 1999.

Part I:

Alternative Thinking about Development Concepts and Ideas

2

Relief and Development: Disjuncture and Dissonance

Ian Smillie

The relationship between emergency and development assistance is an issue that might seem old-fashioned, even passé in the brave new world of reinvented aid agencies—newly decorated with peace-building units, reconstruction departments, and sections preparing sophisticated policies on human rights, democratization, transition initiatives, and civil society.[1] In fact, the need for "linking relief and development" (complete with its own acronym—LRD) has been well accepted by nongovernmental organizations (NGOs), bilateral agencies, and multilateral agencies for almost a decade. Received wisdom notwithstanding, problems remain: serious problems.

The issue of greater synergy between relief and development is important because the development community has seen much of its investment eroded or negated in recent years by war and governmental collapse, and relief agencies have recognized the need for sustainable peace if their work is to have long-term meaning. Understanding the connection is also important because of evidence that emergency assistance can be inappropriate or even dangerous, and that development assistance has in some cases contributed to fueling and igniting conflict.

Through the 1960s, 1970s, and into the 1980s, there was a linear approach to relief and development, with both seen as distinct types of effort, one following the other. The concept of a "continuum," in which the external response to an emergency moves from relief through reconstruction to development, blurred the distinctions somewhat, but it was still based on the idea that at each stage there would be specialized agencies to take and then pass on responsibility for victims. In the early 1990s, the continuum metaphor gave way to more holistic thinking about synergies between relief and development. It is now accepted that relief and development are not mutually exclusive. Linkages can and must be made if reconstruction and development are to be meaningful and sustainable.

There are, however, three challenges encountered by organizations committed to making effective links between relief and development: *timing, funding*, and *understanding*.

Money and Understanding: Quick Impact Projects

The United Nations High Commission for Refugees (UNHCR)'s quick impact projects (QIPs)—an innovative attempt to bridge the transition between emergency and development programming—provide a dramatic illustration of the challenges in doing so effectively. Created to deal with the absence of development agencies in the immediate aftermath of conflict, QIPs essentially aimed to solve a timing problem. However, in stretching time-constrained emergency budgets into unfamiliar developmental territory, they created another problem: Managed by an emergency organization, many of the projects encountered serious developmental problems—an issue of knowledge and understanding.

By the early 1990s, UNHCR recognized that it had a role and a responsibility in helping to set the stage for the longer-term rehabilitation of returning refugees and displaced people, and that this would have to be predicated on the resumption of sustainable development activity. Such activities were most likely to succeed if they were planned and carried out on a community basis, rather than on the specific targeting of returnees, and if they could be dovetailed into the longer-term development programs of government and other agencies. QIPs therefore included community health centers, schools, repairs to access roads and bridges, and the rehabilitation or digging of wells. A review in Nicaragua found that such efforts—conducted in cooperation with NGOs and other agencies—had provided communities with resources that would otherwise have been unavailable. They had boosted the morale and motivation of returnees, encouraging reconciliation, reintegration, and permanent residence. The projects had also developed local capacities and revitalized local communities through training and the injection of cash into the local economy through wages and income-generating activities.[2]

By 1995, however, there were indications that the approach had serious limitations. A review in Guatemala noted that repatriation and reintegration had been difficult and unpredictable, and did not lend itself to the type of boilerplate planning that had been used. The critical issue of land ownership and property title often lagged far behind refugee return, making land-related investment—house building, seeds, tools, fertilizer, and irrigation—difficult and sometimes impossible. Land had also been one of the biggest issues in the Cambodian repatriation of 1992 and 1993. There, some 360,000 refugees were moved from the Thai border on the assumption that there would be agricultural land available for each family, primarily in Battambang Province. It turned out, however, that where land *was* available, much of it was heavily mined. In addition to poor preparation, the land plan collapsed because of the short time frame in which repatriation was organized.

In Cambodia, there were additional problems. A relatively junior officer managed the effort with two assistants in UNHCR's program section. As a result, larger and less complex project proposals stood the best chance of approval and tended to be allocated to the most active and dependable NGOs, rather than allocated on the basis of community needs or potential impact (UNHCR 1993, cited in Law 1995). Many projects were rushed and inappropriate, such as the siting of 250 latrines in one area below the flood plain, causing illness with the onset of the monsoon. Appropriate levels of supervision were impossible, given the staff resources. A team monitoring projects in Battambang looked at twenty in a day and a half. Although there was an agreement between the United Nations Development Program (UNDP) and UNHCR on incorporating longer-term development follow-up and monitoring, this does not appear to have happened in practice. In Mozambique, QIP schools, boreholes, and health posts built in 1995 and 1996 were in disrepair within a year of construction (Lubkemann 1998).

In UNHCR's broader estimation:

QIPs became the major focus of [its] repatriation activities at a time when the concept of the "continuum" model was the basis for multilateral discussions. The continuum idea, from emergency relief through rehabilitation and on to development, was intended to ensure a seamless web of activities. In practice, however, the continuum as applied by UNHCR and its partners often resulted in a disjuncture between their respective activities. . . . The "handover" approach was based on the assumption that UNHCR's initial rehabilitation activities would lay the groundwork for sustainable reconstruction (UNHCR 1997, 7).

Although UNHCR had extended itself further along what might be seen as a relief-to-development conveyer belt (even a "continuum"), it was still a conveyer belt, with one set of actors too widely separated from another by mandate, money, and their understanding of what needed to be done. There was the additional problem of time, which had little to do with local needs and context. In Cambodia, for example, "reintegration was implicitly interpreted to mean whatever could be accomplished with a fixed amount of resources within a predetermined time frame. No clear conceptual framework was used for responding to emerging needs" (UNHCR 1997,7).

By 1998, UNHCR recognized that there would have to be much greater cooperation between relief and development agencies on reintegration strategies. Community needs and participation had not always been given proper weight. Sustainability had been sacrificed to quick disbursement and to the creation or repair of physical infrastructure, without due regard to recurrent costs. The government departments or other international agencies that would inherit these costs had often been left out of the planning, and so the UNHCR projects were left out of *their* planning. Many of the projects were implemented on an ad hoc basis, outside any strategy that might link returnees with longer-term reintegration and development. As a result, much of what had been intended to assist returnees and their communities had become, ironically, a burden (discussions with UNHCR Reintegration and Self-Reliance Unit, Geneva, 29 January 1998).

It is not clear what this implies for the future. In some of their objectives—boosting morale, injecting cash into damaged economies—QIPs undoubtedly succeeded. However, in many cases, the challenges of time, money, and understanding frustrated their developmental impact. UNHCR recognizes its own planning and development limitations and acknowledges it was incorrect in its assumption that multilateral partners would be willing and able to build on activities initiated by UNHCR. Among the perceived culprits is UNDP, which in Tajikistan, for example, "did not continue many of the projects that UNHCR had initiated with grassroots community actors" (UNHCR 1997, 8).

UNDP sees the problem as one of "mandate creep" in which emergency organizations "have sometimes moved into quasidevelopment programs for which they are perhaps technically and organizationally poorly equipped." At the same time, UNDP concedes that

the classical development agencies have been slow to respond or even have been reluctant to participate . . . . The mandate creep combined with the incoherence between programs has been manifested in the unedifying spectacle of public squabbling between agencies in the full light of the international community (UNDP 1998c, 7).

UNHCR has a mandate and decades of experience in defining and fostering protection, and it knows that for refugees, this extends well beyond a bus ticket home. It also accepts the need to "develop a better understanding of its multilateral partners" and believes that it "should be more sensitive to the priorities, agendas, and approaches of development agencies, so as to facilitate activities which are consistent and complementary" (UNHCR 1997, 16). Such felicitous phrases, of course—euphemisms for that old chestnut "better coordination"—adorn many strategic planning documents. It remains to be seen whether the lessons learned by UNHCR in its QIPs development interventions, and by those responsible for taking up the ongoing task of protection, reintegration, and development (such as UNDP), are remembered and acted on.

Haiti: Timing and Understanding

Events in Haiti demonstrate the challenges faced by external agencies in attempting to break the cycle of bad governance, degenerative change, conflict, and external intervention. A rush to act (timing) and ill-conceived projects (understanding) were exacerbated in this case by too much—rather than too little—money. Or too much too soon, and too briefly.

In September 1994, when a United States–led multinational force entered Haiti, restoring the Aristide government to office, the immediate and long-term needs were enormous. Productive capacity had been severely damaged, and there was an urgent requirement for tools, seeds, animals, working capital, and infrastructure development. In January 1995, Haiti received donor pledges of $1.2 billion in reconstruction support, to be disbursed over the following eighteen months.

Within months, several major donors had initiated employment programs aimed at rehabilitating or reconstructing basic social and economic infrastructure: roads, irrigation and drainage, schools and health centers, potable water systems, erosion control and soil conservation projects. With an expenditure of more than $100 million, more than one million person-months of work were created for unskilled and low-skilled workers throughout the country between August 1993 and December 1996 (Charlier 1998). Income was earned, hundreds of kilometers of road were rehabilitated, hundreds of schools and clinics were rebuilt, and thousands of acres of erosion-threatened slopes were protected. In this respect, the efforts were generally successful.

Beyond the immediate outputs, however, a 1997 evaluation found that many of the projects had been hastily planned.

As a result, not enough time was dedicated to ensure proper participation and involvement of beneficiary communities and local authorities. There was not enough consideration for postproject operation and maintenance; and in practice those maintenance considerations—if ever planned (in a few best cases)—have not been implemented thoroughly (Charlier 1998, 7).

The evaluation observed that labor-intensive public works and infrastructure rehabilitation were not only valid, but a high priority. However, like UNHCR's QIPs, they were tied to their emergency origin and lacked the required development perspective and the time frame needed to do the job properly. As a result, they failed to generate lasting employment that might have occurred through the promotion of small contractors and sustainable community improvement committees. All evaluations and studies of postwar reconstruction say the same thing: Projects have to be part of a coherent plan that is based on a sound knowledge of the people, their culture and their history. Organizations must take the time to do it properly and to ensure that there will be ongoing support if this is required. They must involve local authorities and communities at all levels of planning and implementation, and should not start, no matter what the pressure, until they are fully on board.

"It's better to have a working road for four months than not at all," said one aid manager in Haiti. Given the resources available and given the events of the previous ten, if not one hundred years, this is precisely the attitude that Haiti did not need at the moment of its greatest development opportunity. [3]

Disarming the Bad Guys

The United States Agency for International Development's Office of Transition Initiatives (OTI) was created in 1994 as a separate office within the Bureau of Humanitarian Response to reflect the need for a distinct operating unit that could carry out

overt political programs in crisis-prone countries in transition from war to peace. OTI's goal is to enhance development prospects in priority, conflict-prone countries by empowering the citizenry of a country so that they can move toward democratic self-rule (USAID undated, 1).

In its first three years, OTI became operational in Angola, Bosnia, Haiti, and Rwanda and initiated activities in Liberia and Sierra Leone. It funded radio and print media programs, projects run by civic groups aiming to bridge communal divisions, projects promoting human rights and democratic political processes, and projects aimed at training and reintegrating demobilized soldiers. One such project involved the demobilization of the entire Haitian army (*Forces Armées d'Haiti* [FAd'H]) to neutralize the short-term threat it posed to peace and to U.S. peacekeepers in Haiti, to provide the longer-term prevention of possible further security disruptions, and to lay a foundation for the reintegration of former soldiers into Haitian society.

Some 5,482 former soldiers were processed through a program that provided career counseling, vocational training, stipends, tool kits, and a job referral service. In some respects the program was remarkably successful. Despite difficulties with government, it was well coordinated, appropriately funded, and sufficiently flexible to deal with unforeseen problems as they arose. Good quality training was provided to the 4,867 men who graduated from the training program, most of whom received tool kits, and most of whom participated in the job referral service (Patterson 1996). A second evaluation, conducted several months after the program had concluded, found that the primary objectives had been met. Engaging the former soldiers in a training program had helped protect U.S. military forces and had contributed to short-term peace and security. By continuing the program over two years, a longer breathing space had been secured for political, security, and economic transitions to occur. There was only one glitch: "Although the demobilization program gave the former FAd'H some of the skills required for employment, full reintegration is not occurring because of the lack of progress in other areas" (Dworkin et al. 1997, 3).

This somewhat understates the problem. Of the 4,867 men trained, only 304 had found employment, 28 of them as security guards—not a job for which training had been provided. The "lack of progress in other areas" that prevented 94 percent of the men from finding jobs included low economic growth—hardly surprising, given Haiti's economic history—and the possibility of social stigma attached to former soldiers. However, the evaluation observed, employment was only "a tertiary objective of the program (and in some ways more a hope than a real goal)" (Dworkin et al. 1997, 50).

It does not matter, then, that 1,790 men were trained as auto mechanics, probably doubling the number of mechanics in Haiti, or that 602 men were trained in computers for a job market that could realistically employ only a tiny fraction of them. While this expensive and rather cruel hoax was being perpetrated on men who had in their previous lives become hardened and sometimes brutal soldier-policemen, a new national police force was being created. The same evaluation rated the new force as small, ill equipped, undertrained, badly paid, and made up of officers who were too young and inexperienced to handle the job they had been given. Thus, even the short-term benefits of the demobilization program were overshadowed by the difficulties of creating a viable alternative to the FAd'H. Here the issue was not so much "mandate creep" as "mandate shrinkage"—half-finished components moving too quickly along an understaffed conveyer belt. That crime and violence have continued apace in Haiti is perhaps, therefore, not surprising. The big wheel keeps on turning.

OTI notes some of the lessons that were learned in its first three years. One is that exit strategies need to be flexible enough to respond to changes in circumstance and that the two-year limitation on an OTI country operation may not be realistic. The problem of linking real people, who pose real threats, with real opportunities that will keep them out of trouble—the fundamental development challenge—is not mentioned. As a step on the transitional path between emergency and development, the Haiti Demobilization and Reintegration Programme can perhaps be regarded "more as a hope than a real goal," a triumph of short-term thinking, short-term mandates, and short-term funding over entrenched, long-term problems and needs.

"More a hope than a real goal"; "better to have a working road for four months than not at all." With friends like these, who needs enemies?

Three Challenges

This chapter deals with three challenges encountered by organizations committed to making effective links between relief and development: *timing, funding,* and *understanding.* The first challenge, appropriate timing—when to engage, when to modify the intervention, and when to withdraw—is an essential ingredient of conflict prevention, reduction, and resolution. It is also important for knowing if, when, and how to move from basic humanitarian relief to more developmental objectives. Examples of the problem include action too late in Rwanda, departure too soon in Haiti, and transition too fast in countries such as Cambodia and Bosnia.

Money can be a key determinant of timing—in hurrying or delaying humanitarian response and in rushing the move from relief to development programming. It can be the cause of precipitous agency withdrawal, and it is the prime motivation behind the growing demand for "exit strategies"—as with OTI in Haiti—that may not be appropriate to the pace of social and economic change on the ground. Although there are cases in which appropriate timing has allowed for improved synergies between relief and development, timing remains a fundamental problem.

Funding is the second challenge. Emergency funding remains sporadic, arriving in short-term bursts, often after lengthy delays. It can be patchy, and much of it is overtly political. Development assistance too can be patchy, cumbersome, and rigid, often arriving late and without reference to the emergency it follows. Throughout the 1990s, overseas development assistance declined dramatically, exacerbating competition and creating other obstacles to making links operational between emergency and development assistance.

Knowledge and information, related but very different concepts, characterize the third and most important challenge; understanding. Although both knowledge and information may be in short supply, much greater emphasis has been placed on the latter (especially at either end of the relief-development spectrum) than on the former. Inappropriate blueprint-type reconstruction and rehabilitation programs continue to abound, in part because of serious impediments to learning, both within and between institutions. These impediments include a fear of and a consequent aversion to evaluation, and an environment in which relief workers suffer from danger, stress, overwork, and burnout. This leaves institutional memories shallow and provides experienced workers with no time to educate others.

Dual Mandate NGOs: Maximizing Synergies?

Do agencies with capacities in both relief and development have a comparative advantage in maximizing synergies between relief and development? The simple and obvious answer is yes, but simple answers do not always provide simple ways of achieving the obvious. Certainly organizations that have both a relief and a development capacity—CARE, World Vision, Oxfam, Save the Children, and others—have in-house experience that can build knowledge, a flexibility of approach, a nuanced understanding of timing issues, and the possibility of blending donor income to suit the emergency and developmental needs of their beneficiaries. With programs in some of the most emergency-prone countries, the Agency for Cooperation in Overseas Research and Development, for example, has been able (or forced) to adjust its development programming to meet emergency requirements repeatedly in Sudan, Somalia, and Ethiopia, shifting the emphasis as and when conditions have demanded.

Organizations with a dual mandate may have a comparative advantage over others, even in countries where they have no presence at the outset of an emergency. Oxfam's dual mandate has frequently allowed it to move quickly into emergency situations where it had no previous geographic presence and to make emergency investments that would also have long-lasting development benefits. Almost thirty years ago, in postwar Bangladesh, it provided food, shelter, and health care to tens of thousands of returning refugees. This was, and remains, the core of its emergency approach worldwide, not unlike a dozen other relief agencies. However, Oxfam also invested immediately in basic infrastructure, building bridges and providing the ferries necessary to get people, food, and commerce moving quickly. Some of those ferries were still providing useful service three decades later. Seeing local capacities for the delivery of relief, Oxfam also invested in fledgling Bangladeshi organizations, a programming novelty in 1971. One of the largest and most effective NGOs in the world, the Bangladesh Rural Advancement Committee, received its first external grant from Oxfam at this time.

The same is true today. CARE, which ran a massive emergency operation in Bosnia throughout the Balkans war, was able to convert this to reconstruction as opportunities became available, and then moved into development programming and support of emerging civil society organizations.

These examples describe options that were available to organizations with a dual mandate and a perspective that transcended the immediacy of the emergency involved. They were not the sort of options available then or now to organizations with a primary focus on emergency relief, nor would they have been available to organizations with a strong postconflict developmental mindset. Médecins Sans Frontieres and UNHCR, for example, would not have had the time, mandate, or expertise to turn a feeding program into a long-term seeds project. Even if they had started such a project, incoming development agencies would likely have shown little interest in a second-hand seeds project initiated by a departing relief agency. In Bangladesh, the dual mandate, combined with good understanding and a keen sense of timing, gave each organization and its efforts the edge it needed to build real synergies between relief and development.

In Bangladesh, however, funding played a key role, and funding may be the limiting factor in making any generalizations about dual mandate organizations. The major relief/development agencies in postwar Bangladesh were the recipients of huge amounts of unrestricted private donor funds, easy to allocate and reallocate to efforts where the need—short or long term, emergency or developmental—seemed greatest. The same has been true for such agencies in other large-scale, well-publicized emergencies: Ethiopia, Cambodia, Bosnia. But when emergencies have been less well publicized and when unrestricted private donor money has been more limited—Angola, Haiti, Sierra Leone—opportunities narrow.

Dual mandate organizations *can* do more to bridge the gaps between relief and development, and often do. But the question inevitably arises: *Should* they? Should everyone try to do everything? Is "mandate creep" really the answer?

The Aid Superstructure

Imagine an assembly line in an automobile factory with a conveyer belt. Imagine people busy making carburetors—perhaps excellent carburetors—without knowing much about the engine to which the carburetors will be attached. Imagine hundreds of engines backed up, waiting for automobile bodies that might or might not be produced, depending on levels of interest in the sheet metal department. Imagine the body shop producing only right-side fenders and no doors, because the design for the left-side fenders and doors has not been completed, or because somebody else was supposed to make them but did not. Imagine that budgeting for the end product has been organized around the individual components, that wax paper has been supplied for windows because there was not enough money for glass. Imagine a factory producing vehicles for a market, for roads, and for drivers that it barely understands.

There should be no argument—certainly not at the dawn of the twenty-first century—about overlapping opportunities and about overlapping needs for both emergency and development assistance, or about the urgent need for one to inform the other. In this respect, the old debate about a continuum was largely one of semantics, obscuring the larger issue of how emergency and development assistance are actually organized. That they are or can be compatible is, by now, a given. That synergy occurs mainly at the margins of development and relief activity, rather than at their center, however, is a problem of institutional mandates and institutional personalities that, dictated in part by funding, define the limits of outsiders' understanding and their approach to timing.

The conveyer belt image, despite its limitations, is not a bad one. Agencies with different mandates locate themselves along a conceptual assembly line, performing different functions according to need—security, food, water, immunization, schooling, assistance for returning refugees, credit, job training, seeds, extension services. It is not unusual or wrong for services in the depth of an emergency to be provided by different agencies: one drilling boreholes, another handling food, a third perhaps organizing a school for children when the time is right. Similarly, in the postemergency phase, public health may be organized by a U.N. agency, credit facilities by an NGO, and education by government. So, quite logically—and consistent with the concept of overlapping emergency and development opportunities and needs—there may well be different actors working at any given point on the assembly line. While the agencies stay in their position, their beneficiaries move on. However, like the imaginary vehicle factory in which nothing is coordinated and in which individual departments design and produce components at will, the result, if not chaotic, is certainly less than optimal—not just in management terms, but in the results that are intended for the beneficiaries.

If the challenges of timing, funding, and understanding were met, and if the emergency itself was not chronic, would the result be a smoother, more appropriate conveyer belt? The answer, no doubt, is yes, but as with our imaginary vehicle plant, it would probably not be enough. And a larger question is begged: How would it come about? Certainly the answer is not for the carburetor department to start making engine parts, or for the paint shop to produce the last three bits of the drive train.

This leads to a more dramatic concluding question: Can the existing chasm between relief and development be bridged simply with more exhortations for better understanding and more coordination? There may be a fundamental institutional ego problem that cannot be overcome without much stronger leadership and the conclusive demolition of institutional barriers. Virtually all of the new initiatives to link relief and development are located within an aid superstructure that remains basically unchanged after a decade and a half of state collapse, horrific warfare, and millions of violent deaths. In practical terms, funding for transitional peace-building efforts is an infinitesimal fraction of overall aid expenditure.

There is an appearance of activity and change, but the structures of the past—with their problems and dysfunctionality—remain firmly in place. Without major structural change in the way aid is organized and delivered, prospects for more sustainable peace and more sustainable development will remain limited.

Notes

1. This paper is based on work done by the author with the Humanitarianism and War Project of the Thomas J. Watson Jr. Institute for Institutional Studies at Brown University in Providence, Rhode Island. A longer monograph is available (Smillie 1999).

2. The story of the QIPs evolution is available in United Nations Department for Development Support and Management Services/United Nations Industrial Development Organizations 1995; Bonifacio 1992; United Nations High Commission for Refugees 1993, 1994.

3. For a detailed discussion of the transition, see Maguire et al. 1996.

Understanding Development as a Living Process

Allan Kaplan

The concept of development has become bastardized. It has been generally understood as a political-economic project intended to assist "underdeveloped" communities and countries to "become developed," in the sense of "catching up" with "developed" countries. It has been approached largely from an economistic perspective, as the eradication, or at least the reduction, of poverty: Development has implied the building of, or entry into, a modern economy. More recently it has also gained a political overtone: "Developed" is often synonymous with democracy, pluralism, justice, equity, and respect for a universal code of human rights. When coupled with each other, the political economy perspective attains a social dimension, and development implies modernization—the transformation of "traditional" society toward "modern" society.

This is a simplistic rendition of a complex concept, especially today when we are living in a postmodern era, in which ambiguity, uncertainty, and contradiction have replaced former certainties. Many feel that the development project has failed: The gap between rich and poor has increased rather than decreased, and ecological and social problems begin to render our world unsustainable. Development theory has undergone many transformations over the years, and today there is a growing body of thought that is beginning to question not only the various theories but the very validity of the development concept itself, and even the integrity of those who promote development. Questions abound, *but there is little change in development practice* because underlying this practice are certain paradigmatic assumptions that, although largely unconscious, hold practitioners captive. This chapter contrasts these approaches with another possible set of assumptions, which may take us some way toward the transformation of practice.

Some Limitations of "Conventional" Development Thinking

The dominant development paradigm is made up of several key assumptions and practices. The first is that development can be created and engineered. Interventions and projects are designed specifically to "bring" development to those among whom it is lacking. A second assumption is that development is brought by others who presumably are more developed. This constrains the development practitioner to work from the specifications of the world from which he/she has been sent, rather than out of an accurate and sensitive reading of the particular situation with which he/she is actually faced. A third assumption is that development is linear and predictable; so long as the assumptions are correct, outputs can be predicted, based on input. This gives rise to the "development project" which dominates practice and is short term, time bound, and limited in terms of resources and expected outputs. A fourth assumption is that development presumes that understanding will generate change. It does not take much account of unconscious factors, processes of change, culture, tradition, or the human heart. Development places far more emphasis on technical experts and "advisors" and on trainers than it does on change facilitators. This emphasis expresses itself in terms of project specifications, in terms of relative positioning within nongovernmental organizations and in terms of remuneration. A fifth assumption is that development assumes a preferred culture or value system. Most development pundits deny this, yet the presumption continues that there is something wrong and we must intervene to change it, judging the results according to our own norms. The evaluation of development interventions is generally performed in terms of the ends stipulated in the project document, not in terms of the myriad other outcomes that may (or may not) have been forthcoming. Finally, development practitioners are not required to pay attention to their own development as part of effective practice; there is little or no reciprocity in the relationships between "developer" and "developee." A "conventional" development approach is fundamentally about *the delivery of resources*—finances, equipment, technical skills, political clout, even a particular approach to life—from those who have to those that do not.

The Community Development Resource Association Approach

At the core of the Community Development Resource Association understanding of development is the recognition that development is an innate and natural process found in all living things. Essentially, development workers do not deliver development, but intervene in development processes that already exist. Whether the intervention is in the life of an individual, organization, or community, it is critical to understand that the process of development is already well established and needs to be treated with respect. To be able to "read" development in this way, openness is required: an ability to observe acutely and without preconception (although with understanding of development processes) to bring insight to observation.

Equipped with this knowledge and understanding, the practitioner can begin to assess how the resources that they bring will affect the development process. Some common examples of the consequences of the inappropriate introduction of resources include the increase of dysfunctional dependency on the provider of the resource and the inappropriate use or abuse of the resources to the detriment of the recipient. In contrast, it is at times almost miraculous to experience the difference that an appropriate development intervention, facilitated in a sensitive and responsive way, can make to the genuine empowerment of the recipient. Yet this, surely, is the essence of a development intervention—the facilitation of growing awareness and consciousness such that people are able to take control of their own lives and circumstances and exert responsibility and purpose with respect to their future. This approach inevitably implies an activist stance; that is, assistance with confronting the manifestations and dynamics of power. If a development intervention does not succeed in this, it can hardly be said to be developmental.

One aspect of our understanding of the process of development identifies three discernible phases of *ideal, unimpeded* development; these apply to humans as well as the social systems they create. The first phase characterized by *dependence* is a period of great learning and skills acquisition in which others play a major role in providing the environment and resources required for growth. The second phase of *independence* entails a fundamental change in relationship and a period of testing and personalizing capacities and competencies, using them to act and affect the environment in ways that help establish the actor as unique and self-reliant. The third phase involves another fundamental change in relationships toward increasing *interdependence*. The actor now understands that the full realization of one's own potential is achieved only through effective collaboration with others.

These phases are all developmental, and one should not be judged as being superior to another. The experience of each phase provides learning and capabilities that are vital to the ability to engage in the next phase. It is also necessary to recognize that these phases are continually recurring and overlapping in the course of the life of an individual, organization, or community—as one develops, one encounters new areas in which these sequenced phases must be experienced afresh. Although skilled and sensitive interventions can help avoid and even remove hindrances and blockages to the process, development does have a pace of its own. There is an absolute limit to the extent to which it can be speeded up through the application of increased resources and developmental interventions.

A further defining characteristic, one that sets development apart from quantitative growth, is its nonlinear nature. Development does not progress along a smooth line; at critical points in the process, there are periods of crisis and turmoil, when everything that has previously provided stability and meaning is questioned and challenged, and conflict is often symptomatic. Sometimes the crises need to be of such gravity that those involved know that there is no option other than to break the old forms in order to build the new. The seeds of crisis are sown in each phase of development and grow at their own pace as the process unfolds; the passing from one phase to another is prompted by their germination.

There is an apparent contradiction here. Development is nonlinear, unpredictable, and even anarchic; at the same time, there appear to be natural phases, sequences, and modalities that can be said to characterize the process as a particular pattern or arrangement. The contradiction is real, but rather than demanding resolution, it can be seen as the beating heart of development itself, a tension that provides the energy to fuel the process. A constant interplay between order and chaos, between form and flow.

It follows that development interventions are essentially about the development of people and that development cannot be imposed. Ultimately, development is driven from within, so while a development worker must bring specialist knowledge and skill to an intervention, the final outcome of the intervention is determined by the client. Moreover, development processes take significant periods of time, and their flow—in terms of both time and outcome—cannot be determined beforehand. An effective development practice *accompanies* clients through their developmental changes; one-off interventions and predesigned packages are beside the point.

Although all clients develop, none does so in quite the same way as any other. So developmental interventions are not "expert products" or "packages of resources." Rather, they are processes that are created and applied in response to particular situations. They are designed to help people gain an understanding of themselves so that, in time, they are better able to take control of their own future and to arrive at effective solutions to problems, including economic and political marginalization. This is not to say that the development practitioner should not play an activist role—on the contrary, solidarity is vital, as is the creation of enabling environments in which people are more in control of their circumstances and freer to pursue their processes of development.

The New Paradigm: Beyond Resource Transfer

Ultimately, the development paradigm that we are articulating here has little to do with the transfer of resources. On the contrary, development is about *facilitating resourcefulness*, which demands a vastly different response from practitioners. In this alternative paradigm, it is clear that development cannot be created or engineered; as a process, it exists independently of the development practitioner. All that we can do is facilitate processes that are already in motion. When they are not in motion, it would be best—and honest—to refrain. Development cannot be brought: being driven from within, it is not the prerogative of an outsider. As development practitioners, we can assist the flow of the process, but nothing more. Real and honest development work cannot be done to others by third parties—those with a vested interest (however benign) in the future of others whom they resource, influence, or control. If development interventions are not designed through free interaction between development worker and client, then categorically the result is not development work; it becomes at best a patronizing collusion, at worst a cynical manipulation. This has huge implications for current practice with respect to the financing of development. Instead of fearful control, space must be allowed for real and responsive development practice to take place.

Similarly, intervention specifications that are "predetermined" and that do not respond to accurate and sensitive readings of the particular situation will warp and destroy the development process. Because situations change continuously in response to development intervention, flexibility is required. This places a big responsibility on the practitioner and organization and demands new capacities with respect to reflecting, learning, and managing. Development cannot be seen as linear and predictable; we can never know quite what will flow out of a development intervention. An accurate reading of the actual—and largely intangible—developmental place where the client is will help, but never entirely. Output is never based on input but on a complicated array of factors, including the precise relationship between input and the developmental process being intervened on. Our assumptions will always be inadequate. They must of course be made, for they form the foundation of any intervention, but always with due caution.

Development is a continuous process that has no end; the effective development intervention opens things up, rather than closes them down. Equally, development does not begin when we decide to intervene, because it had already begun. The concept of the development project is anathema to the concept of development. It is a figment of an engineering mindset; at best a managerial tool used by a form of management inimical to development work, at worst a donor requirement to fulfill inappropriate financial control systems. Given its place at the very heart of the development system, it demonstrates the misguidedness at the core of that system as well as the system's intractability. It is the repository of all that is wrong with conventional development practice and the greatest stumbling block to effective development interventions.

This does not mean that development practitioners and organizations should be given freedom simply to do whatever they want without frameworks to ensure accountability. *Parameters* should be set for development interventions and should include objectives, time frames, strategies, and evaluation criteria. However, it is important to regard these as *guidelines* for the continuous monitoring, learning, and adaptation of intervention processes—on the part of practitioner, client, and donor. It is imperative that we recognize the development *process* as the issue, rather than the successful implementation of a particular project. And it is critical to understand the project as one fragment of such a process, rather than confuse it with the development process itself.

Processes of development are beset with unconscious factors; realities of tradition, culture, and motivation; and resistances to change. Development practitioners skilled in facilitating processes of change are of far more value to the development endeavor than technical experts, advisors, or trainers. Development always, somewhere, assumes a preferred culture or value system, or way of doing things. This is implied in the very notion of intervening in others' processes. We can mitigate this, but we will never get rid of it entirely, even when we operate out of an alternative development paradigm. It is precisely because of our own unconscious projections and assumptions that we, as development practitioners, have to pay attention to our own development. This is not a luxury or an addendum to other capacities; it is a central requirement of the discipline. At the very least, how can we possibly presume to intervene in others' development if we do not understand our own, or are not prepared to engage in our own?

Participation is an end, and not simply a means; the central point of development is to enable people to participate in the governance of their own lives. The insistence that successful development projects be replicable assumes that different situations are equal; on the contrary, every situation is unique. We can learn principles and guidelines, and develop insights, but the attempt to replicate shows disrespect for the specificity of people's processes of development and their ways of taking control. Within this paradigm, sustainability becomes less an issue of financial sustainability and more about achieving the ability to keep changing, moving, responding, and learning within constantly shifting contexts.

Learning at the Heart of Practice

These arguments give rise to some questions, to which we will attempt to respond with three sets of interlinked "movements." The first relates to evaluation and poverty eradication, which is the whole thrust of the development endeavor. It is all very well making fine points about the development *process*, but how does this relate to people's needs? How does it help that "people gain an understanding of themselves," if we have not been able to improve their material circumstances?

After decades of conventional development practice that has been governed by this economistic perspective, the levels of poverty in our world—economically defined—have increased rather than decreased. Helping people gain an understanding of themselves is done so that they are better able to take control of their own future and arrive at effective solutions to questions, problems, and concerns, including those of economic and political marginalization. There are many ways to combat poverty or achieve political change, but not all of them are particularly or specifically developmental. While the political activist and economic reformer may play roles of incalculable value, and while development practitioners may choose to play these roles as well as their own, nevertheless these are all different ways of dealing with poverty, and not all of them leave people in a better position to move with confidence into their own future. Although the reduction of poverty may certainly feature prominently in judgments on development interventions, it cannot be the only measure, and indeed, it may at times be an inaccurate measure.

We could use all these arguments, and in fact we do, but in a sense, despite their validity, they are slightly beside the point—that there are many forms of poverty, economic poverty being only one. The question arises about how much "other" poverty we create when our goal is narrowly defined as the alleviation of economic poverty. When all values are subsumed to the economy, how much do we lose with respect to social values, to artistic values, to cultural and language diversity, to biodiversity? We must surely recognize by now that the world we are creating with our fixation on the economy is becoming immeasurably poorer with respect to everything that lives outside the economy. The general fixation on the economy creates another, much more insidious, type of poverty: lack of choice. Increasingly, people are being expected to toe the economic line, and freedom to opt for culturally different priorities is frowned on as in some sense deviant. In this way we are all being coopted toward the creation of our own poverty. People-centered development is about increasing, not decreasing, choice. It is about enabling people to become more conscious, to understand themselves and their context so they are better able to take control of their own futures. Thus, judgments on the efficacy of interventions, although they must include the element of poverty alleviation, must go beyond it; development interventions must result, not in a reduction of the world, but in an increase of possibilities.

The second set of questions focuses on how the development process can be understood. Earlier we have referred to the idea of "reading development." Conventionally, we have learned not to intervene until we have done a needs assessment, an inventory, or an audit, and have ascertained the parameters of a situation. "Reading development" implies something more. The experience of the Community Development Resource Association in capacity building—with respect to organization, community, and individual development—has yielded a certain perspective on capacity, which is our entry point into understanding this concept of "reading." From our work with organizations—our starting point—we have ascertained a number of elements that must be present and coherent for an organization to be said to have capacity or to be effective. These are presented sequentially in a hierarchy of importance:

- A *conceptual framework* that reflects the organization's understanding of the world

- An *organizational "attitude"* that incorporates the confidence to act in and on the world in a way that the organization believes can be effective and have an impact, and an acceptance of responsibility for the social and physical conditions "out there"

- Clear organizational *vision and strategy*, and sense of purpose and will, that flow out of the understanding and responsibility mentioned previously

- Defined and differentiated organizational *structures and procedures* that reflect and support vision and strategy

- Relevant *individual skills, abilities, and competencies*

- Sufficient and appropriate *material resources*

We have subsequently—through our own work and in dialogue with other development practitioners working in different areas—affirmed that this hierarchy of importance holds its validity, although with slightly different slants and angles, across both community and individual capacity. If you look toward the bottom of the hierarchy, you will see those things that are quantifiable and measurable: elements of capacity that can be easily grasped and worked with. They are material things; they belong to the realm of the visible. If, however, we turn our attention to the top of the hierarchy, we enter an entirely different realm, that of the invisible. These elements are ephemeral, transitory, not easily assessed or weighed. They are, to a large extent, intangible, observable only through the effects they have. It is these aspects that by and large determine capacity.

"Reading development," then, demands far more than the kinds of techniques we have become used to, for these are only designed to elicit the material, the tangible. In reality, one needs intelligence, acuity, mobility, and penetrating perception to be able to read the particular nature of a specific developmental process. The development practitioner needs genuine observation and listening skills, and the ability to combine an open and nonjudgmental approach with enough understanding to make sense of, and draw insight out of, what one is observing. Such competencies are new abilities that we as development practitioners need to develop—they are not skills in which we can be trained. The conventional development paradigm sees only skills in which practitioners can be trained; the alternative development perspective demands a more developmental approach to building the capacity of its practitioners. It demands the original skills but adds abilities that may best be described, by analogy, as artistic.

The third set of questions is concerned with what constitutes good managerial practice for a new form of development. If we are looking for a responsive development practice that is able to build appropriate and flexible interventions in accordance with nuanced readings, in a context fraught with ambiguity, uncertainty, and continuous change, then a number of things follow. First, you have to develop effective development practitioners who do not work out of books or project manuals, or primarily out of the specifications of the world from which they have been sent, but rather out of a sensitive reading of the particular situation with which they are faced. This does not mean training them in new techniques, but fostering their development through guided reflection on action, facilitated self-critique, mentoring, peer reviews, and so on. Second, they must be allowed the space to be creative with respect to their styles of "reading," reporting, and facilitation. Of course, this plays havoc with bureaucratic organizational styles and requires a very fluid and responsive form of management, which is simultaneously very "hands-on" and "hands-off."

Third, the supervision of these development practitioners—holding them accountable—must take a form that is different from the conventional "judgment by objectives" type of management. We have to know that the job is being done, but supervision of the development practitioner requires that within the organization as a whole, and between development practitioners, and between them and their managers, and between the managers themselves, a *continuous conversation* is kept alive. This kind of conversation can take many forms, some of which may be informal (requiring the fostering of an appropriate organizational culture), some of which may be formal and structured (following set procedures, including presentations of case studies, group discussions around particular programs, and so on).

Fourth, management must ensure that the organization is learning all the time; that it is open and flexible; that it is guided by principle rather than by technique, by experience and practice rather than by academic theory or ad hoc fashion, by its own understanding rather than by its "back donors." Management has to ensure that organizational reflection and learning are not something done in addition to the real work, but in fact constitute the real work itself. This requires commitment and time.

Fifth, and perhaps most important, responsibility and authority must be decentralized, devolved to the outer limits of the organization as far as possible. Frequently development practitioners or fieldworkers are marginalized because they work on the periphery of the organization, while power tends to concentrate in the center. A responsive and flexible development practice can only be achieved by the organization that has responsive and flexible practitioners out there in the (development) field, reading the development process of its clients/counterparts and facilitating responsive interventions. To achieve this, power must move to the periphery.

Conclusion

So what of the ubiquitous and infamous "development project?" Most of us are constrained entirely by donor practice; until that changes, we have little freedom to choose. For donors—key development practitioners themselves—the need for financial control remains paramount. It may be difficult to imagine control being exercised outside the boundary of the project, although moves to program and organizational—rather than project—funding will help. More flexible methods that can satisfy bookkeepers can certainly be found. However, the truth is more profound: If the five indications for development management practice are taken seriously by all practitioners, the development project will gradually metamorphose of its own accord. It will manifest the central aspect of the development process itself: that we first have to let go of the old before we can hope to take on the new, let alone quite know what it will be.

4

The Future of Nongovernmental Organizations in a World of Civil Corporations

Simon Zadek

What's Going On?

Our global economy is driven by a staggering US $22 trillions worth of annual consumption, a doubling in just twenty-five short years. But our twentieth-century hedonism has not been shared by all. More than a billion people are deprived of basic needs. The world's 225 richest individuals have a combined wealth of more than US $1 trillion, equal to the annual income of the world's poorest 47 percent—2.5 billion people. A further 100 million in the industrial world are relatively impoverished. An international poverty index for industrialized countries places the United Kingdom eighteenth out of twenty-one countries, and amongst the Organization for Economic Cooperation and Development's highest rates of adult functional illiteracy and poor health (United Nations Development Program 1998a). At the same time, there has been a twelvefold increase in world trade since 1945. This trade now accounts for about 20 percent of measured, global economic wealth. Of the 100 largest economies in the world today, fifty-one are corporations (Anderson and Cavanagh 1996). An estimated one-quarter of the world's financial wealth is made up of brand value (Clifton and Maughan 1999). The top 200 corporations have sales equivalent to one-quarter of the world's total economic activity (Wheeler and Sillanpää 1997). Foreign direct investment is the largest source of financial flows to the Third World and is increasing rapidly, by 27 percent in 1997 (United Nations Commission for Trade and Development 1998).

There has been an astonishing growth in the number, size, and scope of work of nongovernmental organizations (NGOs). NGOs now manage and disburse a significant proportion of official international development assistance, as well as being the primary recipients of the charitable largesse of wealthier citizens of developed countries, and increasingly also of less developed nations. The measured financial income flows through the "third sector" of most developed countries amount to as much as 3 percent to 5 percent of gross domestic product. This percentage can surely be multiplied by a factor of several times if the wealth of voluntary labor and other nonfinancial contributions are taken into account. The voluntary sector is, as Peter Drucker (1999) points out, the most rapidly growing area of most mature economies as we enter the new millennium. Since the Rio Summit, it has become increasingly the norm that NGOs are visible and active participants in policy debate alongside governments, business, and the increasingly marginalized trade union movement. Opinion polls repeatedly confirm that the public believe NGOs when it comes to ethical issues, as illustrated in studies of who the public believes when it comes to biotechnology.

Large-scale business is increasing its influence over people's lives. This, combined with the "tunneling focus" associated with the intensification of global competition, raises major questions as to the roles business will play in molding tomorrow's society. This chapter explores whether business, and specifically the corporate community, will on balance contribute (enough) to, or constrain, the realization of social and environmental demands by civil society. It also asks whether these corporations can go beyond being the target of these demands and become part of a civil society with purpose and practice that extend beyond narrow market imperatives.

Gamekeepers and Poachers

An international framework of social and environmental standards is needed for many people even to survive a globalized economy, let alone get a fair share (World Development Movement 1998). Standards have historically come from, or at least have been imposed and enforced by, the state. But can the state today reassert itself on behalf of the poor and otherwise disadvantaged? Arguably, this is no longer possible without the overt support of precisely those multinationals that so directly influence a nation's economic progress in globalized markets. NGOs play a role in pressuring the state to create regulatory frameworks, but some NGOs are now engaging with business behind the scenes as well. There is a steadily increasing two-way flow of NGO people into the corporate sector, and vice versa, along with a proliferation of new partnerships and alliances.

Who is now the gamekeeper and who is the poacher? There are cases of multinationals acting with a strong civil perspective, such as British Petroleum (BP)'s departure from the Global Climate Coalition. However, the bulk of the corporate community remains rooted within the traditional "success models" of short-term profitability and return to shareholders. A recent survey of 3,500 corporate chief executive officers in fifty-three countries to identify the world's most respected companies found that amongst the top twenty were Nestlé (seventh), Shell (twelfth), Phillip Morris (sixteenth), and Cargill (seventeenth)—four of the companies most consistently damned for their poor social and environmental performance.[1] In finding General Electric to be the world's most respected company, the survey concludes:

It is not hard to see why General Electric is so widely respected . . . few companies have ever created so much wealth for their shareholders in so short a period . . . . The company had a market capitalization of less than US $20 billion when Jack Welch took over as chairman in 1981: Last month, as share prices recovered from their early autumn swoon, it topped $300 billion. As another respondent put it, this was a phenomenal return to shareholders.

There is hardly a mention of social and environmental performance anywhere in the survey, except ironically in relation to one of the successes of the CEO of Nestlé as having:

. . . defused the long-running row over Nestlé's aggressive marketing of baby food to third world countries which was seriously damaging the company's reputation.

A strong distaste for systematic global, social, and environmental standards prevails even in relatively enlightened corporate fora. A recent report from the World Business Council for Sustainable Development rejected support for any overarching framework of social and environmental rules and associated governance systems.[2] It concluded that the preferred approach to addressing what were acknowledged as being very serious global problems is one in which "diverse players join in ad hoc alliances to solve social and environmental problems in the most pragmatic possible way" (World Business Council for Sustainable Development 1997).

The Potential of Civil Regulation

A growing body of thought and practice is seeking to create the circumstances in which social and environmental benefits go hand in hand with competitive advantage. Gonella et al. recently summarized:

Virtuous but uncompetitive companies *will not* be part of our future. Competitive, but socially or environmentally destructive companies, *must not* be part of our future (Gonella et al. 1998, 1).

This direction seems unattractive for those seeking local, community ownership and more participatory control. It is equally unattractive to those who view the only relevant pathway for strengthening corporate accountability as being through public regulation.

It is possible, however, that civil and public regulation, and even multinationals and localization, are not exclusive routes. The drive to direct companies through "civil regulation" may be one way to gain leverage over globalizing markets and institutions. If leading companies can be remolded to take adequate account of social and environmental factors, they will in turn mold markets in their own image. Where necessary, they will demand regulation to ensure a fair playing field for themselves against their socially less-inclined competitors. Dole, for example, one of the multinationals deeply involved in the banana industry, in responding to the development of a "fair traded" banana with an associated international civil campaign, stated in correspondence to the European Banana Network, the European NGO consortium working in this field:

Dole believes that the best way in which standards can be agreed and imposed is through government regulatory action. Government action tends to ensure fairness and transparency because the standards are agreed in democratic institutions. Private fixing and imposition of standards can be haphazard and ultimately discriminatory. Civil regulation *may* then be one route—and possibly the only route if the power of the multinationals is as great as many civil actors claim—to securing global social and environmental standards rooted in international statutory frameworks.

The strategic question for NGOs is how best to intervene in the never-ending race of corporate competition in a manner that shifts the basis of success toward social and environmental "goods." Ethical trade, social auditing, partnership, stakeholder dialogue, codes of conduct, and social responsibility have become the currencies of the times. Unholy alliances inconceivable just a few years ago are emerging between civil society organizations and corporations, such as bodies with multisector representation—for example, the U.K.-based Ethical Trading Initiative and the International Forest Stewardship Council.

Initially focused in the North, these new waves of engagement are now enveloping southern civil society organizations and are focused in two particular areas. The first is labor standards in the global supply chains of northern-based retailing and retail brand companies, particularly textiles, footwear, toys, and food. An example of this is the recent experience of Levi Strauss in the Dominican Republic in testing a "civil basis" for verification of its supplier code, in which it drew in southern organizations such as the nationally based Centro de Investigación Para la Acción Femenina. The second is community and environmental issues in relation to the extractive industries. In Colombia, BP has engaged with northern (largely U.K.-based) NGOs and local civil society organizations.

At the same time, confrontational forms of NGO activism will continue to flourish (Zadek et al. 1998). Campaigns are seen by some as entry points for dialogue and negotiations to change corporate behavior (Richter 1998). Divergent views of the potential for "civilizing" the business community underpin deepening fractures between civil actors, and parts of civil society are entering a period of massive change. As increasing numbers of leadership companies respond (in part) to civil demands, opinion formers are divided as to the meaning of this response. A survey recently undertaken by Price Waterhouse Cooper (1998) of the views of NGOs toward multinationals suggests that this relationship will improve over time.

David Korten (1997), for example, argues that "ethics" is necessarily pushed out of a competitive market, and so "reformist" NGOs are either simply misguided or part of the problem. Others associated with the International Forum on Globalization also regard "civil regulation" as merely the "acceptable face of the neoliberal project." Jeff Gates (1998), on the other hand, argues that capitalism can deliver against the imperatives of social equity and environmental security if it becomes more adept at producing "close-up" capitalists. His focus is to strengthen rather than weaken the role of the owners of capital, by focusing respectively on "stakeholder ownership" schemes, pension funds, and other intermediaries. John Elkington (1998) similarly sees the potential for an emerging new social contract based on leadership companies taking strategic views as to their likely competitive edge of the future.

What can we expect from businesses operating within the current economic framework? They are generators of economic wealth, yet hold extraordinary power, create havoc and pain in numerous societies, and represent a serious challenge to democratic civil processes.

Why Should Corporations Be Civil?

It is fashionable today to speak of "corporate social responsibility." Companies and ethical gurus alike speak of "corporate citizenship," and campaigners tend to focus on the tougher-sounding language of "accountability." Even the notion of sustainable development has begun to seep into corporate newspeak and strategic and operational planning, the latter albeit still for a small number of companies. Increasingly, public statements by senior managers of leading companies seek to establish a bridgehead between sound business and civil practice. It is notable that there has been a shift in the language of these statements, from:

- If being good is good for business, then we will be good; to

- It is good for business to be good; to

- It is necessary for business to be good.

Recent statements by BP superbly illustrate the third level, for example, "A good business should be both competitively successful *and* a force for good" (1998, 5).

Companies are increasingly under pressure from civil institutions to impose social and environmental standards along the economic pathways over which they have some leverage and control. This includes the spheres within their own organizational and legal boundaries—for example, in relation to their own staff—and increasingly down global production or supply chains. These pressures come in the form of activist campaigning that aims to damage companies' market performance by undermining their reputation (Zadek and Amalric 1998). These pressures are not linked in the main to public regulation, except insofar as the regulatory threat is one basis for successful campaigns. At the same time, this is not a matter of "voluntary" approaches in any meaningful sense. Rather, companies are responding to an organic "civil regulatory framework."

Of critical importance are the organizational and market changes associated with contemporary technological developments and the process of globalization. With respect to the former, we are seeing the most radical shift in the manner in which commerce is organized since Taylorian mechanics entered our organizational vocabulary. The downsizing and flattening of the main rump of most corporations, and the dispersal of many of their core functions into market networks (through, for example, franchising and outsourcing), all raise new demands with regard to quality at every level. The combination of technological developments in the area of computing and communications—and increasingly their relationship—has vastly reinforced the tendencies toward functional dispersal. At the same time, this has tightened market and cost-based competition in ways that place enormous pressure on the need to make these dispersed operations work at their peak of possible performance.

Globalization has both enabled and driven these tendencies further. Opportunities for cost reduction and accessing new markets through physical and cultural extensions of the business process have placed further pressures on the traditional business unit. For example, they have focused the source of value-added and profit on supply rather than production, and brand rather than product leadership. Globalization, however, has not been only the prerogative of the corporations. Civil groups previously focused on narrow local, or perhaps national, agendas have increasingly found voice at international levels. They have taken advantage of exactly the same set of technological and organizational shifts, and have seen how to challenge the globalized brands by "ethical intermediation"—for example, by showing people in Europe what a company is doing in Latin America. A "stakeholder-based company" that is able to build trust and integrity into its key relationships thereby lowers the cost of establishing and maintaining increasingly complex, physically dispersed networks of suppliers, franchisees, agents, and staff.

So How Does Civil Regulation Work?

The traditional thinking behind "civil regulation" is that the reputation of companies can be damaged by civil action to a degree that will affect their business performance. As the perceived ethical behavior of the company increases, so does its financial performance, because staff are more motivated, governments are more at ease in granting planning permission and in playing out other enabling actions, consumers buy its products, and investors are less nervous. The campaigns against Nike, Monsanto, Shell, Nestlé, and the many others of lesser fame have all basically had this relationship in mind: Hit them till it hurts, and then they will change for the better. Indeed, the facts seem to confirm this relationship, with a wide perception that companies like Nike and Shell have responded to civil campaigns.

There are, however, few facts to back this up. Even the very-high-profile civil campaigns against the likes of Shell, Nestlé, and Nike have had no demonstrable effect on share prices or dividends.[3] The exception to this is when the health of the consumer has been involved. Thus, the campaign against genetically modified organisms focused on the company Monsanto only became effective at the point that the headline became about "Frankenstein foods"—that is, a consumer health issue—rather than the previous development focus about the livelihoods of farming communities. However, companies are responding *as if* the financial markets cared. There are a number of possible explanations for this apparently divergent behavior. The first is that companies know better than the financial markets in predicting long-term performance. This would be the view of proponents of the view that "being good is good for business (in the long term)," such as Wheeler and Sillanpää (1997), Elkington (1998), Goyder (1961), and others.

The alternate view is that companies are overestimating the financial significance of reputation losses through perceptions of ethical misdemeanors. There are several reasons why this might be the case. The first is that the growth in importance of the level of intangible assets as a proportion of total assets in the last two decades has not been matched by tools and procedures for fully understanding how such intangibles develop and can best be managed. This has given considerable influence within companies to "reputation teams" dedicated to the protection of brand values, a key element of intangible assets. They may have in turn tended to overrate the importance of reputational value. If the argument that the financial implications of reputation gains or losses arising from perceived ethical shortfalls is correct, then the financial markets will eventually trade down companies that respond as if it is important, and so drive out such practices (Korten 1997).

How and why do companies respond to civil pressure? It is difficult to generalize from company to company, campaign to campaign, and country to country. Shell has over recent years underperformed financially, which explains why it is now moving to restructure, with many redundancies across Europe. BP, on the other hand, has performed rather well financially, and will seek to bring its positive outlook toward aspects of sustainable development to its recent acquisition, Amoco. Nike and Levi's have experienced a drop in earnings because of a maturing of their respective core product range, trainers and jeans. Levi's, on the other hand, may also be using the opportunity to adjust their long-term production patterns, such as moving production out of Europe and the United States. Monsanto's shares have performed poorly, possibly because the markets have not adequately rewarded the company's longer-term investment in research and development. Both of the "ethical business" icons emerging from the sixties—Ben & Jerry's Homemade (1996) and the Body Shop International—have fared poorly in financial terms in recent years, whilst maintaining a strong social performance in many respects (The Body Shop 1998). Coop Italia, on the other hand, and also one of the world's largest credit unions, VanCity Savings Credit, have performed well financially and socially at the same time (VanCity 1998). Many factors, clearly, affect the financial and other bottom lines and their relationship.

There is little convincing evidence that "doing good" per se delivers financial gains to business (Zadek and Chapman 1998). This does not mean that nonfinancial and financial performance are not related. Employee productivity, in particular, is strongly correlated to the ways in which employees are treated, and to a degree to ways in which the companies for which they work treat others. Several studies, similarly, have identified strong relationships between environmental and financial performance (Cohen et al. 1995). However, causality in these and other studies is ambiguous, and in some cases dual directional (see, for example, Waddock and Graves 1997).

In general, the quantitative data and related analysis is so full of *ifs* and *buts* that it yields little of statistical or other significance. Qualitative information seems, however, to yield more interesting perspectives, albeit of a statistically speculative nature. My recent review of the relevant European literature concluded

Being "socially responsible" *is* a determinant of financial success insofar as it reflects the ability of leadership companies to interpret, accommodate, and be vitalized by social values and demands, and reflects the need for other companies to follow the new market contours thus created (Zadek and Chapman 1998, 23).

That is, there is a positive link between social and financial performance, especially when looking at the increased relevance of intangible assets—specifically, reputation, brands, and knowledge networks—as a source of market value and competitive advantage (Zadek 1999). Leadership companies, which *by definition* mold markets in relation to their own competitive advantage, draw insight and energy from the societies within which they exist. Where these energies insistently focus on social and environmental "goods," leadership companies will respond by aligning their business behavior. In some cases, this will create new market conditions that other companies have to follow.

As civil society demands for corporate responsibility grow, leadership companies will seek both to satisfy these voices in the short term (risk-aversion strategy) and to draw from them in the longer term (innovation and market making). But the companies that respond in this fashion are in the main large multinationals, and it is these companies that convert such behavior into new mainstream market conditions. Where civil regulation works, therefore, it tends to strengthen the economic power of these companies by:

- Consolidating their positive position in the public eye (short-term effect)

- Affording them the best predictions of their future operating environment

- Giving them access to societal innovation and vitality, which they can then seek to translate into new market formations in which they dominate

The conclusion that campaigning and other actions to pressure companies to behave better builds corporate power confirms the worst fears of NGOs, which argue that corporate responsibility must ultimately mean a ceding of that power. At the same time, it opens up interesting strategic options for those organizations that seek social and environmental gains by using the economic power of multinationals to lever new products and services, associated markets, and corporate behavior.

Conclusion: So What about the NGOs?

Corporations can be civil, but not at the cost of significant competitive advantage. There is little point in creating virtuous but short-lived organizations. Corporations *can* be civil *if* this allows for the alchemy of using civil values to mold market values, products, and opportunities. The challenge to Nike and others is, at its roots, one that concerns trust. Intelligent, farsighted businesses may see a two-pronged strategy in building their civil credentials. The first is to respond to immediate pressure by adopting negotiated accountability standards and forming partnerships with those organizations that have the trust of key stakeholders. The second is to realign over the medium to long term their brands and overall reputation so that they are marks of quality in the social, ethical, and environmental domains of stakeholders' interests, concerns, and hopes. In some ways, this need not be a bad deal for civil society given appropriate standards of accounting, auditing, and reporting (Institute of Social and Ethical Accountability 1999). The implication of success of this two-stage strategy is that business, and specifically large corporations, will increasingly gain the trust of their stakeholders. However, this in turn means that NGOs may have a diminishing ability over time to challenge business behavior, because as one corporate executive pointed out, if the adoption of accountability standards works, NGOs will not be needed in the years to come.

Does this matter? If companies actually do make a real contribution in pursuing a sustainable development path, why should NGOs be required to sustain the moral high ground as a counterpoint to corporate power? It all depends in part on whether one believes that markets can indeed be remolded to civil interests and the cause of sustainable development. The facts about poverty, inequality, and environmental degeneration highlighted at the beginning of this chapter suggest that improved corporate social and environmental performance may not, within the current structure of markets, deliver the magnitude of "goods" required to right the current "bads." It is more likely that we will experience on current trends an oasis of good corporate behavior and outcomes that benefit a growing but nevertheless small percentage of the world's population. From this perspective, the engagement of the NGO community in the mainstream drive for corporate social responsibility is not bad, but is problematic. There will be a continued need to challenge the underlying structure of increasingly global markets, rather than relying solely on the ability of reformed leading companies to drive the markets that they can dominate toward better practices and outcomes.

The future challenge for the NGO community is how best to maximize the gains available by influencing the short- and long-term strategies of particular companies to secure new types of reputations and market positions, while at the same time increasing pressure on governments and international bodies to reform the global architecture that will be crucial in determining the ability of these and other parts of the business community to sustain and extend their positive contribution to sustainable development.

Notes

1. This report can be found at http://www.ft.com
2. In this, they explore three scenarios. One, named "GeoPolity," is the closest to an overarching framework for global governance, and it is roundly rejected as too inflexible for business to prosper.
3. Work commissioned independently from KPMG as part of work undertaken with the Danish pharmaceutical company Novo Nordisk suggested there was no measurable effect on share prices through civil campaigns against these companies.

5

Understanding NGOs from the Perspective of New Institutional Economics: A Case Study from Ghana

John Cameron

The relationship between the research literatures on nongovernmental organizations (NGOs) and formal economics, even in its development economics form, has been generally tense to the point of hostility. But there is now a need for a more positive engagement as NGOs seek better to understand the economics of their roles in both micro-level income-generating activities and macro-level economic strategy advocacy. This chapter introduces some basic themes of the new instititutional economics (NIE) and uses a case study of an NGO population project in Ghana to illustrate the application of NIE to furthering understanding of NGOs and their activities.

The engagement of development economics with NIE can be dated from the edition of *World Development* dedicated to "The Role of Institutions in Economic Development" (North 1989). The edition included an article by Douglas North, the person with the best claim to being the founder of NIE (North 1990), as did a later collection of writings specifically dedicated to examining the relationship between NIE and development (Harriss et al. 1997).

The essential aspects of broad-ranging NIE that have attracted development economists can be summarized as follows:

- NIE assumes that the operation of market forces has to be understood in a long-term, institutional context in which institutions are held together by the drive to avoid transaction costs associated with frequent recontracting.

- NIE assumes that changing institutions can have high transitional costs—financial, cultural, and psychological.

- NIE is compatible with micro-level information-deficiency models of institutional behavior, including bounded rationality, public goods, and risk and uncertainty moral-hazard propositions. Such models undermine neoclassical economics' analytical conclusions on natural laws of efficiency, equity, and stability properties of open market forces. Instead, they focus on how entitlements are institutionally secured or eroded in the face of unexpected pressures on livelihoods.

On the other hand, there are concerns that the formal underpinnings of NIE can be close to neoclassical economics and its associated "end of history" literature (Brett 1993, 275). Some writers in NIE can appear very close to neoclassical economics in their willingness to assume market-price-driven, individual-utility-maximizing motivations as both universal and desirable. NIE can be timid in not engaging with coercive power and highly unequal distributions and uses rather benign-games, theoretic-style approaches to conflictual relationships.

On balance, however, there has been a positive interest by development economists in NIE in the last decade. This positive interest needs to be understood in the context of the recent besieged history of development economics. Mainstream development economics as it had developed since 1945 came under vigorous attack from neoclassical economists in the early 1980s for its lack of theoretical rigor (Lal 1983). Thinking about economic development was also particularly vulnerable to the widespread loss of confidence in Marxian economic analysis in the 1980s; Marxian thinking had been highly influential in development economics from the 1950s. The 1980s were marked by a great deal of agonizing about whether development economics had any distinctive identity, although a concern with institutional factors was a significant rallying point (Bruton 1985).

Some popular credibility was regained for development economics as a distinctive way of thinking about economics with the publication of *Adjustment with a Human Face* (Cornia et al. 1987), although Samir Amin (1974, 1976) and Amartya Sen (1987, 1989) had done much to keep an alternative view alive throughout the 1980s. The "adjustment with a human face" pragmatic critique of the outcomes of structural adjustment policies in Latin America, sub-Saharan Africa, and parts of Asia threw some doubt on the equity and long-term efficiency gains from freeing market forces predicted by some neoclassical economists. Also, at about the same time, claims by neoclassical economists that the "Asian Tigers" were examples of simple free market successes were widely questioned (Wade 1990).

Around 1990, development economics was finding a distinctive voice again with a strong institutionalist accent and was seeking conceptual frameworks capable of engaging with a critique of neoclassical economics in theory and practice. NIE was a clear candidate for empathetic attention at this moment in the history of development economics. The implications of NIE go beyond formal economics and into wider development thinking, giving insights into themes that can also be found in much of the NGO literature:

- *Change*. Much thinking about development has tended to operate with a model of rapid economic growth and/or distributional shifts in which radically changing institutions play a vital role. NIE suggests that institutions have considerable durability and path dependence because of high perceived costs of change by significant interest groups. Future development thinking needs to include explicit models of the nature and distribution of transition costs as well as the desirability of institutional changes.

- *Sovereignty*: Much development thinking has tended to emphasize the sovereign state as the primary institution in terms of decision making. NIE confirms the need for a much broader vision of institutions at all levels of aggregation, each with its own element of sovereignty and peculiar pattern of transaction costs that hold them together. Development thinking needs to include all institutions, including civil society's, and understand how they operate to condition the operation of market forces.

- *Developmental agency*: Much development economics has tended to assume that state institutions are the essentially, or at least potentially, benign agencies of progress. NIE can be useful in introducing questions about the state, without dismissing it as a developmental agency, as is the tendency in neoclassical economics. Future development thinking must aim for the inclusion of a potential for both developmentally malign and benign behavior by state—as well as all other—institutions in terms of creating and securing entitlements.

- *Relationship to other disciplines*: Development thinking has tended to be economistic in causal focus. NIE explicitly acknowledges the contributions of other disciplines, notably anthropology and history.

- *Observation and evaluation*: NIE is empirically consistent with the widely acknowledged need in the NGO sector to collect both quantitative and qualitative information (especially on relationships, valuations, motivations, and aspirations) to facilitate sensitive adjustments to changing circumstances.

Overall, NIE creates an intellectual space in its general approach to development where development economics and NGO thinking can engage in a mutually beneficial dialogue. Early in the 1990s, a potential connection between the NIE and NGO literatures was spotted by Teddy Brett. He examined the proposition that NGOs are a necessary alternative form of institution in any healthy society. But he is concerned that NIE does not provide a clear rationale for assessing the comparative effectiveness of such institutions compared with those of the state and open market forces (Brett 1993). However, the case that the voluntary sector as a whole cannot be unambiguously justified in NIE terms does not mean that NIE is not useful in comparing between NGOs and understanding the processes of change particular NGOs are undergoing in a specific context.

NIE has a potentially close relationship to current debates close to the NGO literature about social capital. These debates center on the forms and degrees of trust that exist in a society. Concern with trust logically leads to concern with the concept of uncertainty as a social phenomenon. Uncertainty and associated insecurity can help explain why we value entitlements, maintain institutions to avoid uncertain transactions costs, and resist change to avoid uncertain transition costs. Every society has ways of distributing the responsibility for uncertainty between agents/institutions. Uncertainties go well beyond the much explored microeconomics of principal-agent, game playing, zero-sum moral hazard, but pervade the whole of the economy, touching all agents and institutions. Much of a society's social capital in terms of confidence in contracting and people's willingness to accept or reject the distribution of uncertainty exists on the institutional frontier, where cultural understanding and civil society, politics and the state, and economics and open market forces intersect.

NGOs are institutions that work on this frontier and can be seen as wishing to challenge and change the distribution of uncertainty in favor of groups of people who face disproportionate threats to their physical and psychological well-being and livelihoods from sources beyond their control. The following case study is an attempt to use this approach to understand the work of one NGO in Ghana.

A Case Study of Population Policy in Ghana

Population policy is an area in which civil society institutions, state institutions, and market forces institutions meet in a complex pattern of institutional relationships. At the center of this pattern are the fundamental uncertainties associated with human fertility for the individual woman and those claiming an institutional interest in her sexuality.

In Ghana, the central NGO in the population field in 1992 was the Planned Parenthood Association of Ghana (PPAG) (Cameron 1992). The PPAG was established in 1967. The organization became a full member of the International Planned Parenthood Federation (IPPF) in 1969 and, in the same year, the government of Ghana formally recognized PPAG's contribution to national population policy in a population strategy document. During the 1970s and early 1980s, PPAG was a leading national NGO institution. Initiatives were taken in community-based distribution, male motivation, and family life education alongside more conventional static service delivery outlets and women's development activities. PPAG performance was considered as a shining example in a rather lackluster period for population policy in sub-Saharan Africa.

In the mid-1980s, PPAG drifted into an institutional crisis at the national level. Major reorganizational recommendations of the IPPF Overall Program Evaluation and Management Audit (including the appointment of a new executive director) were implemented in 1990. Simultaneously, two significant initiatives drawing on funding originating in the World Bank and the Japanese Development Assistance Program moved into active implementation phases.

The Japanese-funded initiative through the Japanese Organization for International Cooperation in Family Planning (JOICFP) (Project 87/1, "Integrated Family Planning, Nutrition, and Parasite Control Pilot Project" in the PPAG project listing) was geographically concentrated close to Accra and became a high-profile, prestigious venture. The World Bank-funded initiative (a further development within Project 74/2, "Community Based Distribution of Family Planning Services" in the PPAG project listing) was national in coverage. Thus PPAG came into the 1990s with new management at the national level, a "model" project close to the capital, and additional resources for regional staff to expand outreach. The handling of the changing pattern of transition and transaction costs had become crucial issues. In addition to the employed staff, who were all full-time, PPAG's human resource base included formal volunteers and fast-growing numbers of community-based development associations (CBDAs). Less formally associated with PPAG were the many people who served on community and workplace steering groups for particular PPAG activities.

By the early 1990s, PPAG had grouped eight "projects" into three "strategies." The projects originated before the strategies, and only one project had been added since 1980. In effect, the projects had become programs or broad spheres of activity with considerable room for adjustment on an ad hoc basis. The name project survived, but only in name; nevertheless, the term project will be used here in line with PPAG documentation. The three strategies as stated in the project document (PPAG 1992,23) are:

1. Intensify information, education, and communication (IEC) activities to increase knowledge and acceptance of family planning among selected groups, especially in the rural areas.

2. Ensure wider availability and easy accessibility of quality family planning services to men and women in the reproductive age, especially in rural areas.

3. Improve the capacity of the staff and volunteers of the association in Ghana to play its stated role.

All three strategies can be seen within the NIE perspective as institution-building efforts aimed at reducing uncertainty and transaction costs for clients and meeting associated transition costs for both staff and volunteers.

In the evaluation of the project, it became clear that transaction costs were reduced through formal and informal IEC and contraceptive distribution being carried out simultaneously (Cameron 1992). Contacts between staff and between staff and volunteers appeared sufficiently informal that mutual informing and training for greater management effectiveness was a continuing, in-service process to reduce transition costs. Flexibility and responsiveness—which are often considered two of the greatest virtues of NGOs—were observed in PPAG and represented an outcome of efforts to keep transaction costs low and accept transition costs.

However, in more orthodox, logical-framework planning terms, the three "strategic" statements corresponded more to the purpose or effect level of analysis rather than the goal or impact level. There was no evidence of systematic efforts by PPAG to connect immediate activities to wider development objectives. This lack of systematic effort could be restricting both advocacy for wider institutional change and understanding of impact on clients of the uncertainties surrounding fertility. Volunteers appeared to accept that efforts to increase contraceptive use were self-evidently desirable on the grounds of economic development and health (maternal and child health or sexually transmitted diseases) or human rights. This wide range of informal objectives obstructed integrated planning at national and regional levels but allowed staff and volunteers to bring commitment to PPAG from a variety of directions. No clear, shared vision of transition was present.

During the evaluation, discussions with PPAG staff and volunteers highlighted the importance of PPAG adopting an innovative, experimental, responsive, and open approach to activity selection and implementation. Methods and processes appeared to be as important as defining final impact objectives. This emphasis contributed to an inability in PPAG to define a situation in which an activity reached a cost-effectiveness or performance indicator frontier. The resulting uncertainty inhibited reducing or withdrawing inputs from existing activities and transfers to new activities. The uncertainty over developmental goals for PPAG meant that any assessment of achievements associated with a transition to meet its own wider objectives was bound to be fragmented. Transition costs were ill specified and their distribution unclear.

An interesting example of institutional change that affected the pattern of uncertainty over client entitlements was observed in a localized project in nine villages close to Accra that followed a model designed by JOICFP. The project's entry point was the control of infection from intestinal parasites through a mixture of curative health and community environmental health measures. Closely associated with these activities were the improvement of maternal-child health services, family planning advice and contraceptive provision, and income-generating activities. During the evaluation, JOICFP appeared qualitatively satisfied with the progress of the project, and the quantitative indicators on infestation decline and contraceptive distribution were impressive. Field visits to three participating villages suggested an impressively high level of activity (Cameron 1992). A difference in forms of income generation appeared to arise from the differing economies of the villages and the consequent differences in the village steering committees. Thus, the project showed some responsiveness to local entitlement patterns, though not necessarily with a strong poverty impact. The JOICFP inputs in kind (bicycles, sewing machines, training shoes) were not directly inappropriate, but there was no evidence that PPAG had considered the indirect effects or sustainability of these unsolicited gifts.

It is difficult to avoid the conclusion that PPAG proved to be an excellent implementing institution for JOICFP but did not in the end put its own stamp on the project. Arguably, the project activities all lay well within the remit of PPAG, including clinic provision and use of CBDAs, but the question remained of whether PPAG was behaving as an active institutional partner, informing JOICFP of local felt needs and entitlement structures and conditions for sustainability and replicability. In terms of market forces and PPAG as an institution, the self-funding element of PPAG derived overwhelmingly from sales of services, and within that, from sales of contraceptives (more than 80 percent of total self-funding in the 1992 budget). Price elasticities of demand were not known, but a major constraint on any increase in prices was not on the demand side but on the supply side, because Ministry of Health (MOH) prices for contraceptives were lower than those charged by PPAG. Any movement toward greater fundraising would clearly require better information on demand-side price sensitivities and supply-side coordination between MOH-led institutionalized social marketing and PPAG use of open market forces.

The project had expanded, but with relatively little innovation displayed. NIE would suggest that this may be an outcome of a tendency to become locked into existing activities to reduce transaction and transition costs, partially because of the absence of clear objectives as a basis for rigorous comparative evaluation. This trend can also be associated with the move toward decentralization. Strong regional and community-based commitments can develop and exercise effective vetoes over the project's eventual withdrawal from a locality. In this way, the objectives of decentralization and the reduction of transaction costs can ultimately conflict with the objective of being experimental and innovative and accepting associated transition costs.

In terms of entitlements to quality service for clients to PPAG as an institution, staff interviewed in PPAG were confident that they set high standards in client care both in PPAG clinics and through their supervision of CBDAs. The services emphasized nonjudgmental counseling and privacy and confidentiality as strong features of the PPAG approach, ensuring greater certainty for clients. The orientation and training given to MOH staff (279 MOH nurses and paramedical staff and medical students were reported by PPAG to have received orientation or training in PPAG clinics in 1991) may have played a significant role in spreading good practices. If this was the case, then explicit emphasis could, in the future, be placed on the role of PPAG clinics as clearly replicable models for good practice in staff/client relations and the need to induct MOH staff into such practices. From this perspective, a wide dispersal of PPAG clinics in areas served by MOH to ensure access for MOH staff, as much as for clients, would increase the institutional dissemination of good practices, reducing uncertainty over quality of service for clients.

PPAG was found to be effective in providing quality of service at the point of client contact but not so effective in providing quantity-of-service points. It was therefore recommended that greater effectiveness could be achieved by a mix of placing clinics in underserved communities and spreading clinics in served areas to maximize impact on MOH staff. To maximize effectiveness, PPAG could make even greater efforts to bring MOH staff into clinics to observe good practices and reduce both transaction costs in the relationship between PPAG and MOH and transition costs for MOH. PPAG staff interviewed saw their primary effectiveness as lying primarily in accepting uncertainty involved in innovative outreach on the frontier of conventional IEC activities, interacting with communities and individuals while simultaneously assuring contraceptive availability. Field visits to four PPAG activities with differing entry points and discussions with three CBDAs showed PPAG at a high level of technical effectiveness in this kind of activity, achieving both breadth and depth of positive contact founded on mutual respect between communities and PPAG staff.

However, to be considered fully effective in terms of national family planning provision, PPAG needed to be able to demonstrate that its innovations were institutionally sustainable and replicable. A considerable success by these criteria could be seen in the MOH and World Bank commitments to expand massively the CBDA system using the PPAG model developed in the late 1980s. MOH and the United Nations Family Planning Association (UNFPA) were considering even further expansion toward national coverage. This can be seen as an example of PPAG arriving at an attractive formula through experimentation and accepting uncertainty. Finally, it was unlikely that PPAG had been or could be an effective innovator in the field of income generation for women as an entry point for family planning, as the transition costs into such activities would be high, no matter how much such activities were needed and how positive the relationships created. Technically and financially, PPAG was not equipped for a transition to such activities.

It was hard not to be struck by the widespread view among PPAG field staff—and the people they worked among—that there are fast-changing attitudes in Ghana, which may be leading toward new underlying conditions for population policy. One aspect of this change is the growing perception that rural households have reached the extensive margin of cultivable land and that this is bringing a fundamental change in entitlement patterns. Another is the harsh lesson of the economic crisis of the 1980s, with loss of wage and salaried work opportunities. These factors had decreased confidence in the economic future for additional children. Rising costs to parents of education and health care are also encouraging contraceptive use. Also, while women's economic status has probably suffered alongside men's during the 1980s, there has been a systematic, nationwide effort to politicize women's position, downplaying reproductive roles.

There were severe conditions of uncertainty surrounding contraceptive use, but increasing access to quality services based on local outreach may produce rapid change by further reducing transaction, and transition costs may be a necessary and sufficient condition for a breakthrough in many communities. However, such a breakthrough would still be uneven spatially and socially. Some communities, many women, and particular age groups may continue to lag behind in terms of contraceptive use, especially if judgmental attitudes inhibit contact with service outlets. Acceptance and use of contraceptive devices by substantial groups in Ghana will not remove the issue of high fertility rates for many women and possibly Ghana as a whole. In addition, nonmarital sex, sexually transmitted diseases, HIV prevalence, and undesired pregnancies and induced abortions (especially among younger unmarried women) are topics that are difficult to face in any society, and Ghana is no exception—cultural transition costs are high.

PPAG as an institution had a large amount of grassroots experience in the issues around sexuality and contraception across Ghanaian society. The challenge for PPAG was to turn this knowledge into effective advocacy in the policy process. There was an opportunity to turn that credibility into policy advocacy. PPAG needed to key into the current political changes and consider how to turn that experience and credibility into relevant and appropriate government policy. PPAG stood aside from advocacy in the 1980s and ploughed its own furrow in a small number of fields, often very effectively, in order to avoid the uncertain political transition costs to an advocacy role.

This brief case study highlights the ways in which an application of the principles of NIE helps to focus understanding on broadly defined transaction costs between institutions. It also asks how the uncertainty of innovating is distributed between institutions and how the costs of transition to a new family planning regime are to be met. PPAG as an institution can be seen from these perspectives as a key institution, despite its small size relative to the government program.

Conclusion

An NIE perspective provides a useful set of insights on the case study, which demonstrates the importance of institutions that exist on the frontiers between civil society, the state, and markets. NGOs work in the institutional space in this triangle. The NGO ideal position is as a pure civil society institution, negotiating with both market and state institutions to ensure the sustainability of those civil society institutions most conducive to increasing the certainty of livelihoods for the most vulnerable.

However, there are pressures on NGOs to move away from the civil society vertex and toward the state vertex (cooption) or the market vertex (commercialization). An NIE perspective would see NGOs as institutions with a potential role to play in transforming society, but vulnerable to cooption and commercialization as the two competing dominant institutional models. NGOs are not only an important form of institution in themselves with particular patterns of costs, but are also often involved in the creation of institutions that better represent their target groups.

The economic focus of NIE is on transition and transaction costs and uncertain entitlements. NGOs both experience internally and change externally these costs and uncertainties. The impact of NGO activities can be assessed through how they change such costs and uncertainties for their target groups.

The impact of NGO activities on the distribution of uncertainty and in-security is an NIE consideration. NGOs can play a role in reducing the uncertainty experienced by target groups. Although as the total uncertainty in all societies seems to be close to a zero-sum game (Furlong and Cartmel 1997), the reduction of uncertainty for the target groups will tend to increase uncertainty for other groups and institutions in civil society, government and multilateral agencies, commercial institutions, and NGOs themselves.

6

Learning for Growth: Organizational Learning in South Asian NGOs

John Hailey

Learning and knowledge management are crucial capacities for any non-governmental organization (NGO) expecting to survive and thrive in the uncertain development environment of the new millennium. Knowledge is an essential component of effective growth. Creating the learning organization is increasingly seen as being synonymous with capacity building, organization development, and managing change. There are many NGOs that claim to be "learning organizations," but how they promote shared learning and engage their staff in new learning is still unclear. Recent research with NGOs in Bangladesh, India, and Pakistan confirms the important role of organizational learning in building capacity and facilitating change. However, this research also suggests that effective learning is a hard-won goal that depends as much on consensual, participative processes as on management-endorsed training and research initiatives or human resource management systems.

This chapter draws on detailed case studies of the management and organizational issues faced by growing South Asian NGOs. This study was part of a program of research commissioned by the Aga Khan Foundation Canada into the work of South Asian NGOs over the last thirty years. Detailed case studies were prepared on NGOs such as the Bangladesh Rural Advancement Committee (BRAC) and Proshika in Bangladesh; Aga Khan Rural Support Program (AKRSP), the Bharatiya Agro Industries Foundation (BAIF), and Sadguru in India; and AKRSP, the International Union for the Conservation of Nature, the Sarhad Rural Support Corporation, and Sungi in Pakistan. Each case study was prepared by local researchers and based on a wide range of interviews and archival sources. I undertook follow-up interviews with senior NGO staff and was part of an international steering committee established to analyze the overall findings (Smillie and Hailey 2000).

The Learning NGO

The importance of learning as a key organizational capacity has become increasingly apparent in the changing, unpredictable economic and political environment of the 1990s. Learning allows organizations to adapt continuously to an unpredictable future. The survival and success of any organization operating in any turbulent environment is dependent on its rate of learning being equal to or greater than the rate of change in its external environment (Revens 1983). The reality for most NGOs is that the economic and political environment in which they operate is increasingly complex and unpredictable, and that organizational learning and knowledge management is essential if they are to expand and adapt to the changing environment in which they work (Britton 1998). Michael Edwards (1997) concluded a review of organizational learning in NGOs by suggesting that they needed to learn more effectively if they are to survive, and Alan Fowler (1997,64) succinctly noted that unless NGOs learn, "they are destined for insignificance."

The 1990s have been called the decade of the learning organization. Its most articulate advocate, Peter Senge (1990), added systems thinking to the familiar learning disciplines of personal mastery, mental models, building of shared vision, and team learning. His book, *The Fifth Discipline*, has been crucial in shaping our understanding of the concept of the learning organization—in particular, the concept that learning commonly results in a creative process of change that can transform an organization. Senge therefore defines the learning organization as one that is continuously expanding its capacity to create its future. Research into voluntary organizations and nonprofits as learning organizations reflects similar characteristics, and a commonly cited definition of a nonprofit learning organization is one that "actively incorporates the experience and knowledge of its members and partners through the development of practices, policies, procedures, and systems in ways which continuously improve its ability to set goals, satisfy stakeholders, develop its practice, value and develop its people and achieve its missions with its constituency" (Britton 1998, 3).

There is an underlying acceptance among most commentators that learning and change is a product of the creative and adaptive interaction between a set of complex and critical processes operating within an uncertain external environment. For the staff of NGOs working with limited resources in difficult and unstable environments, this has a particular resonance. David Korten (1980) concluded that the success of many NGOs depended on their ability to learn from both the local communities and beneficiaries with whom they worked. However, recent evidence suggests that NGOs suffer from inherent structural constraints that militate against shared learning. Ian Smillie

(1995, 158) concludes that the "inability to learn and remember is a widespread failing of the development community as a whole." This is partly because there is little incentive to disseminate positive development lessons, and partly because the threat of alienating donors or fueling critics means there are powerful reasons to conceal and forget the negative lessons. Alan Fowler suggests that many NGOs have a "limited capacity to learn, adapt, and continuously improve the quality of what they do" and is concerned how few NGOs see error as a source of learning or how few staff can "relate to failure in a positive way" (Fowler 1997, 64).

In summary, most contemporary commentators argue that developing an organization's capacity to learn from experience and research is key to its future effectiveness. Organizational learning is synonymous with capacity building and organization development. The term *the learning organization* has arguably become a metaphor for managing change. Thus, both mainstream organizational theorists and the evidence from South Asian NGOs would suggest that learning and investment in learning processes is a key characteristic of any organization undergoing change in an uncertain economic and political environment. However, this begs the questions, how do NGOs develop the capacity to learn, and how do they promote and encourage such learning among their staff?

One way of answering this is to assess whether organizational learning is the product of informal, participative processes led by the staff or the result of formal learning and training systems and structures introduced by the management. This reflects a wider theoretical debate in the management literature and among organizational theorists as to whether organizations are more effectively managed through formal strategies and management systems (Child 1984; Beer et al. 1984) or whether managers should rely more on informal, consensual processes to motivate staff, improve performance, and effect change (Argyris 1989; Senge 1990).

On one hand, there is a perception that organizations need formal training and staff development strategies in order to ensure continuity and quality in times of rapid change and unpredictability. On the other hand, there is a belief that unless employees voluntarily consent to the espoused values and work practice, they will never be committed to the goals and objectives of the organization. Very crudely, this debate can be reduced to an argument over the merits of control or consent as the most effective approach to managing change, and over which strategy is most effective at promoting organizational learning. The purpose of this chapter is to assess the extent to which NGO learning is the product of an informal consensual, participative process or of a more formal system of management-endorsed learning.

Consensual Learning

This research into the management of nine South Asian NGOs has high-lighted the importance of both learning by doing and the role of personal engagement, dialogue, and participation in helping NGOs learn from a variety of different sources. These informal, unstructured processes lie at the heart of the way many NGOs learn. The ethos of learning by doing and action learning has been central to shaping the way they work and learn.

Action Learning and Community Dialogue

This process of listening and learning has been central to the way many of these NGOs work. Sadguru, for example, has worked with the local tribal communities in Eastern Gujerat, India, since 1974. Its founders, Harnath and Sharmistha Jagawat, spent the first year of the organization's existence walking as many as 30 kilometers a day in order to meet local people, listen to their concerns, and discuss how best to meet their needs. Harnath Jagawat claims that their success as a development agency comes "from learning from our experiences, from feedback from the communities, and from continuous appraisals by external consultants and academics."

Virtually all the NGOs studied relied on similar village-based processes to help internal learning and develop their understanding of the needs of local communities. This is well exemplified in the case of two Pakistani NGOs, Sungi and AKRSP. The staff of Sungi, for instance, identified that their most valuable learning came through constant interactions with local communities, village or cluster-based dialogues, and other participatory processes. In the early years of AKRSP (Pakistan), most early staff training took place through village dialogues between staff and local people. These discussions were recorded and used as the basis for future interventions. But as the organization grew and training needs became more sophisticated, AKRSP became more reliant on formal courses and structured training initiatives. However, staff still look back on these village dialogues as the most effective training they received. Not only did it give them practical insights, but it also led to the creation of shared understanding, a strong team spirit, and a more integrated approach to their work.

Rapid growth has also affected BRAC's ability to learn in partnership with local communities. For example, in an effort to expand the scope and impact of its health programs, staff were "mobilized with motorbikes." However, they were so focused on meeting project objectives and completing their task quickly "by dashing around the countryside" on these new motorbikes that they did not find time to sit and talk with local people. It was soon apparent that "when we walked and went by bicycle, we did much better," and so BRAC reintroduced slower, time-consuming, but more effective ways of delivering health services to local communities. Although the immediacy and relevance of action learning and community dialogue are clearly apparent, it is all too often an *ad hoc* process that is rarely documented or shared at an institutional level. The challenge for many NGOs is how to promote institution-wide consensual participative learning.

Institutional Learning

For many NGOs, institutional learning is also a product of internal processes and developing institutional memory. As Qazi Faruque Ahmed, president of Proshika, Bangladesh, notes

If I, as the head of the organization, had to remember everything, then probably there wouldn't be much remembered. But if you use participation in the decision-making process, then there is much more chance of institutional memory.

Consequently, Proshika has established internal processes to generate feedback and dialogue. It holds quarterly meetings that 200 or so senior staff attend to share learning and review current performance. Similarly, Sadguru holds monthly meetings attended by everyone from drivers and peons to the senior management team to review progress and provide feedback. However, many NGO managers have voiced their concern that such meetings are becoming unwieldy fora with little time for dialogue, critical questioning, reflection, or learning. Sadguru's Harnath Jagawat questions their value and is concerned that they have become a ritual with little constructive questioning and insufficient involvement of junior staff.

Despite these concerns, most NGOs in our sample recognize the importance of personal contact and so use a mix of meetings, retreats, workshops, and seminars to share learning and disseminate new thinking. Some, such as BAIF in India, actively encouraged cross-functional learning by consciously moving staff around the organization. Their policy of transferring staff from research posts to field positions, from single programs to multiple programs, and from specialist to management positions has generated greater awareness across programs and generally enhanced learning in the organization. There is also an awareness that they need to analyze and assimilate past mistakes. Barry Underwood, chief executive of AKRSP (India), talks of the importance of "embracing one's mistakes, and to learn from them," and in the process creating a culture that accepts criticism. In the same vein, one of the senior staff at AKRSP (Pakistan) commented that "If an organization can't experiment and innovate, the spirit of change finishes." Thus, despite Alan Fowler's concern that many NGOs fail to embrace mistakes as a source of learning, the evidence in this study is that NGOs espouse the idea that experimentation, mistakes, and failures are part of the ongoing learning process. As F. H. Abed, director of BRAC, commented, "Little failures are, of course, inherent in any successful program. You must accept that, for they are part of the learning process."

Another challenge facing bigger NGOs that recruit large numbers of new staff each year is how to help recruits to "unlearn and relearn," and so question their preconceptions about development. This is particularly true for new specialist or management staff coming from the educated, committed middle class, who see issues through the lens of a university graduate rather than a villager. BRAC's director of training, Dr. Samdani, argues that any induction training for new recruits must include a "process of unlearning and relearning." This implies creating a new kind of learning environment and using new information in innovative ways so that recruits develop new skills and attitudes and fundamentally modify their behavior and thinking patterns.

NGOs learn through a variety of informal processes. They learn through community meetings, dialogue, and discussions. They also learn from the work of other NGOs, from their mistakes, and through experimentation. However, more detailed analysis of the evidence from the case studies suggests that as these organizations grow, these informal processes are not able to generate the diversity of learning needed to meet the demands of new staff and the challenges of an unpredictable environment. It is debatable whether consensual, participative processes are really able to develop the analytical or reflective capacity and learning competencies needed to cope with change. The evidence from these case studies is that informal processes need the support of formal training structures, management systems, research, and information—disseminating mechanisms to ensure that learning becomes genuinely embedded throughout the organization.

Formal Learning Processes

One of the challenges for any organization is how it shares and disseminates its knowledge and learning among a broad range of staff. Ian Smillie argues that this is particularly important for NGOs because development is in essence a knowledge-based process:

Knowing what works and why is essential to the success of NGOs, yet knowing what does not work is equally important. Knowledge involves awareness, memory and familiarity that develops with experience and learning (Smillie 1995, 158).

NGOs increasingly appreciate that knowledge and the dissemination of knowledge and learning are key to their effectiveness and survival. NGOs in South Asia have dramatically increased their investment in formal training, research, and information systems. AKRSP, BAIF, BRAC, and Proshika have all expanded their specialist research departments. Both Sadguru and BAIF have opened large purpose-built training centers in the last three years. Both BRAC and Proshika have increased their training capacity sufficiently so that together they can train nearly a million people a year. Clearly these NGOs see formal processes of training and analysis as an essential part of their learning toolkit.

Training: A Strategic Instrument

Proshika sees development education as essential to its strategy of integrating its programs and acting as a link between its various development activities. The fact that in one year nearly half a million people attended Proshika's training programs not only reflects the scale of their activities, but also the importance that it places on training and learning. BRAC's preoccupation with staff development and training has also been central to the way it operates. Part of the remit of its training division is to ensure that lack of skills and management competencies do not act as a constraint on BRAC's efforts to grow. Indeed, training is largely seen as a strategic instrument to facilitate program development. BRAC has long acknowledged the importance of training and learning in its success, and sets aside 7 percent of its total salary budget for staff development alone. In physical terms, this has resulted in the creation of twelve training and resource centers, which offer courses to both BRAC employees and the staff of other NGOs.

There is a growing recognition that new management systems can reinforce learning and ensure that training results in increased productivity and improved performance. All the NGOs in the sample had introduced some form of performance incentives, new staff appraisal schemes, mentoring, and more sophisticated career planning procedures. BRAC's oral rehydration therapy program well demonstrates the way financial incentives and rigorous monitoring of post-training performance can be used to promote new learning and enhance productivity at field level. This program was intended to spread new approaches to treating diarrhea among rural families. BRAC had been at the forefront of preparing simple, cheap, but effective and user-friendly oral rehydration therapies that could be used to treat the diarrhea that all too often proved fatal for young children. Oral replacement workers

(ORWs) were recruited to train local women how to prepare and use the necessary salt-gur solution. This depended in part on the success of the ORWs to train local women.

In an effort to motivate ORWs and ensure effective transfer of learning, a financial incentive scheme was introduced. The calculation of ORWs salaries was based on the response of 10 percent of those trained to ten standard questions. The more questions a mother could answer the higher the incentive payment to the ORW. This scheme depended on an objective monitoring of the work of the ORWs, and regular visits by monitors to women who had received training in the last month. As the program developed, one of the main concerns was that a third of those who had undergone oral rehydration therapy training failed to remember accurately the details of the mix for the rehydration solution. This was a disappointing result, so BRAC decided to address the issue through more systematic follow-up and further refresher training for the ORWs. The new initiatives paid dividends, and within two years, 90 percent of those evaluated twelve months after the training could properly prepare the salt-gur solution (Mushtaque et al. 1996, 87). The use of incentives and follow-up monitoring exemplify the application of contemporary human resource management strategies to enhance learning and increase productivity. Experience suggests that it is not enough merely to rely on open-ended participative processes in the hope that staff will become sufficiently engaged in new learning. NGOs are becoming more managerial in the way that they use systematic measures of performance to assess training needs and reward performance.

Research and Learning

Knowledge and learning are inextricably linked with the availability of accurate information, effective data-filtering systems, and access to relevant analysis. Knowledge is as much the product of information, feedback, and analysis as it is of experience and process. Consequently, successful NGOs have made a conscious decision to invest in research, document learning, and see evaluation as part of the ongoing feedback process that leads to new learning. BAIF, for example, believes that development without research is outdated, and that the opposite is also true, research without development is irrelevant. Experience has taught Proshika to complement action learning and practical experience with formal training and research. Its research and demonstration project is attached to the Central Training Center at Koitta to help ensure that research findings are incorporated in training programs. The philosophy of BRAC is that "deep" learning only takes place through "action research." However, although this may be carried out by program staff as part of their daily activities, it is rarely written up, systematically documented, or disseminated. Consequently, there is more targeted support for systematic, rigorous research, as reflected in the way the number of researchers in its research and evaluation department quadrupled between 1990 and 1997.

Formal evaluations are seen as part of the research process in the way they provide longitudinal feedback and offer alternative insights into performance and impact. A program of regular self-assessment and evaluation helps organizations to compare performance over time, ensure records are updated, and learn from past experience. Sungi, for example, before a formal donor evaluation by NOVIB in 1997, undertook its own self-assessment exercise that partly preempted the conclusions of the external evaluation and contributed to a new four-year plan. AKRSP (India) established a separate research and monitoring team in Ahmedabad to undertake in-house research. One of its more innovative initiatives has been to introduce "significant change documentation" to enable individuals to analyze and reflect on their work by recording and reviewing significant events and subsequent changes. NGOs are experimenting with such innovative approaches to assessing work practices, monitoring performance, and evaluating lessons learned, with the intention of systematizing the use and documentation of experience and personal insights. The logic is that organization-wide learning is dependent on the systematic recording and dissemination of such analysis and research.

Conclusion

This chapter has highlighted the role of learning in determining the ability of NGOs to grow and thrive, as well as the fact that organizational learning is inherently associated with organizational development and NGO capacity building. Organizational learning must be seen as a dynamic process that integrates informal processes with more formal structures and systems. The informal processes are those associated with participative dialogue and learning by doing, whereas the more formal inputs are those associated with training courses, seminars, commissioned research, evaluations, documentation, and reporting systems, as well as such human resource management levers as incentives and performance appraisal. The case studies also suggest that the larger NGOs in the sample are actively investing in the development of key learning competencies. These include the ability to filter data and edit information; the analytical skills to deconstruct and reflect on past experience; archival and record management; managing information technology systems and websites; and the capacity to marshal and disseminate information and research in a manner that is appropriate to the needs of staff, donors, and the communities in which they work.

The evidence from these case studies is that the systematic use of formal management-endorsed learning systems is not a management plot to inculcate specific values, limit dissent, dictate attitudes, or shape behavior. Instead, NGO managers have introduced such systems in response to the difficulties of disseminating learning of consistent quality and relevance in a timely and accessible manner throughout increasingly complex organizational structures. As a result, they have consciously invested in such formal processes to develop the capacity of the organization to learn and remember. They are also beginning to appreciate the strategic importance of such processes, and that one of their core competencies is their ability to promote learning and manage knowledge. This gives them an inimitable advantage over other development agencies or government departments, and in turn greater control over their own strategic destiny.

It is also clear from analysis of the case studies that such processes do not work in a vacuum. Organizations scan the external environment for new ideas. F. H. Abed frankly admits he is an "unashamed replicator" of other people's good work, and that much of BRAC's success comes from its ability to learn from other agencies. The learning NGO is marked by a curiosity and an excitement about new ideas and new solutions. Staff demonstrate a willingness to reflect, experiment, and embrace new thinking. They are involved in a constant process of refining and fine-tuning. The evidence from the case studies also questions the myths that learning is a distinctive process that is inherent in the values and activities of NGOs. In reality, NGOs work hard at promoting learning. They invest considerable time and money in promoting and disseminating organizational learning. It does not come naturally or easily to NGOs. They have no particular monopoly in being learning organizations. Such learning is not inherent in the values of NGOs or some innate process. Instead, it is the result of conscious investment in a diverse collection of informal institutional processes and a variety of formal mechanisms and management systems.

Part II:

New Approaches to Influencing Policy

7

Civil Society: Technical Instrument or Social Force for Change?

Jude Howell and Jenny Pearce

For much of the history of development studies, the state-market axis has dominated theoretical debates on development. With the collapse of socialism in the late 1980s and the gradual recognition of the social costs of structural adjustment, there has been a growing intellectual and ideological acceptance of the need to move away from either-or positions toward more creative and constructive thinking about the complementary roles of different actors in the development process. In the 1990s, the concept of civil society has come to occupy center stage in development discourse and practice, reflected in the new triadic conceptual unity of the state, market, and civil society. Civil society was not only perceived as an antidote to repressive government but also as a way of resolving the seemingly intractable tension between the state and market. Donor enthusiasm for civil society soon translated into a series of programs and projects aimed at strengthening the components of civil society.

It is the purpose of this chapter to explore critically the contradictions and dilemmas emerging out of donor attempts to strengthen civil society. In particular we seek to highlight the risk of making civil society a technical instrument rather than a social force for change. We begin by questioning the assumptions underpinning donor visions and expectations of civil society. We then explore the contradictions and dilemmas inherent in donor attempts to make operational the concept of civil society. In the final section we offer a brief case study of Guatemala to illustrate these dilemmas. In particular we argue that although donor funding for civil society in one of the poorest countries of the western hemisphere can protect a fragile public political space, it can also distort the agenda for social change and development of the poor majority.

Questionable Assumptions, Fragile Illusions

It was against a background of discredited state socialism, growing aware-ness of the socioeconomic consequences of structural adjustment programs (Cornea et al. 1987), and pressure on aid budgets that civil society entered development discourse in the 1990s. With its focus on agency outside the state but within national borders, civil society was an appealing concept and tool for promoting good governance policies. In place of the dichotomized debate about the state and market came the new triadic unity of state, mar-ket, and civil society. Civil society had arrived to temper ideological fervors, to mediate otherwise seemingly irreconcilable differences, and to offer an alternative vision of the development process. In addition, it appealed to radical activists as well as powerful international institutions. The enthusi-asm for this new conceptual vision led donor agencies such as the United Nations Development Program (UNDP), the Inter-American Development Bank (IDB), and the World Bank to set up new programs to strengthen civil society, establish civil society posts, appoint new staff, and create special sources of funding. NGO units soon became civil society units, the neat equation leading later to conceptual confusion around the scope of civil society.

These shifts in discourse and practice are in turn premised upon a num-ber of key assumptions about what civil society can deliver. For donors, civil society is a force for and ingredient of democratization, as well as a natural component of a market economy. In legitimizing civil-society strengthening programs, donors make frequent reference to the potential of civil society, to hold in check the state, to serve as the moral pulse of society and to further democratic values. By reducing the power of the state and increasing the role of the market, it is assumed that civil society too will flourish and will in turn encourage further economic liberalization. Moreover, civil society, state, and market are assumed to constitute an organic, symbiotic whole, characterized by unity rather than disjuncture and by cooperation rather than conflict. There is thus an expectation that civil society will function to mediate and balance the power of the state and market, to provide a moral check on the market, and likewise to maintain the democratic integrity of the state. Fi-nally, there is an implicit assumption that external donor agencies can cre-ate, nurture, and strengthen civil society in aid-recipient countries.

Yet these assumptions, which inform donor enthusiasm and policies for civil society, are open to question. A key problem in western donor usage of civil society is the tendency constantly to slip between treating it as an observable empirical phenomenon and as a normative ideal. This is particularly evident in the assumption of a positive link between civil society and democracy. While at certain historical moments voluntary associations outside the state have been a vital force in democratic change, it cannot be concluded that they will always be so. For example, in the 1930s in Germany, "civil society" was as much a breeding ground for fascist as for social democratic organizations. Similarly, the postsocialist societies of eastern Europe and the Soviet Union have given space both to democratic bodies as well as anti-Semitic, neofascist and other antidemocratic forces. Nor can it be assumed that the internal organization of civil society organizations is necessarily democratic. In many cases, such organizations reproduce the hierarchical principles, gender relations, and values of other dominant institutions. The assumption that voluntary associations are essentially democratic in character or purpose is a normative view expressing how voluntary associations ought to be rather than how they are. Similarly, the notion that civil society is a homogeneous, unified whole—a singular actor in opposition to the state—masks the divisions within civil society, the conflicting array of values and purposes, and the unequal power relations between particular groups.

While historical evidence suggests that civil society in centrally planned economies was sharply constricted, it does not necessarily follow that market economies automatically give rise to civil societies, nor that they support or strengthen civil society. Proclaimed by neoliberals as models for market success,[1] the East Asian newly industralizing countries have also been criticized for their authoritarian regimes, their lack of attention to human rights, and the weakness of civil society (Leftwich 1995; White 1988). In postsocialist societies, the civil society organizations that brought about the collapse of repressive states have not always survived with the same purpose or in the same form thereafter. Moreover, with the breakdown of the economic system, the fragility of the new governments, and the changing moral order, space has opened up not only for new democratic forms of organization but also for antidemocratic forces and criminal gangs, which paradoxically are inherently anticivil.

The triadic unity of state, market, and civil society also assumes neat boundaries between the three elements, discrete functions and actors, and an organic harmony and balance. Yet many organizations within civil society receive funding to varying degrees from both state and private sponsorship. In some countries, government officials have set up their own NGOs as a way to work more creatively, access different resources, and gain new opportunities. Similarly, some development NGOs amount to no more than "briefcase companies" founded for the purpose of tax evasion and private gain. Furthermore, the triadic representation implicitly assumes an equal—or at least unproblematic—division of power between the three elements, indeed three separate domains of power. Yet organizations within civil society do not enjoy the same degree of power. Business associations, for example, are more likely to be better resourced and wield greater political leverage than trade unions or community groups. The power of the market thus permeates and shapes the composition of civil society. As Wood (1990) so cogently argues, the juxtaposition of an array of fragmented and diverse institutions within the conceptual space of civil society masks the totalizing logic of capitalism that fundamentally binds these diverse institutions together and gives them meaning.

Donor visions of civil society portray a harmonious and synergistic relationship with the market and the state. Civil society is attributed those functions for which it enjoys a comparative advantage *vis-à-vis* the state, such as the provision of localized and specialized welfare services, grassroots activities, and small-scale projects. With civil society assuming such welfare functions, the market continues to pursue the goal of profit, thus parceling out responsibility for externalities such as income and social inequality. This vision of a harmonious, functional unity, though somewhat caricatured here, glosses over the contradictions and tensions between the state, market, and civil society. Although the state may welcome charities and welfare bodies providing for the homeless, elderly, and sick, not least because this reduces state expenditure, it may take less kindly to advocacy groups that promote causes contrary to government policy or organizations that challenge the legitimacy of the state; hence, the considerable variation in the legal environment framing civil society organization and activity. Similarly, businesses may sponsor community development, but they may be less receptive to challenges from labor organizations or environmental groups for minimum labor and environmental standards. Thus the interactions of state, market, and civil society are overlaid by contradictory purposes and values, the resolution of which may not necessarily favor the sustenance of civil society nor guarantee stability. The alliances and coalitions are not always self-evident nor conducive to redistribution of power and wealth.

Finally, the assumption that civil society can be grown from "the outside" is problematic. Historically, civil society organizations have emerged within specific historical, social, and cultural contexts. Agency has been localized. The outcomes of their initiatives are distinct and unique, thus undermining any claims of replicability and essential content or purpose. Nurturing civil society from the outside presumes a vision that may not necessarily accord with local imaginations, raising fundamental questions about the power relations between external and internal actors. Whose vision of civil society predominates? What organizations are selected for nurturing? What values and morals are deemed worthy of support? Apart from crucial political and moral questions, there are more general practical issues about the capacity of donors to "build a coherent project," given their failure otherwise to act cohesively, and about the availability of resources required to build local capacity. The next section looks more closely at the ways in which donors seek to create civil society through deliberated intervention.

Challenges and Dilemmas of "Manufacturing" Civil Society

With the rise of a new discourse of state, civil society, and market, aid donors began to initiate programs and projects to create and strengthen civil society. Donor attempts to foster civil society in aid-recipient countries have so far taken three forms: namely, institution and capacity building, partnerships and coalitions, and funding for civil society organizations. Institution and capacity building implies a range of activities, such as fostering the emergence of new nonstate, nonprofit associations; supporting local NGOs with funding, technical advice, and training; and encouraging the establishment of a legal and regulatory framework conducive to the development of nonstate organizations.

Partnership approaches involve a range of activities, such as joint initiatives between NGOs, local governments, and businesses to develop local communities; enlisting the private sector in poverty alleviation tasks; and offering donor advice to national governments for enhancing the regulatory and legal environment for the private sector. For example, the Partners in Development Program was set up in 1995 by the Prince of Wales Business Leaders Forum, the World Bank, and the UNDP to promote partnership between public sector institutions, business, and NGOs.

The fragility of the financial base of civil society coupled with donor recognition of falling aid budgets in the post–Cold War context has prompted several donor agencies to consider ways of fostering local philanthropy and foundations. For example, the World Bank developed a joint bank-foundation strategy to create and support country-level philanthropic foundations. The Ford Foundation has played a key role in strengthening philanthropic institutions, both in the United States and in developing countries such as Senegal, India, Chile, and Kenya. In practice, all three approaches overlap to some degree. While institution- and capacity-building approaches can be traced back to the 1980s as NGOs grew in number and influence, the latter two approaches—partnerships and coalitions, and funding for civil society organizations—have emerged in the 1990s.

These three broad approaches to strengthening civil society have raised a number of challenges and dilemmas. How do donors select organizations with which to work? How is civil society created and strengthened when civil society appears to be "missing" and "weak"? To what extent does such a project assume a common purpose and shared meanings and values? What indicators should be used to assess the extent and depth of civil society? To what extent do externally funded civil society strengthening programs create sustainable local organizational capacity?

One of the first tasks for donors embarking on civil society strengthening programs is to identify the range of organizations within civil society with which they might wish to work. Academics can indulge at ease in lengthy discussions about their preferred definitions of civil society, but donors are faced with having to make this elusive concept operational, defining its content, boundaries, and purposes. When the concept of civil society first entered donor program discourse, civil society was reduced to and became synonymous with NGOs. Although such a definition was convenient, as it provided continuity with donors' growing work with NGOs, this neat equation nevertheless defined out of the donors' field of practice a whole range of other institutions that both historically have been and currently are a radical force for democracy and social change. Trade unions, labor organizations, women's groups, human rights organizations, and peasant associations are but a few examples.

As donors became more familiar with the theoretical debates around civil society, their understandings of civil society became more comprehensive, recognizing the role of trade unions, business associations, human rights organizations and environmental groups in their definitions of civil society. However, although many donors recognize that civil society embraces a range of associational forms in a variety of domains, in practice, because of the nature of their activities and their ideological perspectives, they operate selectively with a narrower slice of the civil society cake. For some, this has meant a continuation of former practice, working with grassroots NGOs and developmental NGOs, whereas for others it has enabled them to extend their activities to include other organizations such as trade unions, business, and advocacy groups. The Center for Democracy and Governance unit in the United States Agency for International Development (USAID), for example, defines civil society for operational purposes as "nonstate organizations that can act as a catalyst for democratic reform," thus excluding both orthodox service-delivery NGOs as well as political parties struggling for state power (USAID 1996, v).

Donor agencies may differ in the breadth of organizations with which they strive to operate, but they all tend to define civil society in terms of long or short lists of organizations. Underscoring such a list approach is an equation of civil society with plurality per se, indeed contrasted with the presumed monolithic nature of the state. Yet as Gellner (1994) cogently argued, such renderings of civil society fail to distinguish between segmentary communities and the liberal, "modern" civil societies that Western European and

American societies apparently cherish and Eastern European ones yearn for. Given that in Africa and Latin America much of rural life is still characterized by kinship and communal associations, there is a serious conceptual ambiguity here. Moreover, to the extent that such a plural civil society is also envisioned as an arena of the "good life," rather than as a site of conflict and contradiction in which power is contested, then donor agencies are left without a strategy to distinguish among the diverse range of groups within civil society. Moreover, if mere plurality becomes the goal, as Gellner warned, and autonomy and voluntariness become the landmarks for selecting partners— or indeed if no clear criteria are thought out—then donor reliance on the "feel-good factor" soon becomes inadequate as a means for fostering a common purpose.

Not only do donors fail to distinguish different kinds of plurality, but they also depoliticize, sanitize, and "technicize" the arena of association. Organizations are juxtaposed as though they operate on an even playing field, share similar values, and seek common ideals. The World Bank marking of civil society as the site of "voice" and "participation" masks the political undercurrents and tensions among different organizations. Are the voices of anti-Semitic groups as morally desirable as those of democratic bodies? Are they given equal weight? Are donor agencies neutral toward the diverse groups within civil society? This is not to say that donor agencies are not aware of potential conflict within civil society. Indeed, in the World Bank *Development Report* (World Bank 1997, 114–16), the bank refers to the disparate interests and the differential distribution of power within civil society as well as the limitations of such organizations. Yet such tensions tend to be glossed over, footnoted, or referred to in clauses rather than given the attention they are due.

The public documents of donor institutions and the rhetoric of partnership appear to celebrate the plurality of civil society, but actual practice as reflected in funding, projects, and programs suggests that business associations are more welcome as partners than their trade union counterparts. Suspicion is often mutual. In seeking to work with trade unions in some African countries, USAID encountered resistance, because trade unions saw USAID as supporting privatization. Thus, the neutral appearance of civil society discourse serves to mask subterranean political agendas and render ideological hegemonies almost invisible.

In trying to make the notion of civil society operational and identify organizations with which to work, donor agencies implicitly assume that the concept of civil society has universal meaning, overlooking its historical and cultural specificity to Western Europe. There is an assumed common vision, a shared set of normative meanings and values, and a presumed organizational form. NGOs are viewed as a key—and indeed "natural"—component of any civil society so that where they are absent, they should be created. Such assumptions can lead to blurred understandings about the relative social significance of certain organizations and organizational forms and misguided interpretations of shared activities. Moreover, such universalistic concepts prevent inquiry into the multiplicity of civil societies and the diverse ways in which societies address problems of accountability, trust, and cooperation (Hann and Dunn 1996).

The partnership approach, for instance, optimistically assumes shared notions of the public good, value consensus, and a common vision. When companies work together with the community, it is naively assumed that this is for the public good. Yet for many companies, such involvement may also serve as an effective marketing strategy for pushing their products. For foreign governments, such partnerships may serve to enhance their influence within those communities and strengthen their legitimacy in the eyes of the funders back home. Whereas donor agencies may envisage civil society as a key counterweight to the state and market, local states may resist such visions, fearing that the purpose of civil society organizations may be more to challenge and possibly overthrow governments rather than cooperate in an assumed common project.

The assumed shared meanings also become problematic in different cultural contexts in which the history of state-society relations departs profoundly from the experiences of Western Europe or North America. In many transitional economie—such as the former Soviet republics, China, and Vietnam, where the state previously played a key role in the management of the economy and society, and freedom of association and organization outside of the state were sharply circumscribed—the concept of an NGO may not only be relatively new, but its social and political functions may be far from transparent. For example, in hosting the 1995 Fourth World Conference on Women, the Chinese government and the official Women's Federation had rapidly to come to grips with the notion of an NGO (Howell 1997). The founders of new NGOs soon discover that enthusiasm and charisma may only lead the organization so far. Without a social base, it is hard to establish and consolidate legitimacy both *vis-à-vis* the supposed beneficiaries as well as the local government. Creating NGOs from the outside does not ensure that these will have a democratic content, or aspire to being vehicles of social and political change, or indeed grow roots and hence legitimacy in local contexts. Donors thus face the dilemma of creating entities "from the outside" that are supposed to be "of the inside." Furthermore, the financial dependence of local NGOs on outside funding likewise undermines their claims to autonomy.

Similarly, the concept of civil society does not translate comfortably into other languages and cultural contexts. In Chinese, for example, a range of terms has been used to translate civil society, reflecting variously its Marxist origins, the roles of elites during the late Qing dynasty in taking on state functions, and the notion of urban citizens *vis-à-vis* the state. In Latin America, civil society first established itself as part of the search for radical political change and mostly via the writings of Antonio Gramsci. In Central America, as the case study on Guatemala will illustrate, civil society articulated the yearning for civil rather than military government, but also the radical political project of grassroots movements and their allies. Yet these agendas are not mirrored in the civil society funding packages to the region from external donors.

Also problematic is the donors' image of themselves as neutral actors, brokering relations between the state, business, and civil society, and indeed separate and hidden from the triadic unity. In conflict situations, such as El Salvador and Guatemala, UNDP describes itself as playing a broker role, building a consensus among diverse interests by forming subregional networks of peasant associations, cooperatives, and trade unions. Similarly, in Central America it purportedly persuaded governments that were otherwise reluctant to engage with civil society to meet indigenous leaders. Yet this begs the question from where international agencies derive their authority to act as broker and to pose as neutral observers. Indeed, the prior assumption of a broker role—unnegotiated, uncontested, and unlegitimate—in itself is revealing about the balance of power. The notion of brokering suggests that the broker has no interest of its own, no ideological preferences, no intrinsic values and goals.

Apart from the question of neutrality, which serves to mask the distribution of power, there is also the larger question of the morality of interventionism. Is donor support to civil society another manifestation of neocolonialism in the post–Cold War era, aimed at controlling the nature of political regimes and extending global markets? Do donors have the right, let alone the capacity, to shape other civil societies? By projecting their own visions and understandings of civil society, do they not undermine the ability of local organizations to set their own priorities and agendas, to vocalize their own imaginations of social and political change?

Civil Society Strengthening in Postwar Guatemala

In order to illustrate the argument, this final section looks briefly at the contradictions that are apparent in the civil society strengthening programs of external donors in Guatemala. The concept of civil society was taken up initially by grassroots movements and local NGOs close to them in the mid-

1980s when the first civilian government in three decades was elected and a fragile political space opened for social organizing (Gutierrez 1997, 21). Many of these were led by survivors of the massacres, and indigenous women stood out as protagonists. For at least the first five years of this struggle, many of those organizations that received funding did so from international—particularly European—NGOs. These international NGOs mostly were committed not only to the democratization and human rights agenda of their local counterparts, but also to their desire for radical redistribution and political change. As the Cold War came to an end and international financial and development institutions began to shift their priorities toward issues of good governance, so their agenda in Guatemala shifted. The priority remained Guatemala's integration into the global economy on a competitive basis, a process that demanded structural adjustment, economic liberalization, and state reform. The international aid community began to reach out selectively to local NGOs, mostly to implement targeted poverty alleviation programs, such as the Social Investment Funds of the World Bank and the first phase of the Partners in Development program of the UNDP.[2]

The Guatemalan peace process provided the opportunity for international agencies to extend their involvement in the country. In the wake of the signing of the final peace agreement in December 1996, which ended thirty-six years of civil war, the International Monetary Fund and World Bank Consultative Group agreed to cover almost 75 percent of the U.S. $2.6 billion cost of the implementation of the peace accords, channeling donations and loans from a range of major European and multilateral financial institutions. This gave them considerable influence over the reconstruction and development process that now began. The appeal to an active civil society in Guatemala—where criticism of the top-down political leaderships of the left was allowing previously skeptical groups to accept funding from powerful institutions they had never seen as allies—was an attractive proposition to international institutions looking for a force to support democratization and state reform.

In the wake of the peace agreement, therefore, a plethora of initiatives began in Guatemala aimed at building the capacity of civil society. These civil society strengthening programs have been very progressive in terms of the international protection they have provided for organizational development in the country, and donor funding has certainly nurtured that development. However, there are also some tendencies in this funding that are of concern—namely, the lack of donor conceptual and policy coherence, legitimacy, and dependency, and the promotion of a western liberal-democratic model. The argument is not that donor programs are entirely negative, but that they are certainly not neutral.

First of all, none of the institutions is really clear on what it means by civil society. The World Bank has not in practice evolved much beyond seeing "civil society" as NGOs and the organized private sector, and its agenda is to build partnerships that can help implement the economic modernization strategy for the country. In Guatemala, the most active, radical organizations and local NGOs remain deeply suspicious of the Guatemalan business community, which historically supported military government and continues to resist any increase in what is one of the lowest rates of taxation in the world as well as any discussion of agrarian reform. The UNDP, on the other hand, has broadened its conception of civil society considerably and has been innovative in its thinking on Guatemala. But, in practice, it too looks for the kind of technical capacity and effectiveness that the smaller, radical organizations have difficulty achieving without changing their rationale considerably. The IDB has a major reconstruction and development program in the conflictive and impoverished department of Huehuetenango, which aims at encouraging new relationships between civil society and government. However, what is meant by "civil society" in this region, which has eight different ethnicities, has never been clarified. In order to implement its civil society strengthening program there, the IDB bypassed local NGOs and instead turned to three more efficient international organizations. This was partly determined by the fact that the IDB staff involved in the project have only three years to prove to their skeptical colleagues that this approach can produce measurable results.

Second is the problem of legitimacy. The UNDP sees its role as building consensus between civil society organizations, the government, and the private sector. It is not clear where it derives its mandate for this brokering role, however useful it might appear to be. A problem is that for many Guatemalan organizations, there are still many conflictive issues to be resolved between them and the government and the private sector, including fundamental questions about income and resource distribution and justice for past human rights abuses. The power relationships are very much stacked against them. It is difficult to see how consensus can be achieved without some recognition of and effort to overcome the fundamental inequalities, and without a move toward a more even playing field in terms of who determines the future of Guatemala. The UNDP is aware of these inequalities and seeks through strengthening the civil society organizations to compensate for this to some extent, but in practice it can only fund selectively. These profound issues facing Guatemalan development can in reality only be resolved through local political processes, not external interventions by unaccountable and unelected international agencies, which rely on technical personnel to implement them. Donors can, of course, support local processes positively, and reflection on the limits as well as potential of their role may be a means to gain greater legitimacy for it among aid recipients.

The third issue is the dependence on governments. Despite their new concern for "civil society," most international financial institutions have to work through national governments. International donors are often forced to antagonize governments in the course of civil society strengthening or to retreat and dilute their civil society work. There is evidence that in Guatemala this leads some donors to concentrate on certain civil society sectors that are less controversial for governments, such as women and the environment. In the case of the World Bank, it has opted not to work through NGOs in its postconflict reconstruction project in the department of San Marcos; the Guatemalan government remains very suspicious of the NGO sector and does not see why its own institutions cannot implement donor programs.

The promoting of western liberal democratic models raises a fourth set of issues. Recent thinking on democracy and development in the West has assumed the dominance of the liberal democratic model. When western agencies get involved in democracy programs and civil society strengthening overseas, it appears that they assume a right not only to promote this, but also to make up the criteria for evaluating whether it has been achieved or not.[3]

In Guatemala, there are other visions for the political organization of the society, such as the radical democratic one held by the social organizations and local NGOs that pushed open and defended the fragile spaces for public debate and action in the 1980s. Although these other visions are not very coherent or even theoretically articulated, they undoubtedly have motivated many who participate in Guatemala's popular and social organizations. There is the radical cultural discourse also of the new Mayan organizations that have recently emerged and wish to see something of Mayan culture and practices reflected in the organization of the state from which they have historically been excluded. These popular and Mayan organizations seek a more participatory form of public political life as well as the opportunity to challenge the logic of the project of economic modernization promoted by some of the same agencies that are behind the democratization process.

Many recipients are also critical of the advocacy and lobbying training components of civil society programs. With only a small middle class and low literacy levels, it cannot be expected that pressure groups can easily hold liberal democratic institutions to account. Indeed, it will take a prolonged political struggle to change the priorities of the Guatemalan state toward the needs of the poor majority. At present, however, disillusionment with political parties, including those of the left, is widespread in the country. International donors tap into that disillusionment by offering the organizations of civil society the opportunity to lobby government directly.

However, these organizations are fragmented and divided among themselves. They were able to build a common front against authoritarian government, but it has been much more difficult for them to develop a common strategy for deepening democracy. The only "leadership" on offer appears to be the agenda of international institutions backed by large-scale funding. Gradually, many accept the package on offer and play the role of civil society for the donors. Others seek to retain their agenda for social and political change and are marginalized from the mainstream, dismissed as "extremists," unable to adapt to the new epoch. In this way, radical commitment to social change is eroded, and in its place emerges a handful of well-funded, showpiece "civil society organizations" that are internationally known, highly effective, and technically competent, able to write convincing annual reports for project funding boards, and completely divorced from the needs of the mass of the population.

Conclusion

In this chapter, we have sought to address the question of civil society as a technical instrument or social force for change. What is historically unique in the 1990s is that donor agencies are attempting to create, foster, and strengthen civil society in aid-recipient countries. In doing so, they have inadvertently or consciously foisted blueprint conceptualizations of civil society onto other societies. A particular normative vision of civil society with specific organizational forms and evolutionary processes has been imagined for other societies. The danger of such goodwilled attempts to extend imaginations of the public good and institutionalize these is that the assumption of universal meanings, the channeled energies from the outside, and the technical translation and concretization of such aspirations into manageable projects and programs blunt the political potential of such organizations. They become creations of the outside, embodiments of external norms and goals, and materially dependent on outside rather than local sources.

Notes

1. However, by the 1990s, even the World Bank had accepted that their strong economic performance depended crucially on state intervention (World Bank 1997b).

2. This is discussed in greater detail in Pearce (1998).

3. One of the most controversial countries where western agencies have done this is Bosnia; by arguing that culturally the Bosnian people cannot build democracy themselves, agencies have become ever more deeply involved in a semipermanent form of tutelage.

8

Making the Connection:
Legitimacy Claims, Legitimacy Chains and
Northern NGOs' International Advocacy

Alan Hudson

As U.K.-based nongovernmental organizations (NGOs) increasingly move into advocacy and policy work, they are having to respond to a variety of challenges concerning issues of legitimacy and related issues of accountability, governance, and effectiveness. Legitimacy questions concern, first, the right of the NGO to speak to its target audience, perhaps on behalf of other groups or interests; and second, the wisdom of NGOs moving further toward an advocacy focus.

This chapter is part of an ongoing research project concerning the ways in which U.K.-based development NGOs organize their advocacy activities. I briefly outline the evolution of NGOs and their movement toward greater involvement in advocacy and policy work, explaining the shift and introducing the issues of effectiveness, legitimacy, accountability, and governance, which have arisen and persisted, especially over the last ten years. I then considered questions of legitimacy in more detail before the preliminary findings of my ongoing research are used to illustrate the variety of ways in which NGOs claim legitimacy for their advocacy work. Emphasizing the varieties of advocacy and the range of claims to legitimacy, I argue that in order to substantiate their claims to legitimacy, NGOs need to map out their legitimacy chains. When legitimacy is claimed on the basis of representation, systems of accountability need to be in place. When legitimacy is claimed on the basis of expertise and experience, the relevance of southern operational experience to northern advocacy needs to be demonstrated. Rather than offering a blanket dismissal of northern NGOs' advocacy work as illegitimate, unaccountable, and groundless, I argue that northern NGOs do have a role to play and value to add in processes of international development. The question that

NGOs are beginning to take seriously is, how can northern NGOs and their southern partners best work together in organizing legitimate and effective international advocacy?

NGOs and International Advocacy

In the context of the new policy agenda, NGOs have grown in prominence in international development as potentially efficient service and welfare providers, channels of aid, and facilitators of democratization. NGOs have become important actors in the international political economy, a fact borne out by rapid increases in numbers, membership, activities, and financial resources (Edwards and Hulme 1992b).

In the early 1990s, policymakers in leading northern NGOs became increasingly aware of the limited impact of their development efforts. Despite the fact that more public money than ever before was channeled through NGOs, their impact on the ground was still temporary and small scale. Recognizing this limitation of traditional development activities, leading NGOs began to consider a range of strategies of "scaling up" in order to make more of a difference (Edwards and Hulme 1992b; Uvin and Miller 1996). In the years since the publication of *Making a Difference* (Edwards and Hulme 1992a), the focus of NGO thinking, and increasingly practice, has swung behind efforts to develop more effective forms of international lobbying and advocacy.

Although advocacy takes a variety of forms—from careful research and policy advice, to parliamentary lobbying, to public campaigning and development education—the overall goal is "to alter the ways in which power, resources, and ideas are created, consumed and distributed at a global level, so that people and organizations in the South have a more realistic chance of controlling their own development" (Edwards 1993,164). National and international lobbying and advocacy has become increasingly important within the NGO world (J. Clark 1992; A. Clark 1995; Fowler 1999; Keck and Sikkink 1998). Some large, mainly northern-based NGOs have acquired considerable expertise, authority, and respect and have gained access to decision makers in governments and international organizations. By having a foot in the North and a foot in the South, NGOs are in a good position to link the micro and the macro levels, using their experience in the South to inform their advocacy and policy work in the North. In short, NGOs have begun to move from a "development-as-delivery" to a "development-as leverage" approach (Edwards, Hulme, and Wallace 1999).

Legitimacy Matters

As NGOs have moved further into advocacy and influencing work as part of a development-as-leverage approach, they have encountered a variety of related challenges and criticisms. These challenges question the effectiveness of their advocacy work, their legitimacy as advocates for development, their accountability to those they are perceived as representing, and the suitability of their governance structures for a development-as-leverage role (Edwards 1993; Edwards and Hulme 1995; Hulme and Edwards 1997; Smillie 1995; Sogge 1996).

As regards their effectiveness, questions have arisen about whether a shift into advocacy and influencing work will make a difference to the lives of poor and marginalized groups in the South, and additionally whether it is the most cost-effective use of NGO resources. As regards their legitimacy, NGOs have increasingly encountered the criticism that they are not representative organizations in any obvious sense, bringing their credibility as representatives of the poor and marginalized South into question (Cleary 1995; Nyamugasira 1998). In a similar vein, it has been suggested that NGOs are poorly accountable to the people that they sometimes appear—or claim—to represent and that this poor accountability undermines any claim to legitimacy (Edwards 1999b; Nelson 1997). Finally, encompassing the previous three criticisms, it has been suggested that NGOs' governance structures are poorly suited for a development-as-leverage role (Covey 1992). As NGOs move further into advocacy and policy influence, these questions are not going to go away.

Questions about legitimacy may seem to be little more than a navel-gazing guilt trip for northern NGOs, but legitimacy is central to the effectiveness of NGOs' advocacy work. As regards advocacy, put simply, legitimacy increases the persuasiveness of advocacy, which increases its effectiveness. NGOs have been questioned about their legitimacy from a variety of positions. First, governments, international organizations, and multinational corporations— some of which have been criticized by NGOs for their weak accountabilities (Fox and Brown 1998)—are increasingly asking whether and why they should listen to NGOs. Second, institutional funders are asking why they should fund NGOs that are moving further into advocacy work, and why they should fund NGOs rather than other parts of civil society. Third, as they grow in confidence and experience, southern partners and supposed beneficiaries are increasingly questioning the legitimacy of northern NGOs advocating, supposedly on their behalf. In such a dynamic environment, northern NGOs are clearly challenged to show that they do have a valid role in processes of international development.

Legitimacy Claims

NGO advocacy takes a variety of forms and relates to a wide range of issues; different types of advocacy about different sorts of issues have different implications for legitimacy. An NGO may be considered a legitimate advocate when it is talking about a "technical" issue in which it has a lot of expertise, such as the latest developments in irrigation technology or family planning, but illegitimate when it expands its focus to reform of the World Trade Organization (WTO) or environmental degradation. One approach that sidesteps the issue of legitimacy is simply to make modest claims that are less open to criticism. Similarly, some NGOs—approximately 10 percent of the NGOs I interviewed—steered clear of the term (and perhaps the practice of) *advocacy*, because they feel that speaking on behalf of others is in itself disempowering for the intended beneficiaries. Their preference was for "influencing"—demanding that institutions consulted the NGOs' client group in formulating their policies.

In my research, NGOs claimed legitimacy for their advocacy work on a variety of bases: history; organizational structures; principles, rights, and values; and southern roots. For some—perhaps 15 percent—of the NGOs I spoke with, history was a source of legitimacy for their advocacy activities. Such NGOs spoke of their institutional survival, track record, and reputation. While such attempts to use history to support legitimacy claims might seem simplistic and inconclusive, they do play a role in affecting which organizations are taken seriously. That said, these historical claims beg the question of why the NGOs have survived to establish a track record. A second category of claims was made on the basis of the organization of the NGO itself. Two organizations pointed to formally democratic membership structures that extend internationally. A few others felt legitimated by their U.K. supporter base, and one claimed that its governance structures and staffing policies gave it legitimacy as an advocate. A third group of legitimacy claims relied on the idea that the position being advocated was a basic right, a moral or ethical principle or value, or had been agreed upon in an international code of conduct. Such claims were made by about 15 percent of the NGOs that I interviewed. However, although advocacy is clearly about values—and clarity about the values that underlie an advocacy position is to be welcomed—rather than simply appealing to values, NGOs need to explain where their values come from if they are to persuade others to share and enact them.

In many cases, the values that NGOs hold and promote, and the advocacy positions that they take, derive from experience in and links with the South. For many of the NGOs I spoke with, it was their experience of working at a grassroots level—implementing projects and programs in a wide range of contexts—that gave them the legitimacy to advocate about development issues. In fact, this is the main basis for claims to legitimacy, which, in varying forms, was used by more than 50 percent of the NGOs I interviewed. NGOs that specialize in a particular aspect of development claimed that their technical expertise provided them with legitimacy, and in some cases they took pains to ensure that they did not advocate beyond their experience.

Many of the NGOs I spoke with were well aware of the dangers of claiming legitimacy in terms of representation and cautioned against potentially exploitative attempts to seek out legitimacy through establishing links with southern NGOs and community organizations. Few—perhaps 10 percent—of the NGOs interviewed claimed to be speaking for the South or southern NGOs, but many did argue that they were representing—or, more subtly, promoting—the interests of the South or the values that emerged out of their work in the South. Although many NGOs carefully avoided claiming to speak for the South or represent the South in any simple way, many struggled to find alternative ways of describing what they are about and, if pushed, would fall back on some sort of representational claim—southern issues, values, interests, or concerns, rather than "the South"—to legitimacy.

Legitimacy Chains: Accountability and Relevance

Although NGOs make their claims to legitimacy on a variety of bases, a substantial majority of their claims point—directly or indirectly—to their links with and experience in the South. The strength of these legitimacy claims depends on the ability of the NGO to demonstrate the links, or legitimacy chains, between their operational work and experience in the South and their advocacy work. Approximately 20 percent of NGOs I spoke with suggested that I could have pushed them harder on issues of legitimacy, and were rather surprised that more questions weren't asked of them as they moved further into advocacy and influencing work. Many NGOs are currently thinking about how to develop more synergistic relationships between their operational work and their advocacy, but few have clear systems in place to achieve such a goal. Two potential ways of substantiating legitimacy claims are first, in terms of practicing accountability, and second, in terms of demonstrating relevance.

For NGOs that make some claim to represent southern communities, issues, interests, values, or concerns—however carefully worded the claim is—there is a need to back up their legitimacy claims with appropriate systems of accountability. As Edwards and Hulme suggested: "NGOs do not have to be member-controlled to be legitimate, but they do have to be accountable for what they do if their claims to legitimacy are to be sustained" (Edwards and Hulme 1995,14). As well as being accountable to their supporters and donors for the ways in which resources are spent, one would expect NGOs that make representational claims to try to be accountable for the positions they take. Revealingly, almost 50 percent of the NGOs I spoke with, when asked "To whom are you accountable for your advocacy work?" responded in terms of upward accountability to line managers, donors, trustees, and boards of governors, rather than in terms of downward accountability to those whose interests they claim to promote. Many of the NGOs who responded in terms of accountability to boards of governors regarded my question as to the makeup of the board and whether it includes southern members as bizarre, simply viewing accountability to a board—no matter what its membership—as sufficient. In fact, several NGOs were actually surprised at the mention of downward accountability, seemingly unaware of the concept and unconvinced about its desirability.

NGOs explained their lack of downward accountability in a variety of ways. Some explained that southern NGOs do not have the time or inclination to be involved in in-depth processes of consultation, and others described their legitimacy as "assumed" rather than of a sort that is backed up by formal systems of accountability. More positively, some NGOs, particularly the smaller ones with long-standing advocacy campaigns rather than three-year campaign cycles, claimed convincingly that their relations with partner organizations were so close, and their contact so frequent, that they had developed a sufficient level of trust or "organic accountability" such that formal mechanisms would be unnecessary bureaucracy.

A further reason given for the lack of accountability in relations with partners concerned the difficulties of evaluating advocacy work (Covey 1995; Edwards and Hulme 1995; Fowler 1995, 1996, 1997; Roche 1999; Roche and Bush 1997). As Edwards put it: "When performance is difficult to measure and success is difficult to attribute, accountability becomes very complex" (Edwards 1996, 8). Beyond saying that "We had X number of meetings, sent Y number of letters, had Z level of response from the target organization, and got ten column-inches in the newspapers," NGOs are hard-pressed to know what they have achieved in their advocacy work, and hence what they should be accountable for.

In addition to this "Accountability for what?" obstacle to clear systems of accountability, NGOs also encounter an "Accountability to whom?" issue, an issue which merges into that of how to demonstrate the relevance of southern experience to northern and international advocacy. When advocacy is confined to a specific geographical or thematic issue—health policy in Zimbabwe, for instance—NGOs may feel confident about to whom they should be accountable: Zimbabwean NGOs with an interest in health policy. However, if the advocacy aims to change a policy at a more abstract level—reform of the WTO (World Trade Organization), changes to lending policies of development banks—it can be unclear to whom one should be accountable, and demonstrating the relevance of grassroots work to macro-level advocacy can be problematic. Complex legitimacy chains often lead to diffuse accountability and make the demonstration of relevance difficult.

Most of the NGOs I spoke with recognized that demonstrating the relevance of their operational experience to their international advocacy work is far from simple. An approach that sounded both realistic and useful involves trying to understand and illustrate the links in both directions, trying to look outward and upward from the southern grassroots to broader debates, and trying to think downwards from policy issues back toward southern experience. One of my interviewees acknowledged that there are a lot of layers between the concerns of southern NGOs and their constituents and northern advocacy, but explained that his NGO did not confine itself to simply representing the opinions of its partners, but added value in terms of research and analysis. As NGOs recognize the two-way nature of legitimacy chains, from South to North and North to South, and seek to make the links in both directions, northern NGOs will have to redefine their roles in processes of international development if they are to show themselves as adding value in these processes.

Conclusions: A Global Division of Labor?

Many of the NGOs I spoke with saw a role for themselves as supporting and facilitating international advocacy, and defended their right to take positions on issues of international development as long as they were developed through "real dialogue" with southern partners. Partnerships and dialogues have tended to be unequal (Malena 1995; Smillie 1995), but NGOs should not give up on the goal of genuine partnerships—characterized by jointly agreed purposes and values; mutual trust; respect and equality; frequent consultation; reciprocal accountability and transparency; sensitivity to political, economic and cultural contexts; and long-term commitments.

Missing from many discussions of northern NGOs' advocacy and its legitimacy is any mention of how southern NGOs and their constituents see northern advocacy and the role of northern NGOs. A small number of NGOs I spoke with had made serious efforts to consult their southern partners about the organization of advocacy, and as a result felt less concerned about issues of legitimacy. The southern partners of one large NGO had been consulted and had stressed that the northern NGO ought to take advantage of its position in the North, its access to important decision-making institutions, its ability to recognize opportunities and emerging issues, and its experience and skills in policy analysis and research. These southern partners wanted to be informed about what their northern counterparts were doing, and wanted to be involved in decision making, but insisted that the northern NGO must play its part in international advocacy and not be paralyzed by legitimacy concerns. Other interviewees described an emerging division of labor in the organization of international advocacy, with northern NGOs translating the concerns of their southern partners so that they have maximum impact with Northern and international institutions. The issue comes down to one of deciding what value northern NGOs can add to the advocacy process, when northern NGOs are needed, and when they should step aside—and, importantly, involving southern partners in these decisions.

Perhaps the key question that NGOs need to consider in organizing their international advocacy is whether organizational structures that developed during a development-as-delivery era are suitable for a development-as-leverage approach (Young et al. 1999). NGOs have been slow to restructure their organizations in order to ensure appropriate downward accountability for advocacy and influencing. Some NGOs have embarked on processes of restructuring, considering decentralization, the establishment of dedicated advocacy offices, and harmonization across their federations and alliances. Such efforts seek to move the NGO closer to southern experience, to give the South a voice in decision making, and to develop truly international advocacy rather than a northern-imposed agenda. A related and more common approach to reorganizing international advocacy is to strengthen the southern element in a global division of labor through capacity-building. Such an approach takes seriously the joint responsibilities of North and South in advocating for international development.

However, before rushing into decentralization, membership structures, or poorly thought through capacity building, NGOs must be clear about their reasons for restructuring, avoiding the temptation to follow institutional—at the expense of developmental—imperatives (Edwards 1996, 1999a). In rethinking their roles and seeking to achieve greater accountability, legitimacy, and effectiveness for their development work, NGOs must start from their core values, being honest and clear about what their values are and where they come from. Although often hidden, values are fundamental to the work, not least the advocacy work, of NGOs. Discussions of effectiveness, legitimacy, accountability, and governance (and evaluation) ought to recognize explicitly the values that make an NGO what it is. Effectiveness is relative to the values or objectives of the organization. Legitimacy comes, or doesn't come, depending on the processes through which values are developed. Multiple accountabilities are balanced on the basis of values.

Governance structures, in effect, institutionalize values. As Edwards and Hulme argued several years ago:

The degree to which a strategy compromises the logic by which legitimacy is claimed needs to be carefully considered, and can provide a useful means of testing whether organizational self-interest is subordinating the fundamental aims when a choice is being made (Edwards and Hulme 1992a, 89).

NGOs, particularly their northern components, will not be able to avoid questions of legitimacy as they move further into advocacy. In order to demonstrate their value in an emerging global division of labor, NGOs must institutionalize their core values in their organizational structures.

9

NGOs, Democratization, and Good Governance: The Case of Bangladesh

Mahbubul Karim

It has become common in the post–Cold War world to speak of a "civil society" separate from state and market. Although interactions may take place between civil society and these other two institutional arenas, civil society is increasingly seen to have its own distinct presence as an independent institutional sphere. In the wake of globalizing forces, it has been argued that civil society has emerged as a "third sector" that has acquired the power to negotiate with and exert pressure on the state and market in order to influence policy instruments in favor of the excluded (de Oliveira and Tandon 1994). Bangladesh has a vibrant civil society, including a range of indigenous nongovernmental organizations (NGOs), which are systematically organized and highly active on a variety of fronts. Most NGOs are engaged in the delivery of development services to the poor, but elements of the NGO community in Bangladesh have also, since the early 1990s, played a more political role in seeking to strengthen the country's fragile processes of democratization.

The involvement of NGOs in democratization has inevitably generated some criticism, particularly because most of these NGOs continue to rely extensively on international development funds. In particular, NGO involvement in democratization has given rise to the question of whether it is appropriate that NGOs should take on roles that engage them directly and overtly in the political process. However, alongside these concerns, there are strong currents of support. The main argument in favor of such a role draws attention to the long history of political activism with the third sector in Bangladesh during the twentieth century: first, as a site of resistance to the British colonial rulers; and second, in the period after India's partition, as a site of resistance to the political subordination experienced by the people of East Bengal, which became in effect a colony of Pakistan.[1] The political role of Bangladesh's development NGOs can be situated within this wider history and linked with its specific political, economic, and social conditions. In the three decades since the birth of Bangladesh in 1971, a space has been created in which NGOs have evolved as a distinctive nonparty political formation.

The wide range of NGO agendas, which include protecting human rights, furthering the rights of women and children, developing approaches to empowering the poor, reducing poverty, and furthering sustainable development, cannot ultimately be achieved without putting in place a conducive political environment. This chapter therefore uses an historical perspective to examine the evolution of NGOs in Bangladesh as a nonparty political formation. It examines the problems and prospects of NGO roles as political actors and provides an assessment of the relevance of these roles for wider civil society agendas in the next millennium.

Civil society is essentially a citizens' domain, well captured in Nerfin's (1987) formulation which distinguishes the citizen from the "prince" and the "merchant." Implicit in this symbolic representation is the fundamental characteristic of civil society—its relative autonomy from the state and the market. The "prince," the "merchant," and the "citizen" constitute three distinct sets of institutions, each of which has distinct motivations and structural preferences (Najam 1999). In this way, civil society can be seen as a third dimension of public life—sometimes termed the *third sector*— which operates in an arena that lies positioned between the market economy and the state.

The composition of civil society is complex, and the organizational forms and motivations that it contains are heterogeneous and diverse (Robinson and White 1997). Broadly speaking, civil society is a collective area of conflicting, interdependent, interinfluential organizations (Van Rooy 1999). Within this area, Blair (1997) argues that civil society organizations (CSOs) are a subset of NGOs that are seeking to make changes to policy and wider resource allocation rather than, or in addition to, simply delivering services. A distinguishing feature of these CSOs is their emphasis on organized and group action (Fernandes 1994; Hadenius and Uggla 1996). However, civil society everywhere is not equally conscious, capable, and fervent enough to face the challenges that are now being posed by globalization.

Civil Society in Bangladesh

The colonization of the Indian subcontinent had far-reaching implications for the economic and political systems that were inherited by both India and Pakistan (including what is now Bangladesh) at the time of independence and partition in 1947. The prevailing conditions of underdevelopment and poverty across the subcontinent had deep roots in the colonial histories of plunder, oppression, and domination. As a result, a comprehensive understanding of civil society in Bangladesh is not possible without an historical perspective.

The state of Bengal, to the east of the Indian subcontinent, made a substantial contribution to the liberation of the subcontinent from colonial rule. During the colonial period, an enlightened generation emerged in Bengal in the early nineteenth century which creatively engaged in debate and action on major social issues and contributed to a range of educational, religious, and social reforms; language and literature; art and culture; and media. This generation in practice played the role of what we now call a "think tank" and formed the first conscious and active civil society in Bengal, providing revolutionary inputs to many spheres of life. This facilitated social progress in education and social welfare and also contributed to the rise of nationalism, which formed the basis of the Indian independence movement in the latter half of the nineteenth century and has been termed "the Renaissance of Bengal."

The eastern, predominantly Muslim, half of Bengal became a province of Pakistan at the time of partition and became known as East Pakistan. The area lacked any real resource base other than its people and its highly fertile—though ecologically vulnerable—agricultural land. However, in the political sphere of East Bengal, there existed a strong tradition of political parties and social movements among its citizens, for whom the legacy of 150 years of anticolonial struggle by civil society had left its mark. After 1947, East Bengal effectively became a colony of West Pakistan, and this quickly proved unacceptable to the majority of the population. The resistance that soon ensued generated a violent response from the West Pakistan authorities and produced a further period of political, economic, and cultural domination. This was to last for twenty-four years, ending only with the Liberation War of 1971, which led to Bangladesh's national independence.

Civil society's struggle in East Pakistan was ignited by one specific act of cultural repression: the decision of the West Pakistan government in 1948 to make Urdu the official state language of the whole of Pakistan, including the eastern area, which was completely dominated by people who spoke the Bengali language. In fact, the "Bangalees" formed the majority of the population of Pakistan at that time. Organized civil society in the form of student groups and citizen organizations coalesced into what became known as the "language movement," which achieved its first victory in 1952 with the official recognition of "Bangla" as a state language.[2] However this was not the end of the struggle, which gradually expanded beyond the cultural sphere to take on economic and political dimensions also. It would be very difficult to identify a single cultural, economic, and political movement in East Pakistan—from the language movement in 1948 to the war of independence in 1971—that did not involve a substantial contribution from civil society.

After 1971, a new set of organizations emerged within civil society that came to the aid of the victims of Bangladesh's liberation war, especially those who had to flee the country and take refuge in India. When the war ended, these organizations directed their efforts toward complementing the government efforts to carry out a massive relief and rehabilitation program with international assistance. This enabled many of these new NGOs to sustain their organizational entities for several years after the war. In this way, it became possible for them gradually to change their focus from charity to welfare and development and evolve into development NGOs, combining service delivery with a "civil society" focus (Serrano 1994; Wood 1994).

While this group of post-independence NGOs was creating room for themselves as new actors in civil society, some of the traditional CSOs that had emerged during the period of struggle leading to independence—such as the student political organizations—became effectively coopted into the dominant mainstream political structures. This cooption had serious political consequences as Bangladesh's fragile political system began to veer in an antidemocratic direction. These organizations therefore failed to oppose the highly controversial steps to centralize power that were taken by Sheikh Mujib's ruling Awami League (AL) government in January 1975. The changes included the abolition of all political parties in order to form a single party, which led to abandonment of the multiparty system for a one-party system. The parliamentary system of government was replaced by a presidential form, and all but four national newspapers were banned.

The consequences of these political changes were disastrous for the AL, for civil society, and for the country as a whole. The army took over power through a bloody coup d'état, and Bangladesh lost its democratic process to a succession of military rulers for fifteen years. As Sobhan (1997, 39) observes, during this period, a "spiral of negative events started from which Bangladesh did not begin to emerge till 1990, fifteen years on." The traditional CSOs fell into deep crisis and became riven by internal conflict and fragmented by factionalism along ideological and party political lines. Many of the traditional CSOs were to return to a more active role during the mass movement in 1990 to restore the democratic process, but by this time a new actor in civil society—the NGO community—had emerged.

The typology of CSOs in Bangladesh developed by Holloway (1994) suggests that there are three different general categories in existence. In the first category are membership organizations that "only help themselves," in the second are the nonmembership organizations that "help others," and in the third we find a set of largely spurious organizations that "do not help" at all:

- Membership organizations are indigenous organizations in the community, induced community groups, mass organizations, cooperatives, religious societies, trade organizations, and professional associations.

- Non-membership organizations are local institutions, NGOs, implementing organizations, people's organizations, support organizations, networks and forums, apex organizations, area-based benevolent societies, service clubs, and nonprofit companies.

- Opportunist organizations are those that lack legitimacy as genuine civil society organizations. These have been termed "Come'N'Gos" (set up by unscrupulous individuals for personal profit), GONGOs (government-organized NGOs), DONGOs (donor-organized NGOs), and BONGOs (business-organized NGOs).

The above typology, although neither comprehensive nor exhaustive, provides a useful guide for understanding the general composition of civil society in Bangladesh.

Blair (1997) suggests that CSOs in Bangladesh are potential additional players in the political economy of a country in which he identifies the bureaucracy, political leaders, military, rural elite, and business community as the dominant actors. He classifies these potential additional players in two groups: one he terms *traditional candidates* and the other he terms *newer civil society candidates*. Among the traditional candidates, he identifies two subgroups: one he describes as *coopted* and includes groups of professionals such as lawyers, doctors, engineers, journalists, teachers, labor unions, and students. The other subgroup he calls *missing groups*, and these include the various organizations of market-oriented farmers, sharecroppers, and rural laborers. In Blair's view newer civil society candidates are the various NGOs and umbrella groups that have become concerned with human rights, investigative journalism, the subordination of women, environmental problems, and issues of poverty among the rural and urban populations (Blair 1997).

The NGO Community in Bangladesh

The NGO community in Bangladesh constitutes the largest and most diverse area of civil society. These organizations, which include Proshika, Bangladesh Rural Advancement Committee (BRAC), and Nigera Kori, have developed steadily over the years and have demonstrated a range of effective alternative poverty-reduction strategies, such as microcredit, nonformal primary education, and community health provision. These organizations have also contributed to improvements in public demand for better government services.

In Bangladesh, almost half of its 123 million population exists below the poverty line. Approximately 80 percent of the country's population live in the rural areas and are dependent, in one way or other, on agriculture. The landholding pattern in Bangladesh is highly skewed, with approximately 50 percent of the households functionally landless and 6 percent of the land-owning households controlling more than 40 percent of the total land (Hossain 1997). However, in recent years, there has been a decline in rural poverty for both the moderate and the extreme poor (Bangladesh Institute of Development Studies 1996). NGOs are understood to have played an important role in this change. For example, the findings of the comprehensive Bangladesh Institute of Development Studies poverty analysis noted the success of NGOs in reaching the rural poor in ways that conventional government initiatives have not (1996). The United Nations Report on Human Development in South Asia (Haq 1997) also recognized the important contribution of CSOs to development progress in Bangladesh. The report argues that the vibrant civil society is Bangladesh's greatest asset and refers to the activities of specific NGOs, including BRAC, Proshika, Rangpur Dinajpur Rural Service (RDRS), and the Grameen Bank.

Alongside the strong positive case that is increasingly being made for NGOs in Bangladesh, there are also, of course, many dissenting views. The NGO critics include a range of groups and individuals, including bureaucrats, politicians, the business community, religious groups, and even some of the CSOs themselves. *The Economist* (1998, 30) recently reflected on some of these accusations:

The *mullahs* hate the NGOs for eroding the traditional male-dominated structure, and occasionally attack their offices. Resentment also comes from politicians, bureaucrats and leftists, all of whose shortcomings have been exposed by the success of NGOs. Left-wing critics accuse NGOs of exploitative rates of interests. . . . Politicians complain that NGOs have money and power without accountability, embezzle foreign funds and cook their books.

Such criticisms have provoked a considerable level of public debate in Bangladesh. The same article also summarizes some of the counter-arguments made by the NGOs and their supporters:

The NGOs reply that their accounts are audited, and sometimes not just in Bangladesh but also, to satisfy donors, by auditors abroad. They say they are accountable both to donors and the villagers they serve. The easy availability of donor funds has encouraged some crooks to set themselves up as NGOs but corruption among NGOs is a trickle compared to the rivers in government (*The Economist* 1998, 30).

One of the main recurring and persistent criticisms that is made of the NGOs from many sides is that these organizations' legitimacy and accountability can be questioned in the light of their heavy donor dependence. Except for a few of the larger NGOs, which have achieved a high level of financial autonomy, the sector as a whole continues to rely heavily on the flow of international development funds. Reducing this dependence remains a central challenge for NGOs in Bangladesh.

Democratization and Good Governance

There have been two major focuses of NGO intervention in Bangladesh. One is on the supply side of the development process, such as service delivery to the poor in order to fill the gaps created by inadequate government response. This NGO "welfare" role can be seen as a logical progression from the immediate post-independence period after 1971 during which NGOs worked to meet immediate welfare needs. NGOs gradually developed a strong comparative advantage based on a close knowledge of poor people's situations and needs, and the experience of finding effective ways to reach them. The other main NGO focus is now on creating popular demand for good governance by organization building, empowerment, and mobilization of the poor to enable them to express their rights to access the public institutions, resources, and services.

This latter focus led many NGOs to become aware of the need for action not merely within local communities, but also at the macro level. It also became a priority for NGOs to establish linkages with other CSOs in order to undertake joint efforts for democratization and good governance. The first major step in this direction was the expression of solidarity with the democratic movement of 1990, which overthrew the autocratic regime of General H. M. Ershad and reestablished the democratic process in the country. An alliance of NGOs, the grassroots people's organizations often formed and promoted by them, and sections of the business community also played crucial roles in the mass movement of 1996, which arose because of doubts that the 1996 elections would be fairly managed by the ruling Bangladesh Nationalist Party (BNP). This NGO alliance sought to protect Bangladesh's democratic process further by creating a constitutional provision that would allow holding of all future general elections under neutral caretaker governments.

In the 1991 movement, participation of the NGOs was only one of expressing solidarity with the movement. However, in 1996, the NGOs not only actively took part in the movement but at times played a leading role. This movement led to the resignation of the BNP government and formation of a caretaker government to conduct a general election on 12 June 1996. Before the election, NGOs had implemented a countrywide voter awareness education program covering ten million men and women voters, which significantly contributed to raising voter awareness. It also contributed to the very high voter turnout of 73 percent, which was the highest in Bangladesh's history. The NGOs also played an important role in monitoring the election throughout the country from the platform of the Fair Election Monitoring Alliance, formed by a group of CSOs. Since the 1996 elections, NGOs have kept up their efforts to pursue reform agendas in the areas of local governance, education, health, resettlement of the urban slum dwellers, environment, and water resources.

NGOs in Bangladesh: A Nonparty Political Formation?

There have been considerable levels of debate about NGOs in Bangladesh among policymakers, activists, and researchers. What role should we expect NGOs to play? Should NGOs seek merely to provide services and welfare? Or should they aim at the promotion of development and social change? Or should they attempt to do both? Although the NGOs' role is strongly determined by individual country contexts and histories, these are increasingly shaped by larger global realities. It is, therefore, difficult to find an either/or answer to such questions because, in reality, the boundaries between such activities tend to be blurred. A situation in which an NGO provides *only* service delivery and welfare or *only* development and social change rarely exists.

In the post–Cold War era, there has been an expectation among policymakers that NGOs, as civil society actors, can contribute to democratization and act as a counterweight to state power (Hulme and Edwards 1997). But NGOs cannot be effective actors in the reform of political institutions and processes by maintaining a so-called "nonpolitical" stance. In order to be able to make a contribution to this, NGOs must make themselves politically visible and act as political entities. In no way does this mean that NGOs must turn themselves into political parties and aspire to formal political power. The point is to act as nonparty political formations and to become what Kothari (1984, 219) called "new instruments of political action when a vacuum in the political space exists."

It is therefore necessary for NGOs to ask themselves whether they wish to remain merely as "pupae" within the "welfare cocoon" that they have spun, or whether they should emerge from it to embrace a wider, more political development role. Many of Bangladesh's NGOs have done this. They have made a choice to face the challenges posed by national political crisis and by the new international order. However, the example of Bangladesh shows that to make such a choice does not undermine the need for a significant NGO service delivery role.

The Bangladesh liberation war created a vacuum in the political, economic, and social life of the country, which continued and deepened with the crisis that persisted during the period from 1974 to 1990. After the military takeover in 1975, political parties were formed by the generals, and elections were held to legitimize the army's "civilian" administrations. The parties created by the military rulers did not have any mass roots, because they had been formed by involving opportunist politicians and by buying the support of the rural and urban elites. The result was that politics and people were separated from each other for nearly two decades.

The crisis in the economic sphere went even deeper. An alliance of the civil and military bureaucrats and rural and urban elite ruled the country and paid little attention to the needs of the poor. In reality, their policies were in most cases antipoor, and a recent study found that 74 percent of the Bangladeshi government's total development assistance is still channeled to the nonpoor (Bangladesh Institute of Development Studies 1996). This development vacuum has been filled by NGOs, which have been the lone actors in the rural scenario for the past decade and a half. They have been filling the gap created by government inaction and political clientelism by, on the one hand, promoting grassroots people's organizations and, on the other, directly assisting with peoples' survival strategies through credit and other services. The emergence of NGOs both as agencies seeking to meet the needs of the poor through service delivery and through their evolution as a nonparty political formation is therefore rooted in Bangladesh's political and economic history.

Conclusions

Can NGOs in Bangladesh sustain this role as a non-party political formation in order to spearhead civil society's struggle for democratization and good governance? Globally, the growing emphasis on civil society in the post–Cold War era provides a conducive framework for NGOs to do this. However, at the national level, although NGOs have been able to create considerable political space for themselves, several risk factors still jeopardize their operation. A large section of the bureaucracy remains opposed to NGOs. There is also a growing hostility among politicians—especially members of parliament, irrespective of their party affiliations—who find themselves competing with NGO campaigns and community activities in their constituencies. NGOs have also been accused of being partisan by both the main political parties—in 1991 by the AL and in 1996 by the BNP. The forces of religious fundamentalism are increasingly posing threats to the NGOs, in which women's empowerment activities and links with foreign donors draw frequent criticism. There are also still some opposing views within the NGO community as regards a "political" or a more traditional development or welfare role.

There is much work still to be done by NGOs in Bangladesh, and the first few years of the new millennium will prove crucial ones. An effective continuation of the NGO role in democratization and improved governance will be strongly determined by the following factors: The NGOs will need to attain both a higher degree of institutional sustainability by finding new sources of funding to reduce foreign dependence, and more progress in reaching broader consensus and improving cooperation among the NGO community. NGOs will need to continue to build a longer-term alliance with other civil society actors and will need to create dynamic and fully autonomous federations of local peoples' organizations at the national level. NGOs will also need to find ways to address effectively the attacks that have been made on them by the forces of religious fundamentalism. They will require ways to develop appropriate mechanisms for sustaining their operations in the event of a major shift in government policies concerning NGOs. Finally, NGOs will need to continue efforts to institutionalize the democratic process in Bangladesh which, because of continuing political instability, remains fragile.

Notes

1. Against the wishes of its people who were united by a common language and tradition, the state of Bengal was partitioned in 1905 by the British colonial administration into a western side, which was predominantly Hindu, and an eastern side, which was predominantly Muslim. At the time of India's partition in 1947, West Bengal became part of India, whereas East Bengal was made part of the new state of Pakistan and was known as East Pakistan, separated by more than three thousand miles from West Pakistan.
2. The Bengali language is known to those who speak it as "Bangla."

10

Civil Society, Empowerment, Democratic Pluralism, and Poverty Reduction: Delivering the Goods at National and Local Levels

Harry Blair

By the end of the 1990s, much—if not indeed most—of the international donor community had embraced a democratic development paradigm that looked more or less like the model portrayed in Figure 10.1. Sometimes this was more explicit (for example, Organization for Economic Cooperation and Development 1997; United Nations Development Programme 1997b, 1997c), sometimes more implicit (for example, United States Agency for International Development 1994), but the basic formula shown in the figure became, with minor variations, the principal donor model for promoting democratic development in the 1990s. There are, as should be expected, variations on the theme.[1]

Figure 10.1 portrays a straightforward developmental model, which assumes that the basic macro-democratic framework has been set into place.[2] From this, a number of logical steps unfold, beginning with increasing political *participation* on the part of elements previously outside the mainstream, such as minority ethnic groups, women, urban poor, and landless agricultural workers. In the process of becoming political participants, these elements are mobilized to enter the political arena, contest electoral positions, and win office, thereby gaining *representation* in decision-making bodies. In this series of steps they are motivated and enabled to become actors in their own right in the political arena; in short, they gain *empowerment.* Once empowered, these new players will be able to influence political decision making in legislative and executive institutions to direct programatic *benefits* to their constituencies, which over time will lead to *poverty reduction.* And in turn, poverty reduction, along with the concomitant benefits it brings in terms of health and educational improvements, will lead to *sustainable human development.*

Figure 10.1
Democratic Development and Marginal Groups: Causal Formula

An increase in participation
•→ An increase in representation
•→ An increase in empowerment
•→ An increase in targeted benefits for constitutency
•→ An increase in poverty reduction
•→ An increase in sustainable human development

To put the paradigm in terms of the words used in the title of this chapter, newly *empowered* groups become part of *civil society*, and within a political environment of *democratic pluralism* they advocate policy changes that lead to *poverty reduction*. Northern and southern nongovernmental organizations (NGOs), along with developing country governments and international donors, are the principal outside actors motivating, supporting, and in many ways shepherding the process along.

The central thesis of this chapter is that although this four-part approach shows some (if not total) promise of success at the national level (or state level in such a huge country as India), it faces fundamental problems at the local level, which requires a serious readjustment in direction. To put it another way, what is possible at the macro level becomes very problematic at the micro level. And even at the macro level, it will be argued, the benefits tend to go to elite strata within the marginal groups being benefited. However, with a somewhat different approach, there are prospects for more widespread poverty reduction and sustainable human development at both levels. Empirical evidence is based largely on India and the Philippines, but could be extended to other countries as well, particularly in Asia and Latin America.

Where the Model Can Work: Success at the Macro Level

In countries such as India and the Philippines, the model depicted in Figure 10.1 has enjoyed some success at the macro level, at least in its first four elements. In recent times, both systems have presented an essentially benign democratic context within which marginal groups could hope to influence public policy: India since independence in 1947 (with the exception of the 1957–77 emergency) and the Philippines for more than a decade, after the collapse of the Marcos regime in 1986 and the restoration of democratic politics. It is true that moving through the participation-representation-empowerment benefits in Figure 10.1 does not constitute the whole course. However, if we grant that program initiatives in human capacity building, like health and education, necessarily entail a considerable gestation period before showing concrete results in terms of poverty reduction and sustainable human development, attaining the first four elements of the formula is not doing badly.

The major dynamic in both cases has been civil society organizations (CSOs) acting as advocates for their constituencies.[3] In India, any number of new groups have been able to press their case with varying degrees of success at state and often national levels. Perhaps the most obvious of these have been the farmer organizations that emerged in the 1970s and 1980s as champions of the market-focused middle peasant, demanding increased government support for agricultural production and increased prices for agricultural produce. However, there have been other constituencies as well following similar paths. Dalits (ex-untouchables or scheduled castes) were granted some reserved preferences in the 1950 national constitution for legislative representation, but have pushed further for educational and job preferences at state and national levels. In this they have been emulated successfully to a large extent in many states by the "other backward castes" (OBCs)—the large numbers of Shudra castes that rank just above the Dalits in the traditional Hindu hierarchy.

Women's advocacy groups have also been active in recent years, campaigning successfully for reserved legislative seats (now set by the seventy-third amendment at one-third of the membership in all elected bodies, and also one-third of the leadership posts; see Singh 1994), as well as other preferences. Other successful women's policy initiatives include liquor control acts passed by several states, designed to curb excessive drinking and the domestic abuse it tends to create. Equally spirited but less successful have been other groups such as Adivasis (indigenous ethnic communities, mainly the scheduled tribes), landless laborers, and sharecroppers (Attwood 1992; Rudolph and Rudolph 1987).

Starting from the fall of Ferdinand Marcos in 1986, the track record in the Philippines is shorter. However, in a sense, the opening for civil society's role in politics has been made broader than in most countries, with an explicitly stated fundamental principle in the 1987 constitution officially encouraging civil society organizations to function (article II, section 23; see Brillantes 1997). In any event, significant headway has been made at the national level by women's groups and Igorots (indigenous groups similar to the

Adivasis in India) in obtaining legal rights and protections. In 1997, for instance, a prolonged campaign resulted in passage of a new antirape law in the Philippines—the first serious change in the law regarding rape in more than seventy years (see Reyes 1997 for an account). Also in that year, the Philippines put into effect a law requiring that a fixed proportion (20 percent) of seats in the national legislature be allocated to various underrepresented groups, including women (Montinola 1999).

Such gains are impressive, particularly to the extent that they pave the way for wider future achievements as more experienced groups make further headway for their constituencies and new groups representing more marginal elements find inspiration in their example to launch initiatives of their own to influence the political process. However, there are two problems with this upbeat interpretation.

First, most of the successes tend largely to benefit only an elite stratum among the constituencies whose cause is being advanced. It is, after all, the upper tier of women, Dalits, OBCs in India, or Igorots in the Philippines that will gain from new elective office, educational opportunities, job quotas, and the like. Those who already have some advantages in terms of class, education, or connections (even if only a relative advantage) are going to be best positioned to take advantage of the new possibilities offered. The very much larger mass of more ordinary people in each category will gain very little in the short or intermediate term—and possibly the long term as well—in the absence of some larger social change.

To be sure, there are some exceptions, even among the examples mentioned above with the antiliquor advocates in India and the antirape lobbyists in the Philippines. In the former case, the beneficiaries have been largely lower-class families whose fathers are less likely to binge on drinking. In the latter case, poor women stand to gain at least some further protection from the new law, if perhaps not as much as their more well-to-do sisters. However, for the most part, it will be those already better off in any marginal group who are most likely to become still better off as a result of successful advocacy on behalf of the whole group.[4] The second problem is that even these successes have come almost exclusively at the national rather than the local level, where marginal elements have a considerably tougher time.

Difficulties at the Micro Level

At the local level, success stories are much scarcer (although exceptions exist in some special circumstances). Increases in participation have led to increases in representation (particularly when seats are reserved on local bodies to be filled by members of the groups in question, as in India). However empowerment has been a good deal harder to attain, and the remaining pieces of the Figure 10.1 formula successively more difficult.

The problem is perhaps best explained by discussing the exceptions first. In geographical areas where minorities are numerically dominant at the local level, democratic governance gives these minorities the chance to win office and even control local councils. In this fashion, they can gain empowerment and put into place policies favoring their constituents in ways that will quite possibly lead to poverty reduction and sustainable human development over time. Thus, for example, indigenous groups in the Philippines' Cordillera region have taken control of local municipal bodies, in which they have been able to implement and enforce ordinances protecting ancestral lands from purchase and exploitation by outsiders. They have also invested public funds in human capital development sectors such as education. Adivasis in many parts of India have likewise won control of village councils (panchayats) at various levels where they enjoy numerical concentration.

However, most weak and vulnerable elements do not have such local population densities. Instead they are spread out thinly, and, although they may elect one of their own to office here or there, they can never gain more than a smattering of seats on local councils. Thus urban poor people or fishers or sharecroppers might elect a council member or even several of them in the Philippines, but save in exceptional circumstances, they will not elect enough members to assume control of these bodies. In India, the various reservations established over the years make representations much more assured for the various protected groups, but do not make for control.

The basic obstacle, of course, is that local elites tend to take control of local politics, just as they control most other things in life at the local level, such as economics, religion, and culture. Indeed, this tendency has been observed for so long in both the Indian subcontinent and the Philippines that it has become commonplace (Hutchcroft 1991; Myrdal 1968; Timberman 1990). As is well known, the reasons for this asymmetry lie in the political economy of local existence, that is, ownership or control of the resources needed to survive and prosper: land, capital, employment opportunity, access to government, influence over religious practice, and the like. The uneven distribution of these resources tends to reinforce and accelerate itself as the rich reap returns on their own investments and at the same time pervert government investments to their own use, so that they become the dominant beneficiaries of those efforts as well.

All this leads to the patterns shown in the "Traditional" column of Table 10.1, which illustrates what has historically been the typical case with local level investment of public funds for three different sectors. In education, new money has tended to go to the higher-grade levels, which benefit those

Table 10.1

Three Kinds of Local Public Investment

Sector	Traditional	Poverty-focused	"Universalistic"
Education	High-quality secondary schools	Special education for the poor	Primary education for all
Health	Research hospital in urban center	Clinics for poor neighborhoods	Campaign against malaria
Agriculture	Subsidies for purchasing tubewells	Allocation of surplus land to landless	Improved pest management
Rural credit	Loans to those with collateral	Microcredit for the landless	[not needed]

wealthier strata who can afford to send their children through primary and secondary schooling. Similarly, in the health sector, an archetypal investment at the local level has been an urban hospital in which advanced facilities and therapies are available to better-off elements. And in agriculture, infrastructural investments such as tubewells are not surprisingly going to deliver their water to irrigate the land of those who own them. The poor must put their children to work as soon as possible instead of encouraging them to stay in school; they cannot manage the costs and access obstacles to obtaining scarce medical treatment; and they tend to have land too inaccessible for irrigation (if they own land at all). Therefore, they are most unlikely to see any benefit from such investments. This bias constitutes the major reason why the poor stay poor, to borrow the title of Michael Lipton's (1977) classic account of the subject.

A strong underlying assumption in much current donor support of democratic decentralization is that the formula of Figure 10.1 will enable the poor to gain enough influence over local decision making to launch the sort of initiatives depicted in the "Poverty-focused" column of Table 10.1. Thus, special educational programs can be targeted to poor children, clinics for the poor can be put in place, and land reform can allocate unused state land to the landless. A similar reasoning can be applied to women, ethnic minorities, and marginal elements generally. However, this has not happened for the most part, either in the democratic decentralization programs that have been launched recently in such places as the Philippines and Honduras (in the early 1990s) or Bolivia (mid-1990s), nor has it been the case in a place like the Indian state of Karnataka, which has had one version or another of local democracy in place since the beginning of the 1960s.[5] With a very few exceptions, marginal groups have not been able to redirect public investment along the lines indicated in the "Poverty-focused" column of Table 10.1, nor is there much indication that this pattern will change anytime in the near future.

This analysis does not apply to all programs at the local level, it should be noted, but only to those in which significant decision making is vested in local levels. In the case of rural credit programs, depicted in the bottom row of Table 10.1, the story is different. These efforts were long notorious for being subverted by the local rich, who had the collateral needed to secure loans and the political clout required to default successfully on their loans (see for example Blair 1984). However, the microcredit initiatives stemming most notably from the model pioneered by the Grameen Bank in Bangladesh have been eminently successful in steering resources to the poorest strata. The critical element in these programs, however, is that successful microcredit programs are invariably administered by outside agencies, not by local governments. Situating the loan-allocating process elsewhere precludes takeover by local elites.

It can be argued that marginal groups should be able to press their agendas by playing carefully at the pluralist political game. Dominant elites are scarcely ever monolithic at any level, as the literature in political anthropology and political history make clear. They are constantly riven by faction, conflict, splits, and even violence at times, all in patterns that shift over time with generational change, innovations in resource use, and externalities such as government interventions or international markets. So then surely a deft marginal group—or better yet, a coalition of such groups—can exploit these differences among dominant elites to engineer an alliance with one faction or another in exchange for implementing initiatives such as those illustrated in the "Poverty-focused" column of Table 10.1.

Certainly this kind of scenario can occur, but instances appear to be rare at best. A much more common outcome is that one of the very few things local elites can agree on is that they need not allocate resources to the poor. In short, elite collusion tends to triumph over factional rivalry when questions of benefits to the poor arise.

The "Universalistic" Option

A much more promising strategy for marginal groups, I would argue, is that shown in the "Universalistic" column of Table 10.1, which presents initiatives that will benefit all elements in a political entity: poor and rich, women and men, ethnic or religious minorities, and the majority.[6] The most obvious case for such a contention is the public health sector, in which there are any number of activities that offer benefits that are either indivisible by their nature (for example, malaria eradication, which has to benefit everyone if it is to benefit anyone) or can be made indivisible relatively easily (for example, a sewage system serving all households in order to eliminate cholera and other waterborne diseases). Here it does not take great effort to convince dominant groups that their own interests coincide with those of the poor.

The other two examples in Table 10.1 are a somewhat harder sell, but at the same time make better illustrations of the universalistic option.[7] In education, the rich would have to expand present facilities to ensure primary education for all, because schooling is easily divisible to exclude the poor (for example, by geographical location, requiring books and uniforms, condoning or even encouraging informal rationing mechanisms through which instructors receive side payments to deliver instruction outside the regular program). In the agricultural example shown in Table 10.1, although pest control will distribute benefits more equitably in most areas than tubewells (because the pests will have to be controlled on everyone's land if they are to be controlled at all), equity will be limited to those who own some land in the first place.[8] The latter example might appeal to dominant elites, because they stand to gain proportionally more, but what about the educational illustration, in which they could retain the service for themselves and cut off the poor? This could be extended to other sectors as well, for instance in electrification: Why support a municipal initiative to put streetlights in all neighborhoods when elites could restrict the service to their own areas? Why should elites support programs at all that would give benefits to the poor, when historically they have successfully resisted doing so?

The answer here is that in a democratic setup, *dominant groups can justify universalistic programs to their own constituencies.* In a situation in which a faction of the dominant elite leadership has an incentive to ally with representatives of the lower strata (for instance, to gain a majority on a local council), something will have to be given to the latter if the alliance is to endure for any length of time. Moreover, these concessions will be easier to account for if they can be justified in the name of an initiative that will be good for everyone (the "Universalistic" column of Table 10.1). Such an approach also means compromise for marginal group leaders and their constituencies, to be sure, in effect setting half a loaf as the objective and then quite likely scaling down from there to achieve accommodations with other groups.However, compromise is what pluralistic democracy is all about, and if in the end it cannot hope to meet all the goals of the weak and vulnerable, it can serve their interests better than other political systems have been able to do.

Conclusion

What are the key differences that make it possible, at least at times, to enact and implement development strategies targeted on marginal groups at a national (or state) level, but not at the local level? The principal distinction appears to be that policy preferences, as well as personalities and opportunism, divide macro-level elites, whereas at the micro level, only these latter divisions exist. In local politics, elites find themselves riven by competing family lineages, personal competition, opportunities to enhance status or expand resources at the expense of others, and so on, but virtually never by real policy differences. Thus particular elite factions may ally with marginal groups momentarily in their rivalry with other elites, but when it comes to redistribution initiatives, they find they have more in common with other elites than with the weak and vulnerable. Class interest constitutes the principal policy for all elites in the zero-sum game they perceive themselves involved in at the local level.

At higher levels, these personal aspects are often there and can even at times become dominant themes, as with political dynasties like the Nehru family in India, but there are also policy differences. Some elites favor more restrictive trade policies, whereas others want to open the economy; some are more concerned with nationalism and military strength whereas others favor infrastructural investments, some have religious agendas to push, whereas others are more secular; and so on. It is the addition of these policy differences to the more personal ambitions for power and office that make macro-level elites more willing to trade real program benefits in return for support from marginal groups. Generally, elites find it necessary to build coalitions to press their policy formulas, which necessarily means that several agendas will get included in the package, and some of those agendas could well become programs to benefit marginal elements. This is, after all, the stuff of democratic politics.

This whole process is significantly facilitated in many countries at the national level by the political party system. To the extent that parties are stable institutions enduring over time, this system enables leaders to include multiple interests and enforce discipline, keeping together people of very different interests and classes. Much of the legislation supporting marginal groups in India can be explained in this fashion; both the Congress and Janata parties in various incarnations have conferred considerable benefits on marginal groups as part of their overall agendas over many years. However, the stability and discipline that has been possible at national and state levels has for the most part simply not existed at the local level.[9] Thus, while party can hold class interests in check at least for some periods at the national level, at the local level class generally trumps party. It is for this reason that the most promising avenue for securing real benefits to the poor is not the focused initiatives that are sometimes possible at higher levels, but more universalistic efforts that will benefit all strata on the local scene.

There will be problems. In particular, it will, in effect, be impossible for marginal groups as a whole to catch up with more advanced elements, because at best all will be moving ahead at the same rate from vastly different starting points. Those best off to begin with will continue to do best, benefiting the most from whatever universalistic programs are instituted. Poor children (especially girls) will still be less likely to finish school, even if primary education is genuinely available to all; poor families will endure more illness than rich ones, even if both have the same drinking water or sewage facilities; and sharecroppers will benefit less from effective pest control than large farmers. However, the weak and vulnerable will have life chances that they would otherwise be denied, and individuals within these groups will be able to advance in ways that their parents never could.

These are surely goals worth seeking through supporting efforts to promote a modified version of the formula in Figure 10.1 that would in effect substitute something like "an increase in general benefits for all groups" for "an increase in targeted benefits for constituency." To use an image so often employed by macroeconomists, when we cannot pick out specific smaller boats to lift, we should work on strategies to promote rising tides that will lift all boats. Global warming may do this literally in time, of course, but metaphorically it would probably be most useful to change from NGO support programs specifically targeting marginal elements to donor-sponsored initiatives aimed at more universalistic benefits. To do so would mean diverting some of the benefits that the NGO community would like to see going directly to marginal groups into other hands. However, at the same time, it would also offer a much better chance for assuring sustainable human development for all groups, including the marginal.

Notes

1. The research on which this chapter is based was funded by the United States Agency for International Development (USAID) and is reported in Blair 1998, 2000. This chapter builds on and develops the themes. All analysis is the author's and does not necessarily reflect USAID policy or strategy.

2. It will be assumed in this chapter that such a democratic, market-based environment is more or less in place—that elections are basically free and fair, meaningful competition for elected office occurs, civil society is autonomous from the state, the media are free, human rights are respected, and the judiciary is autonomous.

3. Here the term *NGO* is used to refer to organizations, whether northern or southern, that promote development strategies in southern countries. Organizations functioning as actors in civil society (in this case, advocating public policies on behalf of their constituents) are called *civil society organizations* (CSOs). See Hansen 1996 for an elaboration of this distinction.

4. In the United States during the early years of programs inspired by the civil rights movement of the late 1960s and early 1970s, this tendency to benefit those already better off was known pejoratively as "creaming." Blair 1982 and Shah 1988 make similar criticisms of Indian initiatives to bring benefits to deprived groups.

5. This is one of the central findings of a USAID-sponsored study of these systems (Blair 1988; Manor 1999). For Karnataka, see Crook and Manor 1998. For an account of elite-dominated village councils (panchayats) misdirecting local poverty programs, see Gaiha et al. 1998.

6. I am indebted for much of my thinking on this topic to William Julius Wilson (1987, 1996), who has developed similar arguments for the United States.

7. The fourth example in Table 10.1 doesn't apply here. It will be recalled that the poverty-focused (second column) option is externally administered, and this can avoid control by local elites.

8. Good pest control programs would have secondary benefits for the landless—better crops require more labor and postharvest processing creates more work for hired labor—but the main benefits will accrue to landowners (unlike malaria control, which will protect all equally).

9. Even at the higher levels, most of the parties (Congress and Janata, especially) have often found it impossible to maintain cohesiveness. In the Philippines, parties have been more fluid and ephemeral, with little stability or continuity. In Latin America, on the other hand, many parties are long standing with significant internal coherence. There, parties at the local level could possibly undertake universalistic strategies that subordinate class interests to partisan interest, although such cases are probably few.

11

Stormy Weather:
Microfinance, Shocks, and
the Prospects for Sustainability

Susan Johnson, Karen Doyle, M. Emrul Hasan,
Eduardo Jimenez, and Thalia G. Kidder

Enthusiasm for microfinance interventions in the late 1990s was palpable. Stoked by the 1997 Micro Credit Summit, many more NGOs considered making credit and savings part of their activities. In the past few years, there has been a strong push for microfinance organizations (MFOs) to achieve sustainability, both becoming financially self-sufficient and organizationally independent and self-reliant. As Edwards and others (Chapter 1) point out, the international system is increasingly based around rules and standards rather than subsidized resource transfers. Both microfinance organizations (MFOs) and donors have reasons to seek financial and organizational independence. As donors seek to demonstrate the sustainability of their interventions, they find strong potential allies in the prospect of MFOs that can become financially independent of donor grants or soft loans. MFO business plans may propose self-sufficiency targets, but such plans must come with the caveat that local circumstances are stable and benign for the expansion of microfinance operations. However, a feature of poverty is vulnerability to shocks and instability, and there are few development programs that do not— at some point—encounter these shocks, whether social, economic, political, or environmental, and whether at the local or national level.[1] Finding ways to minimize their impact through the development of institutions and infrastructure in the wider economy and society is an essential part of the development process; work on microfinance is only one part of the story.

This chapter draws on experience of microfinance programs in situations of macroeconomic instability, natural disasters, and conflict and insecurity. It explores the similarities and differences between these cases of instability and reflects on their implications for the achievement of organizational and financial sustainability, and hence on the ability of MFOs to provide services when their members might need them most.

Macroeconomic Instability and the Role of International Capital in Microfinance

Microfinance in the Philippines during the East Asian Financial Crisis

The floating of the Thai Baht in July 1997 in the face of massive speculative outflows dramatically triggered the East Asian crisis. In subsequent months, the shock waves spread to the Philippines as foreign investors lost confidence in the East Asian economies. Although the Philippines did not experience as dramatic a shock, the experience demonstrated clearly how global shocks can affect the work of MFOs.

The Alliance of Philippine Partners in Enterprise Development (APPEND) network comprises nine MFOs working toward self-sufficiency and is supported by Opportunity International. APPEND's partners reported that the impact of the crisis on their clients was extremely varied. Seven reported that their clients had been negatively affected by the impact of the spiraling cost of materials and demands for higher wages by those they employed. Four reported that between 1 and 60 percent of microentrepreneurs had closed down their businesses by September 1998. The main impact of the crisis at the borrower level was an increased demand for funds to enable businesses to keep going and carry on employing those already in work, and an expansion of demand from those who turned to the informal sector for a new source of income. However, the major obstacle that MFOs faced was a withdrawal of their own credit lines when they most needed them.

The APPEND network has pioneered borrowing funds from commercial banks at below-market rates for on-lending. In the face of the crisis, commercial banks decided to decrease or terminate lines of credit and loans made to MFOs. This action was prompted by new regulations imposed by the Central Bank that required commercial banks to reduce their exposure on loans that had no collateral. Despite their good repayment records, six of the APPEND MFOs reported tightening credit lines from banks, with two reporting total closure. Where existing credit lines to MFOs could still be renewed, they were subject to higher interest rates.

Further, five APPEND MFOs had loans from foreign sources—both individuals and corporate investors—who also wanted to renegotiate their loans in the face of the devaluation of the peso and their reassessment of foreign currency risk. These MFOs reported being asked either to pay the loan immediately or to renegotiate loan terms.

MFOs therefore faced a general withdrawal of liquidity at a time when loans were in even greater demand to support their clients through the crisis and enable others to diversify their livelihoods. As a result, five MFOs turned to individuals, locally based institutions, and other NGOs to borrow funds. Two organizations, both rural, had to raise their interest rates to clients in order to cover the rising cost of delivering loans. In the face of the crisis, and despite the reduction in commercial credit lines, MFOs in the APPEND network were finally able to expand the volume of loan disbursements by 40 percent. However, the experience highlighted the reality that as MFOs develop their links to commercial banks and become part of the financial sector, they are likely to be subject to the same shocks as the banking industry and seriously need to consider the conditions under which they source their capital.

The Role of International Capital for MFOs

One explanation of the East Asian crisis has highlighted the lack of transparency in the internal dealings of large private corporations whose business operations spanned industry and banking—so called "crony capitalism." Another explanation has focused on the role of international investors and highlighted the fact that corporations had borrowed heavily in relation to their equity capital and that international investors were looking for the highest return over the short term. As a result, capital was not "patient" or prepared to weather downs as well as ups in the economic system, so the loss of confidence, once triggered, resulted in the net outflow from five economies of 11 percent of their combined gross domestic product in the space of one year (Wade 1998). This had long-term consequences in terms of shattered livelihoods for millions. "Patient" capital, by contrast, is prepared to invest for the long term and weather short-term difficulties for potential long-term gain.

Deposits are the most obvious potential source of "patient capital" for the development of MFOs, but this requires that effective regulatory frameworks are also in place. A clear challenge for MFOs taking deposits is ownership structure and governance. Capital is made patient by the decisions of those who control it. Structures are required that can adequately reflect the interests of different stakeholders within a community. There are many possible approaches, but in Central America and elsewhere, there are pilot projects to institutionalize representation of NGOs or community organizations on the policymaking boards of financial institutions, such as BanRural in Guatemala. The need is to root such organizations in their local circumstances in ways that ensure that wider concerns than investment returns alone enter the agenda.

An intermediate stage between completely soft donor money and "hard" money from the financial markets is also provided by social investment funds, which can be more "patient" in their orientation. For example, TRIODOS bank's "North-South Plan" in the United States has mobilized £11 million by offering depositors modest rates of interest and promising that their funds will be invested in microcredit and fair trade projects in developing countries; it has plans to develop an equity investment product also. Another example is the Wisconsin Coordinating Council on Nicaragua (WCCN), which channels funds raised from rural congregations, religious orders, middle-class individuals, and progressive pension funds in North America to Nicaraguan microfinance partners.

Microfinance in the Context of "Natural" Disasters[2]

The Impact of the 1998 Floods on the Microfinance Industry in Bangladesh

Floods have plagued Bangladesh for centuries, but the 1998 floods were the worst to have occurred in recorded history, affecting two-thirds of the country and causing some 1,100 deaths. Economic losses were estimated at 9 percent of the gross domestic product (United Nations Development Programme 1999a). A survey carried out by the South Asian Network of Microfinance Initiatives and the Credit and Development Forum revealed that some 62 percent of MFO clients had lost their homes and more than 75 percent had their ability to generate income either destroyed completely or temporarily terminated.

The Grameen Bank, Bangladesh Rural Advancement Committee (BRAC), and Proshika employed disaster response policies they had developed during earlier disasters. The Grameen Bank gave grant assistance in cash and kind, as well as interest-free loans from existing group disaster and welfare funds, which were topped up to meet needs and provided to those most seriously affected. Members were also permitted to withdraw all of their money from their savings accounts. This was followed by agricultural and housing rehabilitation schemes in the postflood period. BRAC's relief and rehabilitation activities covered an extensive range of activities—ranging from health promotion to agriculture and infrastructure rehabilitation—under their employment creation program. Over time, BRAC has built up an emergency fund for disasters, with a standard loan loss reserve policy of percent of the portfolio, which it claims could cover a significant portion of anticipated losses. Proshika has also had experience of earlier disasters and was able to invoke its emergency response policies and use its internal funds to respond to the crisis.

However, while these "mega" MFOs had extensive experience and resources to draw upon in situations such as this, smaller MFOs, which account for some 15 percent of total coverage, were not so well blessed. The impact of delayed repayment, loss of interest income, and increased levels of default was severe and exacerbated by the fact that they also lacked access to resources with which to make new loans to their members.

Despite the situation's gravity, there was agreement within the microfinance sector that loan write-offs would not be advocated, and there was commitment to ensure that the government did not promote this. Rather, efforts were made to assess the true extent of losses and make provisions for recapitalization depending on the size and nature of the organization. There was a genuine effort to identify "good" organizations from "bad," with an effort to capitalize "good" organizations. Although rescheduling took place by necessity, with some MFOs allowing moratoriums for short periods, the general shift in policy toward an acceptance that loan forgiveness should not be allowed and rescheduling should occur through organizational assessment was successful. The most critical need was capital for making fresh loans for the rehabilitation of the loan program in order to jump-start their clients and get them back on track. During the 1988 floods, grant funds were not difficult to procure, but this time there was a shortfall of grants from donors. Government delays in making a formal disaster announcement did not help.

The industry as a whole therefore sought to turn the "disaster" into an opportunity by focusing on minimum standards for MFOs to agree upon with government and donors, and promoting the development of a coherent sector strategy to address disasters in the future.

Microfinance in Central America in the Wake of Hurricane Mitch

Although MFOs in Central America were far less prepared for coping with the disaster of Hurricane Mitch in 1998 than their Asian counterparts were with the floods in Bangladesh, the experiences shared many similarities. First, they faced liquidity problems as high demand for credit increased; the upcoming harvest and holiday period was exacerbated by increased demand in the wake of the hurricane. This, accompanied by loss of interest income and late repayment of outstanding loans, coupled with high levels of savings withdrawals, meant that funds were squeezed. MFOs did not have reserves to turn to, nor were additional sources of concessional funding readily available.

Second, the Nicaraguan association of MFOs agreed on definitions for the affected portfolio and minimum standards of accounting, and announced a policy of no loan forgiveness, with new loans being based on past credit history. Two savings and loan cooperative federations were able to transfer funds from those in less heavily damaged areas, or those with reserves, to those facing liquidity crisis. In this context, the benefits of national or regional umbrella associations became clear and smaller. Unaffiliated MFOs faced the crisis alone.

Third, the crisis also highlighted the need for remittance services. In Central America, migration within the region and to the United States is a feature of the way families diversify their livelihoods. After the hurricane, they needed to be able to receive remittances quickly and at low cost. The Nicaraguan and Costa Rican postal services announced a new remittance service between those countries with reduced charges. However, remittances have generally been a much-neglected area of microfinance activity.

Despite these moves to further institutionalize the role of credit, the proliferation of credit-related mechanisms in rehabilitation interventions signaled potential problems. Massive donations threatened to undermine the credit culture that MFOs struggled to establish before the crisis, or simply confused users with the variety of new credit policies involved. There is an important distinction to be made between organizations aiming to become permanent financial intermediaries and those using revolving funds for relief and rehabilitation. Although both approaches may be called "credit," the logic and objectives are different. Revolving funds may seek to avoid a culture of donation, to ensure that recipients make the best use of resources because they have to return them, and to multiply and extend the impact of donated resources. However, they do not necessarily charge rates sufficient to maintain fund value or aim at longer-term sustainability. Such mechanisms can play an important role, but in this case, the MFO credit culture did not have a long enough history to find ways of ensuring the complement of these two approaches; this synergy still needs to be found in practice.

Microfinance in the Wake of Conflict

The expansion of microfinance programming in the 1990s occurred at a time when approaches to programming in postconflict and complex emergency situations were trying to integrate relief and development interventions in ways that offered prospects for longer-term sustainability. In this context, microfinance is often seen as a strategy for addressing relief and development needs as well as supporting economic activity and employment creation in the contexts of months or years of stagnation. This account is based on a review of sixteen microfinance programs in four countries—Bosnia-

Herzegovina, Cambodia, Rwanda, and Mozambique—and supported by information from practitioners in other conflict affected areas.

Practitioners who want to set up sustainable microfinance organizations advise extreme caution, particularly in launching operations in the immediate aftermath of a conflict or when extensive relief and reconstruction operations are ongoing. At the same time, organizations that were operating within the country or region before or during conflict and have knowledge of local conditions and the recognition of potential customers may be in the best position to initiate microfinance services. However, it can be difficult to know whether a conflict has entirely ended or simply subsided for a period. The end of a conflict is sometimes only clear in retrospect when, for instance, a peace agreement has held for a number of years, or political, economic, and social conditions have demonstrated longer-term stability. Microfinance, as other interventions in such settings, is faced with the challenge of operating in environments moving back and forth along the relief-to-development continuum.

Although the absence of all-out or ongoing conflict is essential before microfinance programs can start, the reemergence of open-air markets is a particularly important indicator, as it suggests the return of a degree of entrepreneurial activity and perhaps monetization. A degree of social stability, especially when potential participants include a significant number of internally displaced persons or refugees, is also important. However, although displacement often continues for a long time, there is general consensus that it is more effective and less risky to open a program to a mixed membership rather than to target particular categories of war-affected people. This minimizes the likelihood of creating resentment between groups.

From the review of case study experiences, three findings for operating in postconflict environments emerge. First, the ability to mix relief with development is possible without necessarily having a detrimental impact on loan repayment. When participants understand that grants or relief support from the MFO are a temporary response to a particular crisis, they do not necessarily undermine repayment, but rather allow the organization to be seen as responsive to members' needs. The second significant finding is that major population movements and disruption do not automatically translate into loan loss. Even in dire circumstances, borrowers may demonstrate a willingness to repay loans and express a desire to remain in good standing in order to maintain their access to credit and savings services. Third, where program implementers initiate programs with similar strategies as long-term development initiatives, they do so with a willingness to be highly flexible.

Aware of common expectations for organizational and financial sustainability, program managers in postcrisis settings usually incorporate longterm sustainability goals into program design. Nevertheless, it is often the ability to operate in the short term that takes over. Practitioners anticipate that operating conditions will improve as an area recovers from conflict, but circumstances can change very rapidly, resulting in a range of risks that staff and supportive donors seem willing to accept. They maintain that the benefits provided to potential members through microenterprise development services, as well as the opportunity to take advantage of vast demand, justify program implementation at this stage.

Emphasizing that financial self-sufficiency is a reasonable and essential expectation of any program, but the time frame for self-sufficiency will depend on a range of factors, most of which are beyond the program's control. Therefore, steady advancement toward financial goals is rather unlikely. The renewal of conflict looms as a threat that can disrupt or, in an extreme case, close down a program. Moreover, meeting the current standards for operational efficiency presents a serious challenge because of the high costs of minimizing security risks, operation without banks, and increased monitoring needs.

Many practitioners strive for and understand the critical importance of self-financing, but they also underscore the fact that a willingness to make self-sufficiency goals secondary, at times, is equally important. Pressure toward self-sustainability can be especially problematic in postconflict situations, in which costly safety and security considerations may be put at risk if the early postconflict reconstruction takes much longer than anticipated. Some implementers fear that the speed with which they are expected to become self-financing results in their building weak organizational foundations. Moreover, field staff express concern that headquarters staff and donors do not allow for the uniqueness of the postconflict environment, particularly when they establish strategic plans and evaluate programs.

In general, implementers are resolute in their determination to maintain normal standards of program pricing, scale, and operational efficiency to the greatest extent possible. Almost all programs are found to charge market interest rates and practitioners note that a great deal of education—for government officials, relief donors, and relief staff—is needed to justify nonsubsidized rates. Where programs have subsidized interest rates—examples were found in Bosnia and Angola—they have been a short-term, interim adaptation to facilitate operations during the early stages of reconstruction. Borrowers have responded well to subsequent increases in interest rates if promoters have explained that future interest rate increases are essential to the continuation of financial services and a sign of returning normalcy. Given limited wage employment and fewer informal financing options, members in postconflict environments seem to value security of access over low-cost financing.

The greatest difficulty encountered by programs is in their attempts to achieve *organizational* sustainability. Most postconflict countries are characterized by a lack of experience with decentralized, private sector economic activity and little or no recent history of strong civil sector organizations. In addition, capable middle managers and leaders are scarce, especially in countries such as Rwanda, Mozambique, and Cambodia, where the educated either left or were killed. Developing new management capacity takes a considerable amount of time and investment and may not bear fruit because well trained staff become highly marketable as the situation improves. The lack of suitable, local nongovernmental partners may lead international organizations to attempt to create a local organization from scratch. In some cases, organizations attempt to make the transition from a local relief or social services agency to a microfinance service provider. For staff, the shift from a relief to microfinance mentality is quite difficult, and it can be better to hire new staff to initiate microfinance operations.

Conclusions

Microfinance interventions, in their focus on achieving organizational and financial sustainability, face particular challenges in dealing with contexts of instability. All of these examples show a developing degree of institutionalization of credit mechanisms at the level of both MFOs and borrowers. First, MFOs in Bangladesh and Central America put in place policies of not writing off loans and rescheduling, except as required by particular MFOs. Further, pressure was not forthcoming from other stakeholders either, such as governments, for rescheduling, and loan write-offs. Second, at the borrower level, examples from the postconflict study found situations in which people willingly attempted to repay loans in order to restart credit mechanisms; this signals a degree of acceptance of the role of NGOs as credit providers rather than as distributors of relief assistance. Third, in Bangladesh and in the conflict-affected programs, the combination of relief approaches with credit-based ones was not necessarily a problem. This suggests that as long as the credit mechanism is well enough understood and accepted, relief interventions from the same agencies can also be implemented without confusion arising. However, there was concern in Central America at the proliferation of credit mechanisms in the post–Hurricane Mitch situation and a demand for NGOs to be consistent in their approaches.

The ability to weather shocks is a useful indication of organizational strength. "Mega" MFOs in Bangladesh were able to respond to the crisis, backed by financial resources and the ability to manage the impact of this response on their organizations. Similarly, Philippine MFOs were able to obtain funds from new sources when their usual funding channels dried up; this was a testament to the extent of their organizational development. However, this organizational strength is itself a product of the wider context within which the organization is operating, and the economic and physical shocks did not in themselves threaten the wider organizational fabric. By contrast, the difficulties of operating microfinance postconflict are fundamentally caused by the weaknesses of the operating environment as a whole—the ability to recruit staff and cope with safety and security concerns—and their own organizational development is constrained by this.

A key consequence for MFOs of financial crisis in the Philippines and natural disasters in Bangladesh and Central America was a liquidity squeeze. The "mega" MFOs in Bangladesh had significant financial reserves to draw on and good linkages to the banking system which in the end overcame these liquidity crises. Smaller MFOs did not. In Central America after Hurricane Mitch, MFOs were, to an extent, able to redistribute liquidity among themselves as a partial solution. By contrast, in the Philippines, it was the links to the banking system and foreign investors that were a source of the liquidity squeeze. As MFOs develop toward autonomy as financial institutions, they are inevitably increasing the degree to which they are integrated into both domestic and international financial systems. This requires careful consideration in a globalizing world that is shaping the nature of the relationship between MFOs and wider financial systems. This is not an argument for autarky—indeed, the movement of funds from places of surplus to deficit in response to such crises is a necessary part of building systems that can cushion poor people from shocks. However, if integration into wider systems is to provide this support, the terms of the relationship need to be negotiated in advance. It raises the question of how to make capital "patient" and negotiate the terms on which capital is used for lending to poor people.

Notes

1. Poor households are also vulnerable to shocks, and microfinance programs can assist in developing products—for example, savings and insurance mechanisms—that allow them to protect themselves, however, this chapter does not focus on this issue.

2. "Natural" disasters may be natural in their causes, but their consequences depend on the man-made environment—for example, the extent and quality of flood defenses, the presence of cyclone shelters, and so on.

12

Striving for Influence in a Complex Environment: NGO Advocacy in the European Union

Christian L. Freres

As a result of its growing international presence, the European Union (EU) has become an increasingly important arena and target for the advocacy activities of nongovernmental organizations (NGOs) concerned with development issues. In this chapter, *NGO advocacy* refers to activities aimed at strategically articulating information to democratize unequal power relations.[1] This study explores NGO advocacy in the framework of the EU, because this particular context presents a number of serious challenges and opportunities that are somewhat different from other environments. The focus is on trans-European networks involved in advocacy on nonaid issues within the EU, because one of the main arguments is that the challenges for influencing these types of issues are generally greater than for advocacy on traditional aid matters. The chapter begins with a brief overview of NGO advocacy experience. The following section outlines the EU context. After that, a particular case of NGO advocacy in the EU is considered, and the chapter concludes with some general reflections.

NGO Advocacy: Some Emerging Lessons

Over the course of various decades, NGOs have evolved considerably in the tasks they carry out, their objectives, and their level of resources and public support base. This has resulted in changing roles and activities. To track this change, David Korten (1990), in a much-cited work, developed a classification of NGOs in terms of generations. As part of the fourth generation, in the 1970s these organizations became increasingly engaged in policy advocacy. Advocacy activities signaled a change in outlook, because NGOs had to go beyond their traditional focus to "deal with the political responsibility inherent to advocating on the themes of poverty, environment, human rights and sustainable development."[2] This new outlook started a process that has led to the creation of numerous networks, informal and formal, that have engaged in campaigns, large and small, all over the world (Keck and Sikkink 1998).

Although there have been many successes, it is important not to overstate an optimistic view of advocacy efforts to date. A realistic perspective, based on a rapid and critical overview of experience, would show a relatively low degree of success. In general, advocacy efforts can be considered successful if they are shown to contribute decisively to their intended goals. For instance, the NGOs that sought to stop the multilateral trade negotiations in Seattle in December 1999 clearly succeeded, whereas those that tried to stop the arms trade have not had much success. In most cases, it is not clear if a campaign failed or succeeded because other factors might be more relevant; policy changes often take a long time to be implemented, and the end result may not be the one intended by the NGOs. In addition, success may sometimes be partial, if only one of many objectives was achieved (see Oxfam 1996, 14).

Paradoxically, many "successful" campaigns turn out to produce short-lived benefits that are soon overrun by events or the limited capacity of NGOs to follow through. This was the case of the international mine campaign, which, according to one activist involved, became "a victim of its own success" (Scott 1999,9). This occurred because the decision to ban mines actually led to decreasing public pressure on governments to provide resources for mine-affected populations. Despite increasing interest in these activities, a large number of NGOs do not engage in, or even passively support, advocacy efforts. Many organizations are content to carry out traditional aid programs and projects and see advocacy as interfering with their capacity to raise funds and maintain political independence. Other NGOs may sympathize with the objectives of advocacy campaigns but believe they have too little capacity to get involved in an active manner over a long period, or the goals may be "not urgent" enough (Clark 1991,127). In contrast to these views, Jordan and Van Tuijl (1998) see advocacy—in the broad sense, not limited to lobbying activities—as a key part of NGO identity and accountability (see Covey 1995). Nevertheless, they also note that advocacy actions are not a step above—and therefore inherently more important than—NGOs' development work at the grassroots, but that these two levels or types of activity should be better integrated, in order to link the local and global arenas.

From this very brief review of NGO advocacy, which admittedly stresses the problematic aspects, it is evident that few organizations are actively involved and that the experience so far has been mixed, with some clear successes but also many failures (partial or complete). This general synthesis may be even more visible in the context of the EU because of certain characteristics that I will analyze in the following section.

The European Union Context

The EU—founded in 1957—is the product of a complex and continuously evolving process. It is not a single organization, but a set of institutions, formal and informal, bound together by the common desire of the member states to advance in their integration, in order to "safeguard peace in the region, promote economic development, expand political union and strengthen social cohesion" (Borchardt 1995,23). Although there has been constant debate on how far this integration should go, this has not stopped the process from advancing. On the contrary, the Union has progressed significantly in size—from its original six members to the present fifteen—and institutional complexity, largely as a result of inspired leadership and a series of ambitious agreements and treaties initiated in the mid-1980s. The EU has also become a key reference point throughout Eastern and Central Europe, as many countries are seeking to join the Union. This interest partly reflects the EU having become an important international actor over the past decade. It is the largest trading block in the world, and together with its member states, it is the main source of development assistance today. The EU has also played significant roles in the resolution of international conflicts and has used its influence to promote democracy and human rights around the world. All this has occurred despite the reality that the EU is still considered an economic giant, but a political dwarf, because of its inability on many occasions to speak with one voice on the international scene.

There are three basic characteristics of EU decision making that may provide opportunities for interest groups to engage in the policy process. The first is that institutions are divided, so decisions are taken at many levels. The commission and the European Parliament (EP) are the main community institutions. The commission—the executive body—has been the main target of interest groups' influence activities, but the EP is increasingly important because of its ability to bring new issues into the public debate (Greenwood and Aspinwall 1998). The council is the main intergovernmental body, with ultimate decision-making power in many areas. It is the body that has most responsibility for advancing major policy initiatives. Second, each institution is not in itself monolithic; this internal fragmentation is seen in the various examples of directorates within the commission fighting for control over certain competencies. These two aspects combine to provide many points of access to the decision-making process, the third characteristic.

Theoretically, it would seem that the structure of the EU is relatively conducive to interest groups having influence, but there are other aspects that pose important obstacles. One of these is the weak democratic legitimacy of most EU institutions, reflected in a rather closed process of decision making (with the partial exception of the EP) and limited accountability to EU citizens. In addition, two types of interests predominate in EU decision making: on the one hand, "territorial concerns," which are defended by the member states and have been at the core of the broadest political debates; on the other, business and industry interests, which have been at the heart of community policies since its inception in 1957. Although this situation simply reflects the fundamentally economic nature of this integration scheme, it poses serious challenges for those groups seeking to present alternative views, which are not based on economic self-interest.

At the same time, the relative power of each institution in the EU has changed. Thus, the eminently technical nature of changes introduced in the 1980s contributed to the commission having a leadership role that went far beyond its formal power. This role reached its apex in the Treaty of the European Union in 1992. In reaction, however, the member states reimposed their predominance in decision making, forcing the commission to take a much lower profile. Along the way, the parliament has increased its power, but in a very gradual manner, so that it is still unable to counterbalance the other institutions. As power shifts to the council, access to decision making has become more complex (Gourlay and Remacle 1998). The importance for interest groups of combining their Brussels work with national—and even subnational—activities has increased; however, this has been one of the weakest areas for many collectives.

Related to the above characteristics is the fact that the European Union has developed a complex set of relations with developing countries (see Lister 1998). This is primarily due to the piecemeal form in which its foreign relations have been constructed. As a recent external review of the EU notes, "To find the EU's development policies applicable to any given sector or geographical area it is necessary to enter a thicket of regulations, resolutions, declarations, and communications for which there is no road map" (Development Assistance Committee 1998, 11).

Because of the "original sin" of building cooperation in a gradual and *ad hoc* fashion, the commission lacks "an overall policy statement for EU development" (ICEA/DPPC 1999, 58). In addition, interlocutors vary from issue to issue and region to region. Although internal coordination has improved somewhat with the new commission, which began in September 1999, it remains limited, contributing to a complex and sometimes contradictory decision-making process (ICEA/DPPC 1999; Development

Assistance Committee 1998). On the other hand, because of its need for external allies to support the integration process, and in order to be more efficient in the administration of its scarce resources, the commission (and to a lesser extent, the other EU institutions) has favored "interaction with Euro-groups where possible" (Greenwood 1997, 4). This tendency has contributed to the creation of a multitude of trans-European associations in all areas of public interest.

Research suggests that Euro-groups are more influential on community policy than are nationally based organizations. As one specialist in EU interest groups notes, "A well-organized Euro-group can make itself indispensable to the Commission by bringing representative opinion and other resources from one source" (Greenwood 1997, 4). Thus, many specialists suggest that Euro-groups should have a base in Brussels or close by in order to be able to build up networks of links with other like-minded organizations and with the EU institutions.

NGO Advocacy in the EU: The Case of the Liaison Committee's Intergovernmental Conference Campaign

What has been the experience of NGO advocacy in the EU? The literature includes a number of specific cases (Baranyi et al. 1997), but there is a lack of broader studies. This study is also based on a single case involving the Liaison Committee of Development NGOs to the European Union (LC), one of the central networks engaged in lobbying EU institutions on development issues. The LC is made up of representatives from each of the fifteen member states' national NGO platforms that together include more than 800 member organizations. The LC secretariat has a small policy department in Brussels, which spends about half of its time—to which may be added some of the secretary general's time—on advocacy-related activities. However, in principle, the LC relies heavily on the national platform representatives and their member organizations to carry out much of its advocacy work.

An example of a recent advocacy campaign[3] that illustrates many of the strengths and weaknesses of the LC efforts in this area is the Intergovernmental Conference (IGC) campaign.[4] The LC General Assembly in April 1995 decided to create a working group to advise members on issues related to the IGC. This group was to be responsible for monitoring the conference, drafting position papers, and recommending lobbying action for the LC and national platforms. In addition, the group would act as a channel of information and expertise and was to be available to coordinate advocacy work. In its year and a half of existence, the IGC working group met at least a dozen times, and together with LC staff produced various documents, lobbying letters, and position papers, in addition to a policy pamphlet, "Action Plan for World Leaders." Meetings (for information and lobbying) were held with a large number of commission officials, members and officials of the EP, and other NGO networks at the Brussels level; lobbying also took place in various member states, focusing on national authorities involved in EU policymaking.

There was no outside evaluation of this experience, so the following review is based on my analysis. On the positive side, the campaign involved a number of NGOs and the LC in a new area. It is hard to measure to what extent NGOs became aware of the importance of this dimension to their work. The impression many in the working group had is that although many NGOs began to recognize this, they were not ready to take on extra responsibilities. That is, few organizations had sufficient will to warrant dedicating significant staff time to the campaign. This became evident in the group itself, which lost several members in the course of its short existence. Nevertheless, it is clear that at least for the group itself, the LC secretariat, and the national platform representatives who were most acquainted with the campaign, the efforts constituted a useful learning experience. Some of the obstacles referred to in relation to the EU context were seen in a very direct manner; without that experience, it is doubtful that the organizations would have learned these lessons. However, there are practically no mechanisms for disseminating these lessons, so much learning is lost.

The campaign was also positive in that it presented a different image of the LC to its traditional interlocutors (which are accustomed to a dialogue narrowly focused on aid issues, whereas the IGC work of the NGOs dealt with broader relations with the South). This advocacy also opened contacts with a new set of people in the EU institutions. In sum, relations with the commission and the parliament were undoubtedly strengthened as a result of this campaign. However, there were considerable problems. The most important was the weak response by most national platforms: Follow-through, communication, feedback, and coordination were limited. In addition, the working group and the LC failed to give sufficient attention and resources to media work and public-awareness raising. Finally, although the group originally sought to initiate a dialogue with southern partners, little was actually done. Another key problem with the campaign was that the LC did not have any significant influence on the outcome of the IGC. Although this was not strictly one of the original objectives, many of the lobbying activities were in practice aimed at influencing the policymakers, even if the group realized these efforts could only affect marginal issues.

What were the main impediments, besides the contextual problems of the EU? The group felt it began the campaign late in the process. By the time the first meeting was held, the council had already come out with its Reflection Paper. Throughout the exercise, the working group reacted to council documents and actions and was not able to take the intiative at any time. The late start also forced the group to dispense with many of the participatory mechanisms that would normally form part of this kind of advocacy activity, although in hindsight, this allowed the group to be more efficient.

A second limitation faced by the group was a lack of resources. The LC did not provide as much support as would be expected from such a "priority objective" in its work plan. As a result, at a crucial stage in the campaign, the group did not have any staff support, weakening the possibility to provide continuous follow-through. This may be a general problem of the LC, which is engaged in many campaigns simultaneously and has its staff stretched to the limits (or beyond).

Third, although experts in advocacy in the EU stress the importance of complementing efforts in Brussels with hard work in the fifteen national capitals, few platforms took their responsibility seriously. It is hard to say whether this was because of a lack of ownership or because of their own structural weaknesses, including a lack of advocacy specialists (see Bossuyt and DeBelder 1996).

Final Reflections

There are many lessons to be learned from the specific case analyzed here, but we will focus only on three of them. The first is that it is vitally important for NGOs to understand the EU's institutions and its policy process. In the case reviewed, many NGOs had a very limited knowledge of these aspects, so the group was forced to learn on the job. Some organizations are investing in training of their policy staff, but there are still comparatively few specialists who also have a deep understanding of NGO interests, strengths, and weaknesses.

A second lesson is that European NGOs need to develop attainable goals when starting a campaign focusing on the EU. In the area of aid policy, NGOs have a clear home-court advantage. Often they are sought out for advice through the various formal and informal EU-NGO consultation mechanisms that exist (see Rye 1998). In any case, they have proven that NGOs have definitive expertise and have the capacity to influence policy. This does not translate automatically to other areas of policy, however. Indeed, on issues such as trade, defense policy, immigration, etc., NGOs are outsiders, and possibilities to influence are fairly limited. In these cases, it is important to be selective, focusing on campaigns in which there are greater possibilities of achieving impact, and within nonaid issue areas, concentrating on aspects in which NGOs have expertise or successful experiences.

Finally, it is very clear that NGOs must improve their networking with other civil society groups in the EU and with southern partners. This is easier said than done, because it requires a long-term strategic outlook and the investment of resources over many years. NGOs are accustomed to working on short-term campaigns, many of which have little or no follow-through, so network building is mostly opportunistic and unsustainable. Given their resource scarcities, maintaining large networks is not feasible, so NGOs will have to be selective in their choice of partners (looking for those who show long-term commitment).

The case illustrated here is only one of several in which NGOs are getting more deeply involved in the EU policymaking process in areas outside their traditional domain of development cooperation. This is a case of NGOs attempting to get involved in global governance. In this regard, the EU is developing an international role that NGOs should try to shape. If not, it is possible that instead of aiming to become a global "civil power" (Gourlay and Remacle 1998, 90), the EU may focus its international activities on creating a defense capacity, dedicating less and less attention and resources to developing country interests. NGOs need to confront this reality, not just with criticisms, but also with alternative visions and concrete proposals that are sorely lacking in the EU today.

Notes

1. As suggested by Jordan, L. and P. Van Tuijl. 1998. "Political Responsibility in NGO Advocacy: Exploring Emerging Shapes of Global Democracy." The Hague: Netherlands Organization for Development Co-operation (NOVIB). Available at www.euforic.org.

2. Quoted by Jordan and Van Tujil, no page reference. See endnote 1.

3. This case is based on an internal "evaluation" of the IGC working group in February 1997, my perceptions (I was a member of the group), and discussions with other specialists.

4. The intergovernmental conferences are mechanisms used by the member states of the EU to introduce major reforms, particularly those that require changes in treaties. For instance, this IGC led to the Treaty of the European Union, signed in Amsterdam in June 1997.

Part III:

Innovations in Development Practice

13

The Importance of People on the Ground in International Campaigns

Jennifer Chapman

This chapter focuses on the importance of people working at the grassroots level in contributing to international campaigns. The chapter is one output from a two-year research project that examined how international campaigns work and in particular what they mean to their intended beneficiaries.[1] This focus meant it was important to ground the case studies in particular southern countries. Two campaigns were selected: the promotion of breast-feeding in Ghana and the campaign against the use of child labor in the Indian carpet industry.

Research was carried out in the two countries in collaboration with national and regional nongovernmental organizations (NGOs)[2] I found extensive campaigning had been undertaken on the part of these NGOs, and considerable success had been achieved. These findings have been written up elsewhere (Chapman 1999a, 1999b; Chapman and Fisher 1999, 2000). Key to much of the success was the work of individuals, and particularly the personal dedication, charisma, and leadership abilities of the social entrepreneurs who led or founded the southern NGOs engaged in these issues. These are people who—though at times controversial—have gained a platform nationally, and sometimes internationally, to speak on these issues.

Both campaigns focused on industry. The original conceptual map of the research focused on the *action taken by* international, national, and regional organizations (particularly NGOs), the *effects on* the industry targeted, and the people at the grassroots. However, as the campaigns were tracked, it became clear that to achieve the sought- after change, targeting private sector actors alone would not be enough; therefore, work was conducted at many different levels (international, national, regional, and local) and in different arenas within those levels. The conceptual map expanded both in relation to who was taking action and where it was having an effect.

Particularly striking was the extent to which dedicated individuals and microorganizations at the grassroots were active and taking a key role in these high profile international campaigns. In many cases, these people had no knowledge of the international work and had no idea that people elsewhere might change their habits as consumers because of the issue. In the main, they received no pay for their work, had no opportunity for international travel, and got little recognition except from their immediate community. Yet they were a vital part of the whole process of international campaigns, and their role went far beyond the generally recognized one of supplying information. Without them, real change at the grassroots would have been harder, if not impossible, to achieve.

Most writing on policy processes and campaigning focuses on the work of policy elites at the national and international level. The vital contribution of people at the grassroots *as campaigners*, not as suppliers of information or receivers of messages, is often overlooked. This chapter attempts to redress this balance by giving examples of the type of work undertaken by activists at the grassroots, showing why it is so important, and linking it to the wider campaigns.

The Promotion of Breastfeeding in Ghana

The babymilk campaign to promote breast-feeding in Ghana was promoted by Ghanaian concerned about the negative health effects of donations of formula on babies. It initially focused on the marketing of breast-milk substitutes, drawing on input from northern campaigning NGOs.It advocated for Ghana to introduce its own legislation on marketing based on the international code, and monitored companies' compliance with the international code, using its international links with IBFAN to publicize any violations. Coordinated work in Ghana began in 1987, when a Ghanaian doctor formed the Ghanaian Infant Nutrition Action Network (GINAN), which pressured the government to take action. Work on the control of marketing of breast-milk substitutes progressed quickly initially, with a code committee functioning within a year and a Ghanaian code drafted by 1989, although it is yet to become law because of bureaucratic delays. Concurrently, GINAN has been monitoring the marketing of breast-milk substitutes in Ghana, using the international babymilk code as the benchmark.

Breast-feeding was promoted locally, and health workers were trained. Ghana became involved in the United Nations Children's Fund Baby Friendly Hospital Initiative (BFHI) and the celebration of World Breast-feeding Week, an initiative from the World Alliance on Breast-feeding Action. More recently, work has been undertaken to support nursing mothers via the training of grassroots breast-feeding advisors and the formation of mother support groups (Chapman 1999b). Health facilities must have a mother support group to gain Baby Friendly status, awarded after inspection by the BFHI. However, many in Ghana believe that the mother-to-mother support groups initiated by the community are much more effective than those started by health facilities. One health worker complained that it was a meaningless exercise for the health facility to start a support group; in many cases, the groups were set up specifically for the inspection and did not last. Another complained that if groups formed through the BFHI, they expected to be funded. This was a common problem reported at the International Baby Food Action Network regional conference in South Africa in 1997.

GINAN aims to encourage mother support systems that are made up of ordinary mothers with some skills and experience to help their peers maintain breast-feeding in the home environment. Around Accra, GINAN's base, there are between forty and fifty such groups set up by communities themselves. Many of these have been facilitated by GINAN training women from the community as breast-feeding counselors. After training, some women have started mother support groups to advise on the benefits of breast-feeding; others who are already members of active women's church groups use that route to spread their new knowledge. GINAN has also trained some market women as breast-feeding counselors because they are the major distributors of infant formula in Ghana and are very influential. Not only have many trained market women stopped selling infant formula, they also advise women visiting the market on the benefits of breast-feeding.

The women who run the mother-to-mother support get little outside recognition, but they have become an integral part of the wider international campaign. They have more direct influence over whether mothers in their community choose to breast-feed than any other part of the campaign. A participatory workshop held in Accra found that for many participants, the support of a mothers' group was key to them continuing with exclusive breast-feeding. Members of such groups now believe exclusive breast-feeding gives significant health benefits, as shown in an interview with a member of one mother support group:

I have two children. When I had the first, breast-feeding had not been started in Accra. I gave her breastmilk and water until four months, then porridge and cerelac[3]. I stopped breastfeeding at one year. The second child had breastmilk with no water for six months, then rice and whatever we had that was suitable. I stopped breastfeeding at two years.

I had the first child at hospital. They did talk about breastfeeding, but at that time it was not compulsory.

The difference [between the children] is very big. The younger one has knowledge, everything is different. I didn't go to hospital with the second. I didn't spend much money. The first one was always in hospital. My husband is supportive as we didn't spend much money.

I always go to the mother support group's meetings as we get benefits. The group's leader teaches us how to feed children. If the child is sick I will go to her first as if I go to the hospital I will have to pay.

The best approach to encouraging good feeding practices in the context of AIDS (acquired immunodeficiency syndrome) remains a challenge and does not appear to be an issue that is much discussed in the support groups. GINAN's current position is that the risks to the child's health of mother-to-child HIV (human immunodeficiency virus) transmission through breast-feeding are outweighed by the health risks of not carrying out exclusive breast-feeding.[4]

The following examples are of two support groups run by volunteers, without funding, which instead rely on the motivation and dedication of women at the grassroots. Osu Mothers Support Group was formed by four women who used formula themselves and now believe this was the cause of many health problems in their children. They became active after a clinic nurse told them about benefits of breastfeeding and about other mother-to-mother support groups. There was no group in their area, and GINAN offered to train them in breast-feeding counseling in June 1996.

Since then, the four volunteers have run an active support group. They visit mothers in the local clinic and at home and encourage them to call on the counselors if they need help. During visits they show mothers how to handle babies and ensure correct attachment, and discuss breast-feeding problems, general child health, and many other problems that cause stress and hence affect breast-feeding. This entails considerable dedication of time. One volunteer normally commits three half-days per week and sees fifteen mothers regularly; another sees eight. These women are perhaps unusual in being able to offer so much time. One has given up work to look after her own mother and enjoys the social contact the group gives her. She also appreciates opportunities to meet other mother support groups.

She has seen many changes in baby feeding:

In my mother's time babies never tasted formula. Around the 1970s people stopped breastfeeding as the bottle seemed convenient and diarrhea problems started. It was the fashion; you would see it in the shops. If you see a baby with a bottle it seems to be a nice way to feed. You still see formula in pharmacy shops and supermarkets. Some time ago you would see it on all the corners. That is now uncommon.

The volunteer breast-feeding counselors who formed the Osu Mothers Support Group can take partial credit for formula no longer being sold on every local corner. They have achieved this with very little support. They receive no funding, just occasional transport to functions, promotional t-shirts, certificates, badges, and flip charts. Their main satisfaction comes in being valued by local mothers and seeing healthy babies. They are now planning to spread the message wider and are encouraging the mothers they have helped to form new groups.

By contrast, the founder and leader of La Mothers' Support Group is a health professional. She trained in lactation management in 1995 but at that time had no opportunity to use this new knowledge at work. She felt that the issue was so important that she would give impromptu lectures in the community transport on her way to work and visit neighboring homes in her spare time, looking for newly delivered mothers to inform about breast-feeding's benefits.

She decided to form a mother support group because she found people very interested but lacking knowledge. The first meeting was held in February 1996 with seven mothers to discuss the group's program. They decided to visit houses and talk especially to grandmothers, who tended to encourage mothers to give babies water. They also occasionally visit maternity homes, child welfare clinics, or church groups, where the group members talk about breast-feeding's benefits and their personal experiences. The group also ran a cleanup campaign, sweeping the area and burning rubbish, because they felt a dirty environment diluted the beneficial effects of breastfeeding.

La Mothers' Support Group has widened its focus from just breast-feeding. At meetings, mothers also ask about clinic visits, health protection, mosquito bites, and family planning. Membership has expanded to about forty, with between ten and fifteen attending each meeting. Each member is encouraged to watch for new mothers and to visit them.

The group receives no funding, although, again, they may get help with transport to special events. Many of the original members of the group are small stallholders; one impact is that they themselves no longer stock formula. Other impacts can be seen in members' comments about their babies:

The breastfed children are very bright; they pick things up quickly.

She has always been healthy and has never been to hospital, the others I started giving porridge when they were two weeks and I had a lot of problems, they were always sick and had diarrhea.

My first child I gave water as well and she was always in hospital, with this one I haven't been to hospital and haven't spent much money.

The work of these volunteer grassroots breast-feeding counselors can be put in context when looking at the factors that influence how a mother chooses to feed her baby. The factors that are susceptible to international pressure, such as the marketing of breast-milk substitutes and norms in the health system, are only very small parts of the picture. Nevertheless, these have received most attention from international nongovernmental organizations (NGOs), which frequently concentrate on policy change at a macro level. Many of the other factors that directly influence the mother's behavior—such as her knowledge, the support she receives locally, and her other commitments—are only susceptible to pressure or change at the community level.

However, work at the different levels is interlinked. These volunteer counselors are a direct result of the national campaign, which has benefited immensely from the international one. Without the work of GINAN, it is unlikely that the grassroots breast-feeding counselors would even know the benefits of breast-feeding and would not have received training or moral support. The grassroots volunteers do value the national work on monitoring marketing and the enactment of a national law as they believe "the adverts distract the women." Although the formation of GINAN was a national initiative, it has benefited immensely from the work of the international campaign and the resulting code. It also benefits from being a member of international networks and the resulting exchange of ideas and knowledge.

The Campaign Against Child Labor in the Indian Carpet Industry

The campaign against child labor in the carpet industry in India grew out of two roots—work on bonded laborers and grassroots social development work. The Indian organizations working on this issue aim to make sure that Indian law is implemented—bonded labor, and nonfamily child labor on carpets is illegal because it is classed as a hazardous industry. They are working toward providing and improving schooling for children in the area to provide a viable alternative and advocating for universal primary education in India.

This campaign was initiated by NGOs and activists within India and targets a local industry. However, because it is a major export industry, northern NGOs, consumers, and importers have played critical roles. The campaign started in 1983 with a raid to free bonded children; these raids still continue. Since 1983, a great variety of activities have been undertaken at many different levels, from the international to the grassroots. These include consumer campaigns, legislation, labeling schemes, marches, demonstrations, raids, work on community awareness, and the provision of schools (Chapman and

Fisher 2000).

In this case study, NGOs have not lobbied to introduce legislation (as this already existed) or change policies (although some changes have occurred) but have worked to influence the implementation and interpretation of policies. They have worked alongside the judiciary and government officials to enforce existing laws. They have been able to threaten export markets sufficiently to bring about some changes within the industry without actually implementing a boycott. They have established the labeling scheme (Rugmark) for carpets produced without child labor as a constructive outcome for the consumer campaign, and they have had a significant impact at the grassroots level and on the emergence of civil society. Above all, there is some evidence of a reduction in child labor in the specific industries and areas targeted, although it is debatable whether there has been an overall reduction in child labor.

The campaign has also had significant impact in advancing the debate on child labor as a whole. It has influenced work on carpet children in other countries and work on other industries in India, such as the production of firecrackers and footballs. During the campaign, the need for meaningful alternatives for working children became very visible. As a result, the campaign has also fed into the Indian campaign for universal primary education.

Particularly important in ensuring that children removed from looms were not then reemployed in alternative industries has been long-term work by NGOs at the grassroots. There are many such NGOs, ranging from a few people to large national networks with international links, such as the South Asian Coalition on Child Servitude. For many NGOs, the ultimate success of their community awareness campaigning relies critically on being able to draw on a grassroots network of motivated people.

For example, in one village near the center of the carpet-weaving industry, a woman in her thirties who describes herself as a "houselady" has become instrumental in encouraging families to send girls to school. She is well educated within her community, having reached high school tenth standard, but had no prior activist experience. She describes how she first became involved:

In my everyday life I was seeing how badly girls were treated in the family. It really pained me. I felt I must work on this really sensitive but important issue.

Poverty is very widespread in her village. When she first raised the question of girls' schooling, she was told that the girls were helping their parents with work and could not be spared. Parents were not convinced of the value of educating girls, as girls would eventually join the husband's family. She found various arguments effective in countering this viewpoint:

- Girls, who after marriage found their husbands could not support them, would be able to earn their own livelihood.

- Girls who were maltreated in their new homes would be able to write and inform their parents.

- Education empowers girls and helps protect them against any sort of dominance.

- Educated girls can be instrumental in getting education for their own sons and daughters.

- Educated girls can help other women in the village.

She encountered a lot of opposition from fathers, but some of the mothers were supportive, so she involved the mothers' group in long discussions about whether keeping girls illiterate increased their poverty or helped overcome it. She started this sensitization work alone, and then approached a local NGO a few months later when the mothers' group had formed a consensus. Finally, forty-eight parents decided to send their girls to a school run by the NGO, which opened in September 1997.

She continues her unpaid awareness work in her spare time. She is perhaps unusual, although not unique, in that she started her work entirely on her own. Many more have been catalyzed by local NGOs such as the Centre for Rural Education and Development Action (CREDA), which has trained approximately 1,300 volunteers on the issue of child rights. These volunteers check on who replaces children removed from looms and keep a villagewide vigil to make sure that children do not enter the labor market. CREDA also created 200 village-level child labor vigilance committees, each made up of twelve volunteers who take responsibility for primary school enrollment of children, keep a watch on child labor supply agents, and work closely with the district administration.

For example, one member of a village child labor vigilance committee in the carpet belt has been trained in community mobilization work and may get involved in organizing meetings, demonstrations, marches, plays, folk songs, and handing out pamphlets. Like many of the community mobilizers used by CREDA, he can only occasionally be paid a stipend when there is funding within a program. When the program comes to an end, or if there is a holdup in funding, he continues his activities and lives on his family's farm.

The community awareness work of many local NGOs has achieved considerable success in encouraging parents to send children to school rather than to work. The ultimate success of this work relies critically on local activists who are part of the community, respected by them, and are present and active even during the frequent gaps in funding.

Again, factors that influence how children in India spend their time that are susceptible to international pressure—such as whether loom owners wish to use children for work on the looms, or whether bonded labor continues—are only a small part of the picture; and even here, international pressure can only be a complement to local work. Vital factors—such as the community's attitude to how children spend their time, the children's economic situation, and the alternatives available to them, including education—need action at the grassroots level.

Although micro-level work may seem remote from consumer decisions in the North, the links between international and national campaigning and work within communities are important. It was effective campaigning at the national and international levels that drew wider attention to the problem of child labor in the carpet industry, and the resulting interest and resources allowed a significant expansion of local work by NGOs such as the South Asian Coalition on Child Servitude and CREDA. For example, funds for community mobilization and volunteer training have come from the International Labor Organization's International Program for the Elimination of Child Labor as a direct result of the attention given this issue. At the same time, national and international campaigning depends on direct experience of the stark realities at the grassroots.

It is therefore surprising that some local activists appear unaware of activity at the national and international levels. In a focus group discussion held in May 1998 with members of child labor vigilance committees, none had ever heard of any international or national level work being done on child labor, although they were aware that the issue was portrayed very negatively internationally. Despite carrying out their own inspections of looms, they had never heard about any labeling schemes for carpets.

Conclusion

This chapter highlights the work of just a few individuals. They are not unique; similar work is happening in many places. The reason for highlighting these stories is that the role of southern grassroots activists within international campaigns is little recognized or understood by northern NGOs, even though they are essential to achieving any real change in practice, both on the specific issue targeted by the campaign and on wider issues. Without these activists, changes in legislation or even monitoring of those changes will not necessarily achieve the desired effect.

The grassroots are crucial, but in themselves are not sufficient. This chapter has concentrated on the role of microorganizations and individuals because the need for work at the grassroots is often neglected in international campaigns. This is not to suggest that there is not also an important campaigning role for local, national, and international organizations. For a successful campaign to happen, work at all levels is often needed; furthermore, within each level, there may be a multiplicity of targets. No one organization can undertake work of this complexity that requires many different skills and access to different players. Instead, collaboration between organizations is required. For effective collaboration, it is important that players realize their individual limitations and recognize the significance and value of other players.

This chapter highlights one major limitation for northern NGOs in campaigning work: their lack of influence over changes on the ground. There are others, including the long time frame needed to achieve change, the politics of northern involvement in sensitive issues, and the limits of a narrow campaigning focus when dealing with complex problems (Chapman and Fisher 1999, 2000). However, northern NGOs do have a role to play, including providing resources; access to international experience, organizations, and media; encouraging consumer action; and promoting codes and legislation.

In recent years, a number of factors have encouraged northern-based NGOs to move away from direct implementation on the ground toward policy and lobbying work, with information drawn from project work on the ground implemented by "partners." Policy work is seen as an area in which northern-based NGOs might claim still to have comparative advantage, particularly because of their access to policy elites and international organizations. However, this chapter challenges northern NGOs to understand that in policy and campaigning work, work at different levels is interlinked and there is a vital role for work at the grassroots that can only be carried out by local people and organizations. Northern campaigning organizations need to do more to recognize and reflect that they are not the only—or even the key—player in international campaigns, but are part of a complex web of relationships.

Notes

1. This chapter is based on research during 1997–98 for the New Economics Foundation funded by the U.K. Department for International Development, which supports policies, programs and projects to promote international development. The Department for International Development provided funds for this study as part of that objective, but the views and opinions expressed are mine alone. I would like to acknowledge the help and input that I received from Subodh

Boddisitwa, Thomas Fisher, Shamshad Khan, Charles Sagoe-Moses, and Tina Wallace throughout the research that formed the background to this chapter.

2. The Ghanaian Infant Nutrition Action Network, the South Asian Coalition on Child Servitude, and the Centre for Rural Education and Development Action.

3. A commercial weaning food.

4. It has long been believed that breast-feeding carries a significant risk of mother-to-child HIV transmission. However, recent research challenges this and suggests that although mixed feeding (breast-feeding plus other foods, including water) carries increased risk, *exclusive* breast-feeding does not and gives significant other health benefits (Coutsoudis et al. 1999). More research is urgently needed to see if these results are replicable.

14

Think Globally, Act Locally: Translating International Microcredit Experience into the United Kingdom Context

Ruth Pearson

Global Drift and Microcredit

The notion that development experience—particularly that experience delivered by the flexible and radical nongovernmental organizations (NGOs) of the 1980s and 1990s—has much to teach policymakers in the North has gained credence in recent years (Lewis 1999; Maxwell 1998). Although this approach is refreshing, it needs to be desimplified, not least in the field of microcredit programs for economically and socially marginal groups.

In the wake of the 1997 Microcredit Summit in Washington, D.C., enthusiasm for microcredit as a poverty alleviation strategy in the North has grown, with some commentators seeing access to financial services as the missing link in the new monetized global market. Endorsed by the indefatigable Hillary Clinton, enthusiasts have pointed to the example of microcredit programs in the South, particularly the much publicized examples in South Asia. They have urged northern countries to follow suit and allow those excluded from labor markets to gain access to the financial resources necessary to operate successfully in local trading contexts, thus diminishing the need for dependence on national and federal welfare systems. Indeed, in keeping with the new rights-based discourse of international NGOs of the 1990s, Muhammad Yunus, founder of the Grameen Bank in Bangladesh, declared at the 1997 Summit that

it should be recognized that . . . credit is a human right . . . it also should be recognized that it is a human right which plays a crucial role in attaining all other human rights (cited in Mayoux 1997, 16).

Such global positioning is well suited to an international NGO community poised to reconsider their role in the face of economic and political crisis in East and South East Asia, the former Soviet Union, the Balkans, and elsewhere in the global economy. NGOs recognize that in the face of globalization they have an ongoing mission to provide alternative modes of subsistence and participation for the poorest. As Edwards et al. put it, NGOs

. . . are already developing a number of strategies to help poor people address the realities of their position in global markets and play a creative role in reshaping economic forces . . . . [including] improving access to credit, services, and economic opportunities (Edwards, Hulme, & Wallace 1999, 120).

Indeed, the current flurry of position papers to celebrate the "Plus 5" anniversaries of the various United Nations World Conferences of the 1990s are focused on the elaboration of alternative strategies and alternative modes of delivery of development policy and practice for the twenty-first century. However, there is a danger that the ghost of globalization will bring a new orthodoxy of universalism. Many international NGOs were born and have matured within the protective policy framework of post–World War II international development cooperation, but it is important that these organizations do respond to the increasing globalization of development discourse by suggesting that there are standard global solutions to problems of poverty.

Microcredit and Poverty Alleviation: The Example from the South

Most development agencies—both official and nongovernmental—are making poverty reduction the central objective of their activities. It is therefore not surprising that microcredit to support microenterprise has attracted a central place in strategies to achieve such ends. Following the celebrated successes of the Grameen Bank in Bangladesh and other well-known "success stories" in the microcredit field, such as the Bangladesh Rural Advancement Committee and the Self-Employed Women's Association in India, a wide range of national and international NGOs—with varying degrees of experience—began offering financial services. The strategy aimed at supporting the entrepreneurial activities of the poor as a response to their perceived lack of working capital for micro-level enterprises.

The new policy interventions were also responding, if less consciously, to the increasing monetization of Third World economies and the growing importance of access to money, even at the level of subsistence and survival. Many women working as unpaid family helpers or low-paid day laborers in both rural and urban economies face an increasing demand for money, as do the growing numbers of female-supported households in urban areas (Pearson 1998b). Under the earlier political economy orthodoxy, the state strove to provide basic household services directly, particularly health care and education; in the poststructural adjustment era, many of these services could only be accessed via money, meaning that women's reproductive role as well as their productive role became monetized (Pearson 2000, forthcoming).

Microcredit provision became a priority in the 1980s during a public policy climate that was focused on enabling the individual to participate in the market rather than organizing the state to meet the individual's needs. The macrocontext of the growth in popularity of microcredit is often ignored, and most literature focuses instead on the inadequacy of existing financial institutions to meet the needs of the poor who by definition had no security, had no regular income, and relied on small and multiple transactions—an unattractive and high-cost sector for conventional banking institutions. Many NGOs have entered this service gap with little analysis of the changes in economic policy that had generated this demand.

It was quickly established that women were often the majority of borrowers. Again, the attention was on women's higher repayment records, their amenability to peer pressure and discipline, and the added assumption that if credit was targeted at women, it must by definition be "empowering." This issue has generated considerable description, dispute, and debate (Goetz and Sen Gupta 1996; Kabeer 1998; Mayoux 1997). However, the focus has been on intrahousehold relations and bargaining, rather than on a gendered analysis of the monetization of subsistence and survival. Nor has attention been given to the gendered responsibilities for household welfare that make women guarantors of household subsistence, or the fact that at the level of trading involved in women's loans, the boundary between production and consumption is extremely permeable.

Adapting Microcredit for the Excluded of the North

This lack of attention to the dynamics of local economic relations of subsistence and accumulation finds an echo in the ways in which southern microcredit models have been adapted for use in the North. From the mid-1980s onward, innovative and pro-poor financial institutions (such as Shorebank in Chicago) were developed by the not-for-profit sector in the United States, aimed at providing poor households and poor communities with credit for housing, business, and consumption. Groups organizing minority city communities, such as Women's Self Employment Program in Chicago, developed a series of training and credit programs for disadvantaged people and built a strong urban credit movement that is still effective and innovative today. In fact, many of the successful microcredit programs in North America were established in large urban conurbations with immigrant and minority communities. The 1992 Community Reinvestment Act made corporate funding available for community regeneration and economic empowerment projects aimed at reducing long-term welfare dependence and exclusion from education, employment, and other markets.

However, the history of microcredit in the United States shows how myopic it is to lump all minorities together. The most successful programs were organized with immigrant communities—those from South East and East Asia, Central and South America—economic cultures in which trading was the norm for subsistence. The communities, particularly among first- and second-generation migrants, had no experience in their countries of origin of extensive state provision for welfare and no history of multigenerational welfare dependence.

However, in other sections of the minority community, such schemes had a different trajectory. Microcredit projects, based on the peer-collateral model developed in South Asia, were first enthusiastically adopted in Governor Clinton's state—with very mixed results. Peer-lending technologies—insisted on by the Clintons in Arkansas—turned out to be far from successful. These mainly African-American communities were extremely debt averse with no entrepreneurial experience or reference groups to guide their initiatives. Local organizations found that they had to adapt the programs to provide very different options, such as intermediate and sheltered labor markets for those with no work experience, and training for available public and service sector employment. Some projects still operating on the peer collateral model found it nearly impossible to move loan funds and organize effective business starts and repayments (Goldstein-Gelb et al. 1998).

Those adapting models to the U.K. context cannot therefore assume unproblematic transfer from one context to another (Pearson 1998a). First, there is the question of the different ideological, political, and economic role of enterprise within different cultures and economies. In the United States, the rhetoric—and part of the reality—is that everyone is an entrepreneur. The United States is a nation of immigrants; it celebrates self-sufficiency and "rags to riches" mobility. Welfare has never been largely accessed by the middle class, who had private insurance and occupational pensions. The trends toward flexibility and job insecurity hit much earlier. Entrepreneurship is seen as part of the concept of national citizenship, and bankruptcy is seen not as a total failure but as a signal to draw a line and try again (Stuart and Collinson 1999).

In the United Kingdom, the situation is quite different. The small "corner shop" culture tends to be confined to the margins of the economy, particularly in localities where such activities have been the preserve of ethnic minorities. Self-employment and microenterprise has often been seen as "cheating" by those on the right and as "exploitation" by those on the left. The right sees it as a way of making money on the side—the gray economy—claiming welfare benefits and then doing work "cash in hand."[1] This is compounded by the hostility toward new immigration from the Commonwealth. The left see self-employment as exploitation, as labor that enjoys no appropriate entitlements—no benefits, no health and safety surveillance, no regulation of working and wage conditions, and no job security. In this conceptualization, microenterprise is represented as the extreme end of labor flexibility, where all kinds of non-regulated income-generating activities are lumped together—home working, contract working, itinerant building and decorating, gardening and housepainting, domestic services, and child care. Historically in the United Kingdom, the whole of the policy approach from the left has been to regulate to ensure that exploitation of workers in these sectors is minimized and benefits are paid, while promoting employment opportunities in the "mainstream" labor market. There has been little interest from the traditional left in policies to promote and revalue enterprise activities for the working poor. An exception to this has been the Prince's Trust, established in 1986 to support unemployed or underemployed eighteen- to thirty-year-olds by extending loans and grants to start up a business. The Prince's Trust also supports potential young entrepreneurs by providing a business mentor to assist with business and financial planning and to facilitate relationships with the commercial financial institutions. Although this organization was long regarded as an example of charitable support rather than as a promoter of self-help solutions, it has achieved a high level of voluntary and government grant support and continues to be seen in government circles as a model of microenterprise support with marginalized groups (Treasury 1999).

However, this initiative, which predated the current policy debates, illustrates the problems inherent in incorporating support for small entrepreneurs into the politics and policies of Britain. In much of the current debate about welfare reform, the left in the United Kingdom continues to insist on an undifferentiated notion of the deserving poor. The concern with globalization and labor flexibility has reinforced the focus on labor market regulation and entitlements for workers rather than extending it to discussions about new forms of work (Giddens 1999). Until fairly recently, there was little discussion about the potential for self-employment as a desirable route into mainstream economic and social activity. However, particularly since the election of Tony Blair's New Labor government in 1997, there has been increasing policy attention given to tackling poverty and social exclusion in the United Kingdom by (re)insertion of marginalized groups into labor and enterprise markets. The policy emphasis has been largely on supply-side initiatives, particularly the various "New Deals" (for the young and long-term unemployed and partners, the disabled, single parents, and people older than fifty). These initiatives have combined a range of labor market and training guidance services with mentoring, work experience, subsidies, training, and employment opportunities designed to enhance the employability and employment readiness of such groups. Interestingly, in spite of the current global debates, consideration for an enterprise route to economic activity was only belatedly and partially introduced, and has yet to be widely promoted or supported (Fisher 1999). The U.K. prime minister observed that

. . . many people are trapped on welfare who could be making a local living. . . . We need to look at how small amounts of credit and capital can be made available for promising business ideas in Britain's poorest areas. . . . (*The Observer*, 31 May 1998)

The New Economics Foundation, an independent think tank with a commitment to bottom-up community-based economic policies, responded with a report calling for a new microcredit agenda for the United Kingdom (Conaty and Fisher 1999). The report highlights an important policy dilemma for both South and North as to the suitability of microcredit as a tool for poverty eradication. Should credit be provided for potential entrepreneurs for whom access to finance is the key obstacle preventing the establishment and growth of otherwise viable businesses, or should the priority be "regenerating particular areas or facilitating disadvantaged or marginalized groups" (Conaty and Fisher 1999, 14)? The significance of this distinction can be highlighted by a study of two very different microcredit initiatives in the United Kingdom: the nationally based Credit Mikros (Street UK) initiative and the locally based Full Circle Fund operating with low-income women in Norfolk, East Anglia.

Street UK intends to provide credit to the self-employed and microbusinesses that are either too small or too risky to be served by mainstream banks and other financial institutions, as well as those operating in the (illegal, unregulated) gray economy who are trading while continuing to receive welfare benefits. It anticipates that its clients will cover the whole range of home-based or local-based traditional businesses, including street traders, domestic and household services providers, crafts persons, and computer programmers. It is based on a successful project funded by the United States Agency for International Development in Poland, called Funduz Mikros. This project works with

fledgling enterprises which have been trading for at least three months and are operating in the informal or black economy. . . . [It gives small loans of £1000] initially for
basic equipment and working capital, with subsequent loans for investment and expansion purposes. It utilizes group collateral methodology developed in the south,
with each group of four to seven entrepreneurs providing mutual guarantees, though
it also makes loans to individuals outside a group at higher interest rates and with
external personal guarantors. Funduz Mikros provides no pre-start up or planning
support, dispenses with business plans, and interacts with loanees on the basis of site
visits by loan officers with laptops (Conaty and Fisher 1999,27).

The project is requesting £7 million of grant subsidy from the Treasury,
which is excluded from calculations of financial sustainability,[2] and will serve
approximately 16,000 clients with a total loan portfolio of £40 million. The
proposal argues that a national initiative of this kind has the ability to draw
on critical innovations in microfinance internationally and to provide a scale
of operations large enough to provide the strategic push for microcredit
necessary if such initiatives are to contribute significantly to social regeneration
and inclusion (Conaty and Fisher 1999). This project in some ways reflects
the confusion of economic regeneration and social objectives, promising to
create substantial numbers of "unsubsidized" new jobs, create widespread
access to appropriate capital and financial services, support gray economy
entrepreneurs into the formal economy (reducing welfare payments), and
develop appropriate public/private sector partnerships. However, it does not
discuss the risk-taking propensities of the target population and their degree
of preparedness to reduce reliance on benefit payments. Moreover, it assumes
that there are sufficient numbers of self-employed and microregistered
enterprises, self-employed gray market activities, and current start-up
businesses that will generate sufficient demand to make such a national project
sustainable.

In contrast, the Women's Employment Enterprise and Training Unit
(WEETU)/Full Circle Program is a pilot initiative that has developed a peer-
collateral credit and training program for low-income women in rural and
urban Norfolk (Pearson 1998a; Pearson and Watson 1997). This program
was developed with inspiration from southern examples, but on the basis of
an existing organization with a track record of working with its local target
group, and a substantive understanding of the dynamics of the local economy
and labor markets. The proposal was initially greeted with incredulity from a
number of the key business and enterprise institutions in the area, particularly the Training and Enterprise Council. This body continued for some
time in the 1990s to work with a model of the economy that was entirely
growth oriented and that therefore considered microenterprise projects for

low-income, often benefit-dependent, women as part of social rather than economic policy. Like Street UK, the Full Circle Program used successful international experience (from South Asia and North America) to provide evidence of the viability of such policies as well as guidance on procedures and services. It also used the support of key figures, including Mohammed Yunus of the Grameen Bank (Yunus and Jolis 1998) and OXFAM International to build confidence and support among funders and key opinion makers. Although it is run by an independent not-for-profit organization in the voluntary sector (WEETU), the project has funding and other support from a range of other stakeholders, including local authorities; social investors (particularly the Charities Aid Foundation); international NGOs such as OXFAM International; and commercial banks, such as Barclays.

The pilot phase of this program illustrated the difficulties of working successfully with the pilot group and the necessity of a deep understanding of the dynamics of local economies and structures. It has become clear that the demographic structure of East Anglia—one of very low immigration and ethnic homogeneity, and restricted geographical mobility—makes enterprise very alien to low-income people, particularly women. In these circumstances, women are decidedly risk averse, and the risks involved in taking out loans and setting up small enterprises that are to provide part or all of household income appear threatening, particularly to those whose lives have been characterized by dependence—on men, on kin and family, and on the benefit system. However, the risk is not confined to income sources; it is also social and cultural. A would-be woman entrepreneur in a conservative society risks losing face if an enterprise fails, particularly if she is from a social class to which regulated self-employment is a largely unfamiliar venture. There are also risks attached to committing oneself to a particular path in a context in which positive decisions, rather than accommodation to circumstances, tend to be the norm. There are hazards in doing something different and therefore making oneself visible and vulnerable.[3]

Two simultaneous strategies were required before the project could mobilize the potential microentrepreneurs in the Full Circle target group. First, the model of group collateral was adapted to provide ongoing mutual support through business training and lending circle formation as preparation for the point at which individual women take out business loans from the loan fund.[4] Second, the project took on a policy development and advocacy role with central government to address the greatest obstacle in developing entrepreneurial potential within this group: the problem of the inflexibility of the welfare benefits system.

WEETU/Full Circle has therefore advocated a "welfare waiver," which would provide an appropriate level of protection of basic income for women and their dependents at the point at which they initiate self-employment. This is predicated on the importance of giving women in the local economy time to establish themselves and to be confident that they can begin to support themselves and their households from their incipient business, before cutting off their income support and other benefits. This approach is built on an understanding of the role that credit and training for self-employment could have for (some) low-income women. However, it also accepts the results of U.S. research, which shows that this is not the path for all women, and will not necessarily be appropriate for the rest of a woman's working life, but may well be an intermediate step back into the mainstream employment market (Pearson 1997).

The two approaches described here illustrate the complexities of the U.K. context as an arena in which to introduce microfinance and poverty alleviation policies and highlight the difficulties of adapting models that have been developed for other economic and social contexts. However, they also show the complicated and unclear role of NGOs in the emerging policy arena in the United Kingdom. If community-level microfinance projects (assumed to have a social rather than a commercial role) are to be relegated to the margins of the movement to provide appropriate financial services (which may indeed be a very appropriate place for them), what kind of accountability and connections will such an institution have with the voluntary and community sector? If credit is the only missing link in the ability of already entrepreneurial individuals to transform their activities into the profitable regulated sector, what sense does this make of the analysis of multiple levels of social exclusion and social capital, which has been at the forefront of policy discussion? If the purpose of a nationwide project is to create partnerships with private and public organizations, what is the appropriate forum for discussing and establishing such partnerships? In short, if microlending is to be heralded as an effective policy-alleviation and employment-creation tool in the United Kingdom (as it has been in other parts of the world), then is it sensible to see this as a socially sensitive but commercially operated initiative, unconnected with local circumstances or individual situations? And if it is a commercial solution that is required, cannot this be accomplished by the commercial banking sector together with the newer social banking institutions that have been established in recent years?

WEETU/Full Circle's case is that more than credit is required: Alternative visions, training role models, marketing, systematic business planning, accounts and bookkeeping, and economic and financial literacy are needed at the very least in order to make microcredit a useful tool.

Conclusions

In the North, just like in the South, it is important to look at the socio-economic context to understand how and why microcredit works or does not, what it can do and what it cannot. It is also important to understand why women might be successful users of microcredit services and what that tells us about monetization and globalization, intrahousehold gender relations, and responsibilities for household survival and maintenance.

It is also important to be aware of international and intranational differences, rather than assuming microcredit is a stand-alone universal poverty alleviation tool. It may be, as Mohammed Yunus claims, a human right to have access to financial services. However, as feminists have long pointed out, it is also why you need the service and what you do with it that is significant in terms of the implementation of human rights. The freedom a financial loan might give to one person may well mean further loss of freedom and choice for another. The kind of activity that might be successful among recent African migrants in the United Kingdom might also work for second-generation Asian immigrants, but may not work for recent arrivals from the subcontinent nor for the hand-to-mouth white "underclass" in suburban Britain. Moreover, as we have shown in Norfolk, for populations that are dispersed and relatively ethnically homogeneous, the assumption that trading in home-produced goods and services is a straightforward and obvious way to sustain a household is sorely misplaced.

NGOs do have a role here. My argument is that NGOs can test the water. By definition, they are small, locally responsible, and flexible. They can pilot initiatives and work out how they can be designed to meet local circumstances. They can also test alternative regulatory frameworks that can provide the basis for adaptations to national regulations—in financial matters, income support and benefits, small business support services, and training strategies. They can serve as institutional mentors to inspire other organizations and institutions to develop their own appropriate projects and strategies. However, such a role does not require NGOs to establish grandiose national schemes, nor does it require the deployment of universalistic assumptions. It requires that initiatives of this kind are properly integrated with local demographic, ideological, and bureaucratic conditions based on local research into the demand and supply sides of both labor and commodity markets.

Notes

1. The difference in perception of the entrepreneurial working poor is perceptively discussed in Connolly (1989).

2. Personal communication from Ros Copisarow, Founder of Street UK and former chief executive of Funduz Mikros, Birmingham, January 1999.

3. Interestingly, participants in this project from already nonconforming groups—ethnic minorities and women with disabilities—are twice as numerous as the proportion of these groups in the local population.

4. Initially, the groups of between four and six women who were to take on responsibility for monitoring and guaranteeing each other's loans were called "borrowing circles." At the suggestion of the participants, the name was changed to "lending circles," on the grounds that "We lend each other support, advice, friendship, and understanding—we are not just here to borrow money."

15

NGOs and Local Organizations:
A Mismatch of Goals and Practice?

Sarah Crowther

Nongovernmental organizations (NGOs) often work with and through local people's organizations. Helping local people organize activities in a more or less formal manner is an integral part of participatory approaches, but one that has received considerably less attention than that given to participatory methods.

NGOs justify working with local organizations in ways that echo established justifications for participation. Organizing is seen as a means and an end: a tool for development agencies and a right for local people. Organizing is expected to increase effectiveness in project management and quality, for example, by enhancing communication, mobilizing local resources, and encouraging local cooperation (Esman and Uphoff 1984). It is meant to improve people's access to NGO resources and services and expand distribution of project benefits—for example scaling up people's access to credit by creating credit and savings groups. Supporting local organizations is seen as a way to build sustainable structures for local people's own management and subsequent expansion of development activities.

NGOs also claim that building local organizations will empower local people, boosting their capacity to act for themselves in many practical ways. Organizing is meant to help more vulnerable local people find greater equality within local relationships. Wood et al. (1991) reported success when a project gave poorer men in Bangladesh control of sources of irrigation water that better-off farmers needed. As well as being able to negotiate satisfactory payments and arrangements with the other farmers, some of the groups' members reported gaining social status and respect from better-off farmers. Some NGOs espouse Freirian philosophies, in which organizing and participation are almost synonymous—the experience of participation in collective action serving to raise consciousness and strengthen solidarity among the weak so they can act in the face of local opposition (Fals-Borda and Rahman 1992). Local organizations are seen as a route to stronger civil society by helping local people engage in dialogue or even partnerships with government, market institutions, and NGOs themselves. Eventually, local people's own organizations will link into people-centered global networks and come to influence globalized notions of development itself (Korten 1984; Korten and Quizon 1991).

To achieve these diverse ideals of quality, sustainability, and greater equality, NGOs often draw from a fairly normative range of organizing practices: from initial awareness raising, to group formation and resourcing, and toward formalizing as an identifiable local organization. However, despite keen attention paid to the ideals and forms of organization, there is little attention to the actual experiences and processes local people go through in attempting to get organized and what it then takes for them to stay organized. Closer attention to organizing as a process indicates that mistakes are made in practice and repeated, and the potential outcomes of many normative organizing practices are out of line with NGO justifications for work with local organizations. This chapter looks at organizing by asking about local actors' experiences of the subjective, social, and political processes involved. This perspective gives an observer a different view of organizing and throws some of the potentially serious errors in certain NGO organizing practices into sharp relief.

Organizing as a Negotiated Process among Local Actors

Organizing is a process in which local actors manage constant negotiations among themselves and constantly adapt their activities. It brings together a range of interested individuals and parties. Organizing is political and dynamic and founded on relationships among local actors, rather than on the organized activities themselves.

When local actors organize, they may create or adopt defined roles, structures, and systems (such as voting methods for decision making). This can be called the *form* of organization. Actors adopt various forms to help negotiate relationships and manage the complications of organizing. In much NGO practice, efforts are concentrated on helping local people adopt certain forms of organization that the NGO considers ideal or appropriate to the local situation.

In this chapter, the forms of organization are seen as secondary to the processes local actors go through in organizing their activities. In exploring processes, the initial starting point is to ask why people want to act, and then why they might want to act in an organized way. Much of the time people can act alone, so what makes them inclined to organize with other people instead? If people are inclined to organize, what else in their lives enables them to get organized and stay that way in constantly changing situations?

Subjective Interests

Why do people want to act in the first place? Put simply, if someone feels a subjective interest in a matter or resource, she is more likely to act in some way relating to it should the need or opportunity arise. Subjective interest should not be assumed to mean self-interest, however. A person may feel driven to act by a threat to the lives or welfare of other people in the local area.

But when does a having subjective interest in something incline a person toward organizing with other actors? In many situations, people could feasibly act alone, but there are advantages in organizing their activities—for example, because collaborating with other people will increase their resources. Advantages of organizing come and go with changing local situations, and actors' inclination to organize to serve their subjective interests will also come and go with those advantages. Perhaps more significant in the long term are situations in which actors need to organize to further their subjective interests. One could practice hockey alone, but one needs to organize a team in order to play a match of hockey. A single person can graze a cow in land behind his or her house, but some level of organized activities is needed to manage the common property resources of pastoral rangelands. In political processes, candidates are often required to have the backing of an organized group or party. An individual cannot act alone in any of these cases but needs to organize with other actors if he is to stand any chance of being effective for his interests. While he remains interested in that particular matter or resource, the inclination toward organizing with others will also remain.

Perceptions

Actors' perceptions of a situation and of potential actions are fundamentally subjective and social. People's perceptions are created and influenced by their sense of identity with respect to both other people and their town values and ethics, and these influence their judgments about possible future outcomes. Rational calculation of personal costs and risks and of potential benefits is part of people's judgments (Curtis 1991), but such rationality is only one aspect of the complex social processes involved in how people perceive their situation.

Perceptions are crucial in relation to how people are inclined to act, and particularly to whether they are inclined to organize. Social and group identity will influence willingness to associate, how and with whom. Attitudes to organizing are often tied up with ideological values around collaboration, exchange, or social status. Previous experiences and received wisdom, as well as cost to time and resources, will influence judgments about organizing (Hirschman 1970). Organizing is risky because it increases interdependence with other local actors and uncertainty about likely outcomes. Moreover, getting organized is only part of the story. Staying organized involves new layers of identity as group dynamics build, values change with experience and personal interaction, and new experiences and costs emerge to shift people's judgments toward and away from organizing. All this is taking place within a constantly changing local situation and changes in each actor's life. In many cases of organizing, people can only stay organized because they are able to manage some of the influences on perceptions—perhaps by creating a group identity or finding ways to reduce personal costs by excluding those from the organization who cannot contribute much.

Relationships

Organizing builds new layers of relationships on an existing dynamic mesh of relationships between local interested actors. In this light, organizations will be full of inherent tensions between diverse parties. Organizing is only possible when those tensions are reasonably well resolved or kept to a manageable level, for example, by keeping groups socially homogeneous (Olson 1971). The need to manage tensions between interested parties gives rise to many of the forms of organization that are visible to outsiders. However, the parties negotiating over disparate interests are unequal, and resolutions may be forced on weaker actors who have little option but to cooperate if they are to be involved at all (Quiggin 1993).

Realization

When actors are inclined to organize their activities, they must still realize (or make happen) both the organizing process (for example, bring a reporting system into force) and the eventual activities themselves. People need assets of skills, resources, and a repertoire of actions or the ability to innovate, even if acting alone. The particular assets required by organized actors to realize activities give those with appropriate assets advantages over those without. Individuals with appropriate skills and assets often become key to effectiveness and subsequently powerful within any organization. Those actors who gain organizing experience gain skills and new contacts and rapidly outstrip those who are not involved. The gap between actors who can realize organized activities, and those actors who are not able to, grows fast.

NGO Organizing Practices: A Mismatch?

From this view of organizing as a negotiated, unequal process between interested parties, I can reexamine certain NGO organizing practices. A feature of current practices is the emphasis NGOs often put on building formalized organizations, giving attention to form over process. Certain forms are encouraged because the NGO thinks that they will help ensure effective, sustainable, and just organizations. An NGO also needs to be able to monitor what is happening among local actors in its organization and track the use and value of NGO resources. Many of these formal, visible forms are also necessary for the NGO, so that managers can serve their own needs for monitoring and reporting to distant colleagues, and account upward to funders for their resources. A second feature is a widespread emphasis on consensus and community building that is a common theme in much participatory work.

NGO Organizing Practices and Actors' Subjective Interests

NGOs try to heighten people's subjective interests in matters that the NGO considers important. They increasingly use participatory methods to seek out local people's existing subjective interests. Thereafter, NGOs often create channels through which local people can access NGO resources and services. These access channels are often structured in ways that mean local actors need to organize—for example, only giving resources to recognized women's groups, or only recognizing local representatives on a development planning committee if they were elected by a known organization.

NGO Organizing Practices and Actors' Perception

NGO practices often target local actors' perceptions regarding organizing. They may emphasize area-based approaches or attempt to build "community" identity—for example, encourage and reward altruistic values, or publicize the long-term benefits of organized activities, enhancing actors' immediate benefits with training opportunities or public praise. NGOs often try to reduce the costs of organizing by providing local workers who take on administrative and logistical tasks. However, formalizing organizations increases the costs actors have to bear, especially for those trying to manage the process, such as leaders (Curtis 1991).

NGO Organizing Practices and Actors' Relationships

NGOs are themselves interested parties in the multistranded meshes of relationships in a local situation. However, by creating a need to organize, or a situation in which there are advantages in organizing, an NGO is also creating new layers of relationships among local parties. Diverse parties must come together to organize when they have not previously had a relationship. When an NGO has created a need to organize, but access is only available to a few actors, new, competitive relationships can become intense. One party's success is another party's loss. Some NGOs will only recognize one local organization that is supposed to represent the whole "community," without exclusion. When there are local conflicts, as there always are, stronger interested parties can use their strength over weaker parties to organize more effectively and silence or exclude the weaker. If NGOs require an appearance of "community" consensus, the actual conflicts between interests must be hidden, whether by subterfuge or by the strongest actively excluding any conflicting parties from relationships with the NGO.

NGOs often use organizing as a way to support and protect relatively weak parties. The forms that NGOs often require of local organization are meant to increase leaders' accountability to their fellow actors and that of the organization to the wider public. NGOs set conditions for organizations—for example, quotas for women's representation or expecting richer members to subsidize poorer members (Fall 1991).

NGO Organizing Practices and Actors' Realization of Organized Activities

NGOs provide resources and support in cash and kind to help local people set up their organization in the form the NGO thinks is appropriate. Forms frequently include written constitutions and reporting, bookkeeping, membership and attendance records, and named and elected post holders. Organizations are expected to advertise and hold meetings on a regular basis; often NGO representatives also attend. NGOs are sometimes criticized for introducing new notions of organizing, rather than using local actors' existing repertoire of processes and forms, which are "ignored and wasted as an organizational resource" (Bagadion and Korten 1991, 81). NGO requirements can demand specific and sometimes new skills from the local actors. Those actors who can learn and innovate have an advantage, and people with less experience of NGO conditionalities or less able to innovate could be excluded from organized activities.

Indications from this Perspective

This perspective on local organization shows organizing as an iterative process of negotiation between interested social actors. As people interact with NGO staff and development activities, their subjective interests, perceptions, relationships, and potential to realize activities change. However, people's experiences of the NGO are only ever part of a far more complex range of experiences and relationships in local society.

I have hinted at key points at which NGOs need to look more closely at their organizing practices. Some issues demand closer attention. Regarding the *quality and sustainability* of local organizations, many current NGO practices for working with and through local organization:

- Raise people's subjective interests in accessing NGO resources and services, which are arranged so that people need to organize, thus increasing the likelihood of people organizing

- Influence people's perceptions so that they are more inclined toward getting organized, but have less relevance to people staying organized

- Require local actors to have a range of specialist skills and resources or the potential to take risks and innovate.

Although actors may be more inclined to organize because of NGO practices, there is a strong chance that actors will create organizations simply to "hoop-jump" through the NGO's conditions. If this is the case, these organized activities are very likely to stop when the NGO stops actively supporting them (whether by providing resources of interest or influencing perceptions and negotiations). The form of the organization may remain as a name, constitution, and addition to local actors' repertoire that may be useful in future, but organized activities themselves will often cease once the NGO is no longer there to stimulate actors' interests and inclination.

Some aspects of NGO organizing practices push local people to organize in ways that may not be in their best interests. Regarding the search for *greater equality* among local people and relative to outside forces, the following quote from Dennis Wrong, a major writer on political science, is a timely reminder to development scholars and practitioners:

Organization, then, is a collective political resource that is at least as unequally distributed in the population as are the individual resources of wealth, prestige, expertise et al. (Wrong 1979,131–32).

The following points are significant:

- When people need to organize to access the NGOs resources, services, and activities, actors who cannot organize will be excluded.

- When NGOs influence people's perceptions in order to encourage organizing (for example, building group identity), people may organize when they could have acted alone quite adequately.

- Some practices add risks and costs to the processes of organizing, so that poorer and more vulnerable people are less inclined or able to organize.

- NGO activities create new relationships within existing dynamic meshes of local relationships (especially when people need to organize to access NGO resources). However, when there is competition for limited resources, these new relationships can promote conflict, creating conditions in which a stronger local party may force weaker parties to cooperate in ways that do not serve the weaker party's interests well.

- When NGOs can help actors resolve conflict in relationships, those actors may be more able to organize. However, when the NGO puts pressure on local actors to be cooperative and harmonious, conflicts can be driven underground or factions actively excluded from organized activities to create an appearance of cooperation and "hoop-jump" through the NGO's conditions.

- Local actors with sufficient assets to organize, who are more free to take risks and innovate, will be more able to organize activities that meet NGO approval. These innovative actors will have an advantage over people with less flexibility in their assets, who must avoid risks. This is the case for many poorer people.

- When an NGO relies on observing the forms of local organization in monitoring or evaluation, actors can adopt the forms the NGO prefers, but the NGO will not be aware of the actual processes and negotiations going on between unequal local parties. In this case, weaker parties are greatly disadvantaged.

Good practice and established relationships between local people and knowledgeable local workers should offset many of these weaknesses in current organizing practices. However, this analysis indicates a mismatch between the possible outcomes of NGO involvement and NGO justifications for working with and through local organizations.

Roots of the Mismatch between Goals and Practice

Let me conclude the chapter with some observations about the roots of this apparent mismatch.

Ideology

NGOs' drive to encourage local organization is often ideological. There is a deep-seated belief that organizing will increase cooperation among local people and, at times, this belief seems to outweigh theoretical or empirical investigation of NGO practices. NGOs do not have practical, analytical frameworks to appreciate what local people are likely to do, or what they actually do when faced by an NGO's activities in their area. Nor do NGOs have frameworks to appreciate the iterative, negotiated processes of local people organizing. Without useful methods for appreciating local processes and relationships, NGOs will always have difficulties incorporating local realities into their practices. They must fall back on practices that are assumed to be appropriate because they are associated with favored ideological movements.

From a more subjective perspective, the crucial point in NGO ideology is perhaps around the assumptions about the nature of local relationships. When local relationships are seen as essentially harmonious, NGOs will see organizing as a process that is essentially positive, if difficult to achieve. By looking at organizing as a negotiated process between interested parties, tense and even conflictual relationships—issues that NGOs must take seriously—are highlighted.

Such underlying and implicit assumptions concerning the nature and role of local organization preclude further inquiry into forms of organizing which do not fit with these ideal-typical models but which are central to the livelihood strategies of peasant smallholders. Local "organizing practices" are often denied their importance and labeled as corrupt, informal and "disorganized" or in an essentialist way as "traditional" or "indigenous." So, the whole concept of "local organization" as used in development studies appears to be enclosed within a debate which, due to the specific and constrained way in which it has evolved, remains far removed from the everyday practice of the people (Nuitjen 1992, 189).

NGOs' Need for Visibility

Local people's lives are opaque to outsiders. Complex meshes of relationships, inequalities, and power battles are barely visible, and often hidden. Change is hard to see—the impact of an NGO in influencing change even more so. Organized activities are considered desirable and become a proxy indicator for development progress. However, processes and relationships involved in organizing are themselves often barely visible to outsiders. Two neighbors who meet by chance on the road and take the opportunity to discuss informal arrangements for water sharing, are not visible. However, several people meeting in an agreed and advertised public place are visible. The event can be observed, recorded, and reported on to distant parties. A formal water users' organization, with a name, official recognition, and elected post holders is even more visible from a distance. Visible forms of organization, such as annual elections, become proxy indicators for effective organizing.

Why have visible activities become so necessary for NGOs? First, NGOs need to find ways to make sensible decisions about their local activities in spite of the opaqueness and complexity of local realities and relationships. NGOs need to make workable and timely decisions about how staff should act, and to negotiate effectively with other bodies, whether local groups or international funders (Mosse 1998). The complications of doing this within rationally planned project structures are well known (Pottier 1993; Thin 1995).

There is an unbridgeable, but largely unappreciated, gap between the neat rationality of development agencies' representations which imagine the world as ordered or manageable and the actualities of situated social practices, an incommensurability tidied away in sociological jargon as "unintended consequences" (Hobart 1993,16).

NGOs need to simplify local realities if they are to act locally. Dealing with what is visible is one way to do this.

Second, NGOs need visible activities because of current funding relationships. NGOs need to report and justify their activities to colleagues and funders who do not have direct contact with the local situation. These distant parties need to be able to see evidence of NGO activities going on at the local level. Staff need to be able to track, monitor, account for, and justify the use of resources received and passed onward to people at the local level. Large, bureaucratic, institutional funders must be assured that NGOs are trustworthy and making good use of what they receive (Hulme and Edwards 1997; Wallace et al. 1997).

In the current funding context, it is unlikely that NGOs will be able to escape the need for visible local activities. One solution is to make the processes local actors go through when organizing more transparent. NGOs can start by acknowledging the significance of these subjective, social, and political processes. Rather than looking for harmony, they will do well to look for tensions. They can look for the disadvantages to weaker actors of organizing, rather than focusing on advantages. Simple analytical frameworks can provide illumination on some of these issues, and asking about diverse subjective interests, perceptions, relationships, and realization is one place to begin.

NGOs must find ways to appreciate the subjective, social, and political processes involved when local actors organize. While they continue to rely on normative practices for working through local organizations, they risk raising the costs of participation and increasing inequality among local people.

16

Microenterprise and Microfinance: The New Kids on the Block

Pat Richardson and Karen Langdon

The belief in the wide potential of income-generating activities and micro- and small enterprise (MSE) development programs for poor and otherwise disadvantaged communities across the globe has accelerated in the last ten years. A further push for the adoption of MSEs has come with the proliferation of microfinance institutions and microcredit initiatives, promoted as a "proven tool" in the search for "pro-poor" interventions (Department of International Development 1998; Gavin 1997; Kidder 1997).[1]

This shift in attention has arisen from political, economic, and social changes both globally and locally. For example, MSEs are seen as significant providers of jobs in a context in which the public sector has contracted and jobs created by the formal private sector have been limited. They also appear to offer a seedbed for future successful formal enterprises and an opportunity to indigenize economic wealth through locally based and controlled activities. In a social context, MSEs are seen to provide accessible economic options to disadvantaged groups and, in some sense, to "empower" those groups and individuals through their involvement (Dignard and Havet 1995; International Labor Office 1972; Schumpeter 1934).

This broad acceptance of MSE activities has been reinforced by development approaches that have shifted from "charity-giving" to an emphasis on self-help and the pursuit of sustainability.[2]

NGOs as Providers of Support to MSEs

Support for enterprise development in most countries is provided by a myriad of different private, public, and "third" sector organizations, and examples of effective enterprise support agencies from within all of these three different groupings can be found (Richardson and Langdon 1998). Research in both North and South has demonstrated that the most effective MSE support organizations are those that mirror the attributes of the MSEs themselves (see for example Gibb 1993; Gibb and Manu 1990).

Nongovernmental organizations (NGOs)[3] are seen to have characteristics much more in line with the attributes of small businesses in that they are flexible, are customer focused, and tend to adopt a holistic and grounded approach. Also, many NGOs operating in the field of MSE support have set up and established themselves in the same localities in which they work, or at least have local offices that employ local or national staff. This identification with and grounding in the community is often a critical attribute for effective community economic development activities and a great strength of NGOs. Therefore, it is not surprising to find that NGOs are prominent among enterprise support institutions and indeed are seen by many—notably donors—as being one of the most appropriate forms of organization for such work (Harper 1998; Otero and Rhyne 1994).

Although enterprise support activities and income-generation support projects are widespread among the NGO population, agencies have not entered this field of work by the same routes or at the same time. Some have developed their enterprise activities to such an extent that they are seen as specialists in this area, particularly those focusing on the provision of microfinance. Organizations such as the Kenya Rural Enterprise Programme (K-Rep) and Kenya Women's Finance Trust (KWFT); Independent Business Enrichment Centres (IBEC) and Get Ahead in South Africa; AMKA (Export Marketing Enterprise Agency) in Tanzania; Foundation for International Community Assistance (FINCA) in Malawi; and Zambuko in Zimbabwe are recognized internationally in this respect.

Other NGOs have incorporated enterprise-oriented activities into their broader portfolio of development work. At one end of the scale are the larger national NGOs, such as the Bangladesh Rural Advancement Committee (BRAC), PROSHIKA, and Association for Social Advancement(ASA) in Bangladesh; Self Employed Women's Association (SEWA) in India; and the international NGOs such as Oxfam, CARE, ActionAid, and World Vision. All of these NGOs have their roots and original remits within a much broader social and economic agenda and have only become very active in the enterprise support arena within the last decade. As a result, many have established new sections or divisions within their organizations to focus specifically on MSE support services. At the other end of the scale, there are very small NGOs with an original and primary mission that has always been more socially oriented and that have added MSE to their existing core work.

New Wine in Old Bottles:
Tensions of Supporting Enterprise Development

Although many NGOs are emerging as extremely effective providers of support for MSE development (Richardson and Langdon 1998), there are others that are experiencing a set of conflicts and tensions, especially balancing the satisfaction of community development goals with the simultaneous need to help develop successful enterprises. From our work with four staff in a wide range of NGOs, it is clear that the tensions or constraints they face in designing, delivering, and facilitating enterprise development support activities are complex and interrelated. This chapter examines some of the key tensions. For ease of discussion, they have been grouped under five areas: personal values, organizational motivations, and orientation, competencies and attitudes for effective enterprise support, markets and competition, and sustainable institutional building and service provision. The first three issues are more prominent within NGOs that historically have been rooted in, and are still primarily oriented toward, social development goals. The latter two tend to be of concern to NGOs that have been set up specifically to address microenterprise support or which have separate divisions responsible for such activities.

Personal Values

One of the most fundamental challenges facing many NGO staff at the personal level is their negative view of entrepreneurs and thus resistance to supporting enterprise as a means of development. In our enterprise training programs for staff with public and voluntary sector backgrounds in Africa, India, and the Middle East, we explore the nature of enterprise and small business and approaches for fostering its emergence at both the community and national level. We ask participants to characterize what they understand and feel about "businessmen and businesswomen." Their responses are wide ranging but usually reveal a fairly negative image: one of exploiters of resources, including people; individuals who are outsiders or anticommunity; those who are protective of family or class/caste interests; and generally people to be mistrusted. Such negative, or at best neutral, views of business owners by these participants is always surprising, particularly given that they are the very people in-country who are responsible for enterprise promotion and support.

For those with a public sector background, their concerns focus sharply around issues of uncertainty and risk taking, innovating and being creative, and taking responsibility. For those with a primarily voluntary sector experience, their concerns relate to business people being profit-oriented or money conscious, creating advantage for themselves at the expense of communities, being selfish and individualistic rather than focusing on collective benefit, and dealing with symptoms rather than the structural causes of disadvantage.

Reflecting on this experience, it would appear that many people who have become drawn into enterprise support work may have a set of values that are in contradiction to what they see as the "values" of business. A common response to this situation has been for NGO staff to design support for particular *forms* of *collective* enterprise. The view is that if individual businesspeople are avaricious and not to be trusted, then this can be mitigated in supporting MSEs by encouraging groups of people to work together within or explicitly for communities and collective benefits. In particular, there is a high incidence of the type of projects involving women's income-generating groups in almost every donor's portfolio of initiatives throughout Africa, Asia, and the Middle East (see for example Dignard and Havet 1995).

When we have discussed these apparent tensions between personal values and the needs of enterprise support practice with staff and colleagues in both northern and southern NGOs, it has been interesting how the whole issue is placed within a broader discussion about societal values and prejudices. Several individuals have said that this "value conflict" at a personal level merely mirrors similar tensions within their broader society. It is felt that traditional values and attributes—such as conformity, acceptance, control, and priority of the collective over the individual—have long been rewarded in their societies. This is particularly strong in Jordan, Malawi, Tanzania, and Zimbabwe. Increasingly, these "collective/social" values are being challenged by the promotion of diversity, being critical, devolution of control, and the elevation of individual responsibility and action as elements needed for effective sustainable development in the future.

Organizational Motivation and Orientation

The personal values of staff working in enterprise support organizations are also closely interlinked with the primary motivation, orientation, and culture of the organizations in which they work. It is not surprising to find that tensions arise between the organizations' primary, or perhaps original, social goals and the economic activities they subsequently take up. Many NGOs are established to address a specific need in poor communities that has nothing in itself to do with enterprise development—for example, sourcing clean water, provision of health care, or the establishment of schools. This essentially social goal can be challenged—or at least its primary status diminished—when the NGO then seeks to support the community by addressing economic issues through enterprise development interventions. How this is perceived by the organization depends on the circumstances that lead the NGO to get involved in enterprise development.

People have to have money to survive; hence, the NGO may have to accept that "self-help" through enterprise is one of the few economic alternatives that exist, even for the poorest within their communities. In these circumstances, it is a "no choice" option for many NGOs, a last resort rather than a positive choice. For such NGOs, a preferred option would be for the community—or members of that community—to have the opportunity to secure waged employment, and if waged employment opportunities do arise, then income generation and enterprise development activities are quickly scaled down.

Other NGOs positively recognize that microenterprise is a valid option in community economic development, but in doing so, they seek to find ways of making the exigencies of microenterprise more acceptable in relation to a "social" development agenda.

If the intention is to prioritize the well-being of people, then the NGO will be the primary driver of the enterprise activity and seek to provide the community with opportunities for work within enterprises without the attendant risks of being "in business." So we see the proliferation of enterprise projects in which the NGOs are in effect the "owners," or in which people are encouraged to follow enterprise ideas identified by the NGOs. For example, in Jordan, there are several examples of local NGOs setting up income-generating "projects" for poor women, providing education and training, a space for women to work, and equipment needed. The women decide how much time and how many items they produce. The NGOs sell the goods on behalf of the women and pay the individuals according to how many "pieces" they produce. This is seen as a successful women's enterprise development, but this is questionable when the business is essentially the NGO's enterprise.

Competencies and Attitudes for Effective Enterprise Support

Tensions about competencies relate both to the knowledge base of NGO staff and the manner in which they engage with their local communities.

The expertise and practice of many NGO staff is grounded in health, horticulture, education, social welfare, and public sector management rather than economics, business management, and financial or marketing skills. This provides another potential level of discomfort for staff, because many do not feel able to offer appropriate advice and guidance for the creation and survival of viable MSEs. Creating viable MSEs is a difficult task, as organizations with experience in the sector would confirm.

In MSE support, it is acknowledged that "knowing who" and "knowing how" are as important as "knowing what." Enterprise development not only requires NGO staff to acquire new knowledge about enterprise; but also requires them to engage in more networking with others in the community. NGO staff must therefore recognize a broader range of public and private stakeholders in the environment and to help individuals and groups within the community build networks for themselves. This is essential for the development of self-sustaining MSEs; however, it involves NGO staff handing over responsibility to the communities, a shift from the direct "do for" interventions that are typical of many social development activities to a much more "hands off" facilitating role. Such a shift can be interpreted by NGO staff as not taking responsibility for the community. In an effort not to expose vulnerable communities to even greater risk, the temptation is for the NGO staff to stay "close" to the MSEs and to be the sole direct deliverer of support.

Markets and Competition

MSE development by its very nature is outward looking, driven by the need to find new and larger markets. This external orientation is seen by some NGOs at best to contradict and at worst to undermine their focus and commitment to local, geographically specific communities.

As NGOs help an increasing number of people in local communities to set up in business, the challenge of local market saturation emerges. Inevitably, poor people have limited resources and so tend to set up enterprises based on local markets, which they both know and can realistically serve. In poor communities, these local markets can soon become saturated, and NGOs are faced with having to encourage people to look for new ideas and markets outside their immediate locality. Staff have to further develop their enterprise competencies by increasing their knowledge and experience of nonlocal markets.

Looking more widely outside the immediate community for opportunities is quite a logical and, indeed, necessary step from an enterprise development perspective. However, such actions can create tensions for NGOs that have strong local identities. Encouraging individuals and groups to look externally can be viewed as counterproductive for the local community. As people move out of the area to seek new ideas or new markets, this can lead to the erosion of a local community, especially if these individuals tend to be the younger and mobile members, which inevitably they are. Furthermore, if NGOs are seen to encourage certain individuals or groups to move outside the local area, then this may be frowned on by the community; this in turn undermines the credibility of the NGOs. For example, women face significant personal and logistical challenges to their mobility when, as enterprise owners, they need to travel away from their village to seek supplies or new markets for their businesses. The disapproval of fathers, husbands, and elders in the community can discourage and forbid such travel and have negative repercussions for NGO staff who are seen actively to encourage such activities.

This conflict between the needs of individual enterprises and the needs of local communities seems to be most acute in rural or remote communities that have very limited options for enterprise development. NGO staff in the south of Jordan; in rural India, Malawi, Tanzania, and Zimbabwe; and in the southern islands of the Philippines have voiced this as a major difficulty that they face in supporting MSE development in their communities. They nurture new enterprises, which then move away to urban or periurban areas to survive and grow, leaving behind a further depleted community.

Sustainable Institution Building and Service Provision

Much has been written about the evolution and sustainability of NGOs and MSE support institutions, especially as providers of microfinance (see for example Harper 1998; Havers 1996; McGuire and Conroy 1997; Otero and Rhyne 1994). NGOs appear to face three main areas of conflict or tension in juggling the needs of the poor in their target communities and the need to deliver services on a sustainable basis.

As we noted earlier, many NGOs have become involved with supporting enterprise development as a last resort. Very poor people frequently require more than simple access to credit to start up viable enterprises. However, "credit plus" support, be it training or technical support, is resource intensive in terms of staff time and skills. Consequently, there is pressure on the NGOs, especially from donors, to focus on the more able, who can start and grow enterprises with the minimal of support. This fundamentally challenges the NGOs' commitment to helping the poorest people in their communities, particularly when there are no alternative economic options available for them. This conflict between "cherry-picking" and helping the most needy in the community arises again and again in our evaluations of microenterprise and microfinance NGOs.

A second source of tension with respect to sustainability again concerns the loss of clients by NGOs. Enterprises not only need new markets to grow and develop, they are also likely to require a more extensive range of business support services. This can present a challenge for some NGOs and their staff on two fronts. First, NGOs have to make the decision as to whether they can directly deliver such services themselves or whether to refer their "clients" to other providers where they exist. The latter is often not an option, and so NGOs face the dilemma of having constantly to upgrade and extend the services they offer. If other service providers do exist, then NGOs have to "hand over" their clients to these providers. However, some NGOs seem to find it difficult to effect this "handover." Facilitating and signposting to other agencies, especially other NGOs and service providers, appears to be viewed as a "failure," essentially "loss" of the client to outsiders.

A third source of tension concerns sustainability of NGOs rather than of the enterprise they help. The more specialized enterprise NGOs may understand and accept that their clients or beneficiaries will need to "graduate"; however, they as organizations are faced with the issue of sustainability. NGOs need clients to help underpin the financial sustainability of the services they provide. For example, NGOs require a certain volume of customers taking and repaying a certain level of loans if they are to cover the overhead or transaction costs of delivering their microfinance services.

Another way for NGOs to achieve or maintain the sustainability of their services and their institutions is to increase their customer base—that is, for the NGOs to "scale up" and extend their services beyond the local communities in which they have originated. This may be an option in theory, but the practice has proven much more difficult. Trying to bring in an ever-increasing number of new clients from poor communities is a major task, and it is often easier to keep those you have already got, even though they may need the services you offer for longer.

This particular tension—what is best for the sustainability of the community versus the sustainability of the NGO—was identified as a major and widespread problem in a recent review of enterprise development by the authors (Richardson and Langdon 1998) and by many others (Fowler 1997; Korten 1987; Sahley 1995).

Challenges for the Future

The above discussions highlight a number of tensions that face NGOs as providers of MSE support within a community economic development context. These tensions, although not unique to NGOs, are particularly relevant for these organizations, given the primarily social origins and motivations of many of the NGOs involved in MSE and the associated values, attitudes, and competencies of their staff.

Some of the more "socially" derived tensions experienced by NGOs do disappear as more specialist enterprise services and separate NGOs evolve and a "breed" of more focused specialist enterprise advisers emerge. However, even in these more focused organizations, it is likely that many tensions will remain. The dilemma between prioritizing the development needs of the local community and those of individual entrepreneurs and enterprises within those communities is a difficult one to resolve. The dilemma between assisting the less poor who have the potential to start and grow modest enterprises (which in turn will help the NGOs to sustain the services they provide) versus prioritizing the poorest of the poor also presents a continuing conflict for NGOs. This is particularly the case when poverty continues to be widespread and few, if any, alternative options for generating income exist (see Johnson and Rogaly 1997).

Reconciliation of such tensions and dilemmas is not always necessary to ensure effective support of MSE activities. However, recognition that these tensions might exist and understanding what this might mean for NGO staff certainly is.

As practitioners and researchers in the field of MSE for the past fifteen years, we feel that a constructive way forward is to break down the boxes of the social and the economic, and the camps of those for and against enterprise development. It is important to recognize that enterprise development—be it self-employment, part-time or full-time employment, enterprise/ownership in the informal or formal sector—forms only part of a complex web of activities that comprise the livelihoods of poorer people throughout the world. As such, it is equally critical that activities that support such enterprise development are flexible, varied, and evolve over time to meet these diverse needs.

In conclusion, there is one indisputable fact that all enterprise support agencies have to acknowledge and prioritize if they are to support effective enterprise development: No matter what the form or scale of an enterprise, it needs to make a profit. How that profit or surplus is made and who benefits from it may be aspects that the NGO can influence for the further benefit of the community. However, an enterprise can benefit no one if it does not have a sufficient customer base to make a profit and survive over the long term.

Notes

1. This chapter draws on the authors' experiences over the past ten years working in the Foundation for Small and Medium Enterprise Development (FSMED), at the University of Durham, UK. FSMED (formally the Small Business Center) has experience of working with a wide range of different MSEs as well as enterprise support organizations throughout the world, including a large number of NGOs. The issues raised and discussed in this chapter stem, in particular, from the authors' recent work with NGOs in the United Kingdom, India, Zimbabwe, Jordan, Malawi, South Africa, Kenya, and Tanzania.

2. See Langdon (1999) for an overview.

3. There is a lengthy debate about the use of different terms and definitions about NGOs (Edwards and Hulme 1995; Vakil 1997). Our comments here are derived from and concern NGOs that are intermediary organizations engaged in fund-

ing or offering other forms of support to communities and other organizations. They are involved, although not always exclusively, in the direct delivery of support for MSE development, and they include small local NGOs as well as local offices of larger national and international NGOs.

17

NGOs and Peace Building in the Great Lakes Region of Africa: States, Civil Societies, and Companies in the New Millennium

Pamela Mbabazi and Timothy M. Shaw

A major concern for most countries and communities in Africa in general and in the Great Lakes Region (GLR) in particular at the start of the twenty-first century is the issue of stability—whether economic, political, or social—because this largely determines the level of human development and human security. Recent events throughout the GLR and Uganda's own mixed peace-building experiences offer important lessons to state and nonstate actors both in Africa and beyond. Alongside governments, civil societies and multinational corporations (MNCs) have made contributions to ongoing peace-making efforts in the GLR. Together, this triad of distinctive actor types determines prospects for sustainable peace and security, democracy, and development—that is, *peace-building governance.* [1]

Our focus in this chapter is, therefore, not only on the role of states but also on two (not always compatible) varieties of nonstate actors in such governance: private economic agencies, especially MNCs, and civil societies, especially nongovernmental organizations (NGOs) (Shaw and MacLean 1999; Shaw and Nyang'oro 2000). In terms of MNCs, as we will see below in the case of Mbarara, there is a growing presence of large and small companies, from global banks and consumer manufacturers to several local milk producers. In terms of NGOs, a diverse range are identified whose activities have an explicit impact on peace building in the GLR, extending from global/national Red Cross Societies to the national/local Uganda Women's Efforts to Save Orphans (UWESO). These mainly offer relief services to refugees and assist orphans and widows who are victims of war. NGOs whose activities have an implicit impact on peace building include AIDS Support Organization (TASO) (an AIDS [acquired immunodeficiency syndrome] support organization), Organization for the Disabled and Aged (OURS), Federation of Uganda Women Lawyers (FIDA), Family Planning Services Project, and Concern Worldwide. These are mainly engaged in social service program delivery—for example, water, health facilities and education, advocacy, poverty alleviation, resettlement, and community development.

By contrast, the main aim of private companies, both national and global, is to make profits. However, they also offer employment, provide markets for and process previously undervalued agricultural products, and contribute to the development of infrastructure, as we will see in the case of the burgeoning milk industry centered in Mbarara.

The preliminary study of peace-building governance on which this chapter is based was carried out in the southwestern region of Uganda, a country whose current regime has been a key player in the recent developments in the GLR. The position of Uganda is pivotal because it forms the link between the conflict in the GLR and the wars in southern Sudan and the Horn of Africa. A sample survey of nonstate actors was undertaken: these included NGOs, and international agencies as well as private enterprises. The area was taken to be representative of the GLR based on its geographical location, the socioeconomic characteristics of its population, and its political systems (Shaw 1998).

Our thesis here is that the agency of nonstate actors such as MNCs and NGOs needs to be recognized and facilitated if human development and security are to be realized in the GLR at the start of the new millennium. It is increasingly recognized in the burgeoning literatures, debates, and policies about "peace operations" that effective and sustainable peace building require partnerships or coalitions between states and armies on the one hand, and civil societies and economies on the other: an agreed, dynamic division of labor to advance confidence building and entrepreneurship. Certainly, Mbarara at the century's dawn is enjoying something of a boom, with the private sector generating new investments, new banks and hotels being constructed and opened, along with milk and soft drinks factories. Additionally, the not-for-profit sector is building and running educational and health facilities, augmented in both areas by the new university.

Western Uganda in the decade of the 1990s may, then, constitute something of a model in terms of constructive postconflict divisions of labor among state(s), companies, and NGOs, encouraged by the Musevni regime's "realism" following the traumas of the Amin and Obote II years. That is, peace-building governance has advanced human security, which makes human development a possibility once again.

The Great Lakes Region at the Dawn of the New Millennium

The very term Great Lakes Region (GLR) has recently taken on a new meaning as a result of efforts of leaders in the nine countries of the Horn and Central Africa (from Eritrea and Sudan to Congo and Tanzania) to agree to move toward a common political and economic front. In reality, however, the GLR grouping includes only parts of some of these territories and could expand its membership further if Somaliland and Puntland were recognized and included. Certainly, this region shares a rich variety of ecologies (mostly centered on water), ethnicities, histories, infrastructures, languages, and religions, with a distinct identity apart from neighboring regions like the Mediterranean and Southern and West Africa.

Very low levels of human development/security (United Nations Development Programme [UNDP] 1999b), together with the abject poverty of the mass of people, have contributed to latent discontent among the populations scattered throughout the GLR. Arguably, this is one of the major reasons that countries in the region have failed to achieve either national or local stability. The cumulative impacts of (interrelated) globalizations and structural adjustments have not helped either, exacerbating declining human development index scores.

Uganda was unstable in the period after independence, through the Idi Amin and Milton Obote II eras, until President Yoweri Museveni came to power in 1986. Since then, the National Resistance Movement government has striven to create avenues for peace, reconstruction, and development. This has been partially achieved by, among other strategies, improving the socioeconomic infrastructure; providing universal primary education, along with both secondary and tertiary education; and adopting a number of poverty-alleviation programs that seek to improve living conditions for people in rural areas. In most of these sectors, NGOs have played a fundamental role as "service providers." For example, many roads have been rehabilitated by NGOs such as Africare; the health sector has been supported by organizations like DISH (Delivery of Improved Services for Health) and WHO (World Health Organization); and in education, World Vision and CARE have been of great assistance.

In Rwanda and Burundi, the well-known or notorious "ethnic" struggles between the Hutu and Tutsi led to massive genocide in the 1960s and in 1994 and created a war that attracted the attention of the international community in supporting efforts toward peace and justice (Gourevitch 1999; Uvin 1998). Kenya and Tanzania have experienced relative stability since independence, without military coups and with relatively stable economic transition processes that encouraged gradual human development. These two countries have participated less vigorously in both the GLR grouping and the Inter-Governmental Authority on Development (IGAD), appearing in some instances to be mere observers. For example, even in the current Congo crisis, they have not been direct contributors of military forces, although elements of the conflicts have spilled across their borders and both Nairobi and Arusha have been center of refugee responses and legal and diplomatic efforts at peace (Malkki 1995).

Ethiopia and Eritrea, on the other hand, have again become trouble spots in the region with the recent border dispute, which has been further accentuated by Sudan-sponsored, cross-border terrorism as well as instabilities within the regime in Khartoum. However, it is the Democratic Republic of Congo (DRC) that is the major vortex for conflict in the GLR, initially sparked by the overthrow of President Mobutu by opposition groups led by Laurent Kabila, who was by then supported by Uganda and Rwanda. After his takeover, the Banyamulenge uprising brought renewed chaos, culminating in the present crisis.

Conflicts in the GLR are extremely complex in terms of their dimensions and actors, even if they are not so-called complex political emergencies (CPEs) (Cliffe 1999). Mixed-actor coalitions result in shifting patterns of conflicts and alliances in the GLR among states, NGOs, MNCs, gangs, and other informal groupings (Shaw 1998; Shaw et al. 1998). Among the immediate as well as remote causes of these DRC conflicts have been the struggle to share power, the existence of the Banyamulenge in the Congo, vast mineral wealth, and competing security coalitions (Duffield 1999a):

Central Africa is bound by a web of political, economic and personal intrigue, every bit as complex as early twentieth century Europe. Further to that is that in the centre of this complex web lies Congo with vast countless riches, which have become the springboard for the insurgencies plaguing the governments of Sudan, Angola, Zimbabwe (our insertion), Rwanda and Uganda and an ethnic mix with spine chilling potential for the conflict (Mark Turner, *Financial Times*, as reported in the *New Vision Daily*, 23 November 1998, 14).

For a few years in the mid-1990s, the various state and nonstate actors in and around the GLR exhibited a remarkable degree of companionship in a struggle to work together to maintain security and development. Their honeymoon, however, along with notions of an African renaissance or alliance under the guidance of "new Africans" (Shaw and Nyang'oro 2000), has been cut short with the proliferation and escalation of interrelated conflicts inside and around the DRC. These conflicts have indeed threatened the very existence of the embryonic GLR grouping, raising the question of whether it can aspire to become a "security community" or continue to be a cauldron of anarchy.

NGOs, Peace Building, and Realism in Africa

As this and similar volumes make apparent, there are multiple definitions of both civil societies and NGOs from a variety of disciplinary and theoretical perspectives (Murphy 2000; Schechter 1999). Included in many commonly accepted definitions of NGOs is that they are nonprofit-making, voluntary organizations seeking to improve the standard of living of the less advantaged in society, from local to global. It is also widely accepted that there is, however, a major divide between those interested in advocacy and those interested in service delivery (although some do both) and between indigenous, intermediary, and international NGOs (Dicklitch 1998). Many NGOs are now concerned with reconstruction work as part of involvement in peace-building/peace-support operations in a variety of roles, from early warning and confidence building to postconflict reconstruction and reconciliation.

However, almost all "African" conflicts and states have extra-African dimensions, and such linkages may be nonstate and intergovernmental. Such extracontinental influences not only include major global agencies such as those in the United Nations system and the international financial institutions (IFIs), but also international NGOs (INGOs), such as CARE, Médecins Sans Frontières, and Oxfam. The burgeoning African diasporas in the North, especially in the North Atlantic region, from Liberian to Somali, also play important roles. In short, several aspects of "globalization" affect local or regional conflicts and their containment or resolution, especially the cumulative impacts of structural adjustment concessions and conditionalities. These aspects, along with corruption, ecological variability, and "ethnic" tensions, have served to transform not only the definition of the "state" in Africa but also state-economy and state-society relations. Hence the new importance of nonstate agencies, which increasingly are expected to "pick up the pieces"—notably in terms of basic needs like education and health—in support of often diminished and impoverished states.

NGOs in Museveni's Uganda have mainly been involved in development and relief programs intended to enable the country to recover from decades of anarchy and decay, and the AIDS/HIV (human immunodeficiency virus) pandemic. The major concern of the rural population is to survive and ensure that basic services are accessible. NGOs, therefore, are mainly addressing these demand-driven expressed needs. NGOs have also been instrumental in filling gaps where the government's performance has been deficient. An inefficient, bureaucratic, rigid government mode of operation has not delivered what is expected. In Uganda, NGOs have moved to provide services in areas largely ignored by the government. Most missionary hospitals, for example, are situated in remote and inaccessible areas of rural Uganda, such as Kagongo and Mutorere in the southwest. NGOs have also brought services to marginalized social groups largely ignored by the government, such as older people, street children, orphans, and widows. They have provided a range of services, including counseling of traumatized children in the war-ravaged areas of the North; tangible aid, such as food; clothing and shelter; vocational training; student sponsorship in the formal educational system; agricultural inputs; medical services; family planning; and credit. NGOs have therefore gained a reputation for being able to promote peace through the provision of basic services and helping to raise community expectations for the maintenance of peace and stability.

NGOs, Decentralization, and Peace Building in Uganda

Since 1992, decentralization has been one of the strategies adopted by the Ugandan government to foster good governance and promote peace and stability, especially around its border districts. Decentralization in the Ugandan context entails the transfer of resources and decision-making power to lower-level units. In Uganda, these are local governments or NGOs that are (ideally) autonomous, democratically elected, and independent from central government (Rondinelli et al. 1983; UNDP 1997a).

For the previous three decades, governance in Uganda was characterized by dictatorship, corruption, centralization, and personalization of power. During this period, the state dominated both the economy and civil society. Local governments were virtually powerless, and all decisions were made at the center with few mechanisms to check the abuse of power or to enforce the accountability of public officials. In addition, there was a dependency mentality in which citizens tended to look to the state as the provider of everything. This had the effect of weakening local initiatives for development. Decentralization, therefore, has been advanced as the policy framework that can help reverse these negative tendencies, enhance good governance and empower civil society.

The advent of the National Resistance Movement (NRM) regime and the restoration of relative peace and stability has attracted a substantial donor presence in the form of bilateral organizations, multilateral organizations, and NGOs, as well as a degree of private direct foreign investment. The international agencies have participated in postwar rehabilitation and reconstruction. NGOs in particular have tried to fill the gaps of an inefficient central government administration and have been involved in charitable and relief work, community development, advocacy, and social sector service delivery. Religious NGOs have been more consistently active than government throughout the turmoil of Uganda's postcolonial history, especially in health and education service delivery. Our argument is that NGOs—both indigenous and international—have made a major contribution to the building of peace in Ugandan society by providing services to the population (Dicklitch 1998).

NGOs have been identified as the best avenues through which community participation for rural development can be mobilized and promoted. With the onset of decentralization, districts have tried to put in place mechanisms to ensure that there are no overlaps and conflicts. The district officials have tried to intervene in the operations of these NGOs to ensure that they are at least in tune with developmental aspects of beneficiaries' traditions, beliefs, and structures. Such approaches have been observed to contribute to sustainability. However, more information is needed to uncover the ways in which NGOs and local authorities have networked to facilitate service delivery to local communities. NGO, community, and local government interfaces need to be understood clearly in order to determine service delivery effectiveness and sustainability; that is, governance for local human development and security.

In Mbarara District (Western Uganda), as in other areas throughout the country, an NGO forum has been created at the district level, charged with the responsibility—among others—to register and coordinate NGO activities within the district. This has helped to curb the "briefcase NGOs" that have appeared, as well as streamline the operations of the existing genuine NGOs to ensure optimum performance. With closer supervision, it is hoped that NGO service delivery will be more responsive to the needs of poor beneficiaries. The question remains, though, as to whether the district officials will have any meaningful influence on these NGOs, especially, as the saying goes, because "beggars can't be choosers." It has, however, been noted that NGOs initiated by community members are more in line with local contexts than INGOs, although in most cases these local organizations lack financial sustainability.

Large defense budgets for most African governments have been a key reason for the neglect of basic service delivery and the increasing involvement of NGOs. Peace building in contemporary Uganda can be taken to mean creating conditions that would promote sustainable human development and security to advance stability and enhance progress (UNDP 1998b). One of the innovative strategies adopted by the Ugandan government to try and address the question of poverty and underdevelopment and ensure sustainable human development has been the formulation of a comprehensive development plan for Uganda over the next twenty-five years. Vision 2025 is a process that constitutes the first steps toward building a national participatory process for the strengthening of human development and security; that is, peace-building governance.

Funded by the UNDP, Vision 2025 was launched in Mbarara in November 1996. It made explicit acknowledgment that the people have a vital role to play in the transformation of their economy and consulted the population on a range of issues, from human development to social services. Given the understandable emphasis on peace building in the GLR, it was thought necessary to find ways to reinforce the efforts of countries and communities in this area. The government of Uganda put in place several strategies aimed at achieving such aspirations, among which include free and compulsory universal primary education; vocational education; improved national research capacity by strengthening the National Agricultural Research Organization (NARO), National Environment Management Authority (NEMA), and higher education institutions; functional literacy programs; as well as improved social services. The aim is to increase employment opportunities, encourage political dialogue and social participation in peace resolutions, and attract investments in the country to create economic opportunity.

Given existing government and NGO initiatives and participation—including international support and community involvement as well as the participation of NGOs and MNCs—such aspirations for achieving a better future by the year 2025 may yet be achievable. Alongside these, however, many threats remain that might still cripple any such aspirations; for example, an increasing debt burden despite the Highly Indebted Poor Countries Initiative (HIPC); donor fatigue; unhelpful foreign policies of the bigger powers, including donor conditionalities; rampant corruption and embezzlement; AIDS; ecological decay and vulnerability; and massive poverty and increasing insecurity in the GLR.

Companies, Universities, and "Peace Building"

Despite these problems, at the start of the twenty-first century, redevelopment and reconstruction continue apace in Uganda, especially in Western Uganda. Mbarara—now a university town, as well as the place where Rwanda's new leaders went to school as refugees—has become a regional center, not only for Western Uganda, but also for the GLR as a whole. It is a center for both informal and formal exchange, overland communication of people and goods, and agricultural and light industrial production. Symbolic of the redevelopment is the construction and operation of five new dairies in Mbarara. Many companies and entrepreneurs have made heavy investments. As this is a cattle-keeping region, there has been an influx of private individuals, in some cases in partnership with foreign investors, constructing and operating milk-processing plants. As the Ankole people are pastoralists and own private land, small- and large-scale (male) farmers have been able to augment their regular income dramatically by bringing urns of milk to market on bicycles or in pickups. The results in terms of improved livestock and housing (for example, tin roofs) are quite apparent. In addition, all these factories have links across several borders, especially for marketing their products. Mbarara milk is now drunk in Tanzania, Kenya, Rwanda, Burundi, and DRC. Is this another definition of new regionalisms (Boas et al. 1999)?

Characteristic of novel developmental possibilities, and affected by ubiquitous globalization (Scholte 2000), is the Coca-Cola plant in Mbarara, commissioned in 1998, which also aims to serve the whole region. What will be its impact on basic needs, employment, environment, electricity, health, and water supplies? In effect, emerging regional possibilities involve profound local to global issues in a variety of sectors. Are they antidotes to conflict and adjuncts to peace and confidence building?

Regionalisms and Peace Building

As in several other crises on the continent, the one in the GLR has been the focus of both local and international NGO—as well as state—interventions in efforts to promote peace and restore stability in the region. The revived East African Cooperation arrangement and the related "New African" alliance, for example, have provided helpful venues in Arusha and elsewhere for conflict prevention and postconflict investigations (Whitman and Pocock 1996).

Ideally, mixed-actor coalitions in and around Africa may advance what Wheeler (1997, 405–407) refers to as "non-forcible humanitarian intervention," that is:

the pacific activities of states, international organizations and non-governmental organizations in delivering humanitarian aid and facilitating third party conflict resolution and reconstruction.

It should be noted however, that the sustainability of the de facto Central African security alliance around Uganda is problematic for both internal and external, and regional and global reasons. It is a function of economic and ecological—as well as strategic and organizational—factors. Much as Uganda has been widely seen as a "success story" by the international community of late, this masks a different picture for the majority of Ugandans as they continue to live in absolute poverty—absence of human development—as well as endure a lack of human security. So, what are the prospects for the new millennium?

All in all, Uganda and the GLR at the end of the twentieth century indicated a range of possible futures, from the optimistic scenario of emerging markets to the stereotypical nightmare of exponential "anarchy" (Shaw and Nyang'oro 1999, 2000). Uganda is very much a swing state that displays two tendencies: an air of optimism about sustained redevelopment in the South, but diversions and the costs of continued conflicts in the North. The same applies to the related crisis in and around the DRC. Such divergencies undermine economic, political, and strategic confidence and deter sustained regional development.

Conclusion

Regrettably, too much of the burgeoning discourse about "peace keeping" and "peace building' in Africa ignores the active roles of both African state and African (as well as non-African) nonstate actors (Shaw et al. 1998). This chapter has suggested that the "agency" of NGOs (and MNCs) needs to be recognized if such "peace making" on and around the continent is to be sustained in the new millennium. Peace-building "partnerships" or coalitions cannot be effective, let alone extended, unless Africa's official and nongovernmental organizations are recognized, respected, and included. NGOs in the GLR have played a fundamental role in providing services to the population in the region, especially when the governments have failed to do so.

In our own research on peace-building governance, it was apparent that most of the NGOs in southwestern Uganda are mainly engaged in reconstruction activities and postwar rebuilding. Although many of their activities do not have a direct impact on peace building, they have made a big contribution to meeting (very) basic needs. Our conclusion therefore is that because several NGOs—indigenous, intermediary, and international—are so engaged in all these activities, peace building without them may be problematic. Arguably, then, sustainable peace building/development does require the involvement of NGOs (and MNCs) on a continuous basis.

The existence of institutions to carry out studies and make recommendations about how peace can be defined, achieved, and sustained in the GLR is very important for peace building and sustainability in the region. The development of appropriate tertiary-level institutions is very desirable.[2] In addition, it is recommended that a special working group of "eminent persons," agreed on by states and nonstate actors in the GLR as well as their extraregional "friends" or "associates", be set up to study, plan, and make specific recommendations for peace building in the whole GLR. This would be more broad based and more regional than the distinguished diplomatic role played by first Nyerere and then Mandela in Burundi. That is, it would reflect the necessary involvement of the trio of actor types at the regional level in peace-building governance for the GLR. There is clearly a pressing need to formulate long-term aspirations for all the countries, communities, and companies in the GLR. This can be done through coordination of institutions, research and publications using a suitable participatory model like the one adopted by Vision 2025 for Uganda. In short, out of the cauldron of the GLR in the late 1990s may yet emerge novel and sustainable forms of regionalisms appropriate to Central Africa in the twenty-first century to advance human development and security.

Notes

1. This chapter and the research on which it is based have been supported by a collaborative seed grant from the International Development Research Centre (IDRC) in Ottawa, whose invaluable assistance is gratefully acknowledged. They have laid the foundation for continuing cooperation on issues of regional conflict and peace building between development studies programs at Mbara University of Science and Technology (MUST) and Dalhousie University.

2. MUST, for example, aims at focusing on the current issues of ecological, economic, health, political, social, and strategic concern related to sustainable peace building. The faculty of development studies at MUST in particular aims to become a hub for peace-building activities, research, and networking in the region. Research, workshops, and seminars are accommodated at MUST as a pivot for coordinating other universities and think tanks in Africa and beyond, and thereby attract serious studies and plans for peace building in the GLR at the start of the new millennium. The faculty of development studies at MUST is well placed both geographically and institutionally to advance and exploit with like-minded analysts and organizations promising directions in the field of "development studies" in so far as reconciliation, reconstruction, and regionalisms (that is, peace-building governance) are concerned at the dawn of a new millennium.

18

An Actor-Oriented Approach to Micro and Small Enterprise Development: A Namibian Case Study

Stephen Biggs and Frank R. Matsaert

Recent literature on small and microenterprise development has focused on the need to understand socioeconomic contexts in which development interventions are planned and take place (Lyon 1998). This includes looking at social networks, linkages, and transactions in many arenas, and the effects of development interventions within them (Buckley 1997).

A criticism of microfinance development is its preoccupation with narrow economic criteria as indicators of success (Johnson and Rogaly 1997). Recent work has indicated that the impact of these interventions is more complex and dependent on interrelations between various actors and networks (Goetz 1998). Goetz suggests program outcomes focus on not only social norms, networks, and gender relationships, but also on values and positions held by the male and female development workers in the implementation. Pearson (1998a) argues that microfinance programs cannot be understood without analyzing their history and links with external actors. The importance of institutional linkages is clearly a critical factor for institutional survival (Von Pischke and Adams 1992).

There is clearly a need to develop approaches that take into account the complexity of social, economic, and political linkages and relationships in enterprise development interventions. One of the challenges is to develop methods that can analyze the complexity of relationships between different actors in processes of change. In this chapter we present an "actor-oriented approach" that was developed for planning and analyzing capability development in research systems (Biggs and Matsaert 1998) and that we believe could be usefully applied to enterprise development interventions. To demonstrate

Figure 18.1
Actor Linkage Matrix: Example

		1	2	3	4	5
		Poor rural women	Poor rural men	Village level development workers	Senior managers	External funding agency officer
A	Poor rural women					
B	Poor rural men					
C	Village level development workers					
D	Senior managers					
E	External funding agency officer					

its use, we have used the case study of an enterprise development project in Namibia (Matsaert 1998).

The actor-oriented approach is based in the work of Long and Long (1992) and the tradition of such writers as Clay and Schaffer (1984) and Apthorpe and Gasper (1996). Their writings highlighted the significance of relationships between a wide range of actors in the economy and the agency role of people within development organizations. The actor-oriented approach we are suggesting tries to take these ideas forward and provides a framework for planning and analysis that takes into account key relationships, linkages, and flows of information.

The approach uses two main tools: the *actor linkage matrix (ALM)* and a *determinants diagram*. The matrix can be used in a variety of ways: for institutional assessment purposes, "scenario projections," monitoring and replanning purposes—and for developing location-specific indicators. The determinants diagram is more useful in assessment and planning situations (for further details on the approach and these tools see Biggs and Matsaert 1998).

The ALM (Figure 18.1) illustrates relationships between different actors involved in a situation of social change. The actors are listed down the side of the page as matrix rows, and the same actors are listed along the top as columns. The matrix cells are the full range of possible interactions between all the actors represented. If one took one row and worked across the columns, this would represent flows of information going from the actor in the row to all other actors. Figure 18.1 represents a hypothetical rural enterprise project with five sets of actors (rows A to E). Cell A3 represents the flow and social control of information flowing from poor rural women to village level development workers. Cell C1 represents control over information going the other way.

At one level, the matrix can be used to direct attention to exploring a number of features that sometimes get overlooked in project planning. For example, the act of compiling a list of actors can reduce the probability of key stakeholders being omitted or of missing important differentiation within groups. However, we are not arguing for a complex and cumbersome matrix, as that would be missing the point of the exercise. Each matrix should be highly location and time specific (Hyman and Dearden 1998). By listing major actors involved in project activities, one is able to include in the same conceptual framework both the village level "beneficiaries" and other village actors as well as the "beneficiaries" in the organization(s) involved in creating and "implementing" the project. In this the framework has similar features to some types of stakeholder analysis (Gass et al. 1997; Grimble and Wellard 1997; Overseas Development Administration 1995) but has the advantage of gauging the nature of interactions more holistically.

The matrix can be used in various ways. The content of each cell could be text that describes the social nature of the interactions. Alternatively, the cells might be given shading (see figure 18.2) to represent the existence of meaningful information flows regarding project objectives. The list of actors and the content of the matrix could also differ depending on the project purpose at hand. For example, a matrix that describes a current situation would be different from a matrix constructed for scenario forecasting.

The second tool of the actor approach is the determinants diagram. This takes a specific cell from the matrix, describes the flow of information in the cell, and analyzes the reasons why these flows take place and what determines control over the flow of information. Different arrows pointing at the cell represent major influences. This visual representation enables important political and social determinants that influence the flow of information to be explicitly recognized. The diagram can be used to improve communication between the actors involved. Some of the activities of the project might be addressed to changing these influences, whereas in other cases, the influence is recognized, but it might be beyond the project to make any change. The determinants diagram is illustrated later in the chapter (figure 18.3).

Small Enterprise Development in Namibia

This section examines a case study located in the Kavango Region of northern Namibia: the Lisikamena Credit Scheme (LCS). We begin by providing background on the case study area. LCS's objectives, loan services, and development are then examined and the actor linkage approach applied to the project until its first evaluation in mid-1996 (Strauss 1996).

Namibia is characterized by a dual economy with a very high level of income inequality among its small population (World Bank 1997a). LCS is situated in the northeastern Kavango region. The Kavango ranks as one of Namibia's poorest regions, with low levels of education, food security, and life expectancy (UNDP 1996; GRN 1996). The agricultural system is dominated by dryland subsistence farming (mainly millet) and livestock rearing, which rarely produces enough for subsistence throughout the year because of extremely variable rainfall (Devereux et al. 1996). This means that off-farm micro-enterprises (MEs) represent a high priority for many households' livelihood strategies augmented by migrant male labor (KFSRE 1998a; MAWRD 1997).

The small enterprise sector in Namibia remains largely underdeveloped, and is concentrated in the capital, Windhoek (Hansohm et al. 1998). In Kavango, there are estimated to be approximately 4,000 MEs, and small to medium enterprises (SMEs) (ECI 1998). Many of these enterprises are involved in retail and trading within urban areas, selling items such as crops, milk, beer, and traditional foods (Nesongano 1997). On the manufacturing side, there is a tradition of rural blacksmiths in the region (KRFSE 1998a), and industries such as baking, sewing, thatching, basket making, and boat building are common. Around some of the main road arteries to the south of the region, there are also a significant number of woodcarvers, and within Rundu (Kavango's main town) there is a carpentry industry, represented by the Mbangura Woodcarvers' Cooperative.

The sizes of enterprises involved in the sector varies (Mead and Liedholm 1998). The smallest MEs exist only *temporally* at the end of the month to sell surplus agricultural produce in the main markets of Rundu. These MEs generally represent poorer rural households (KFSRE 1998a; LCS 1998). Larger MEs are *permanent* and involved in trading higher-margin processed foodstuffs, for which there are greater barriers to entry. These permanent microentrepreneurs have higher levels of income and turnover (Matsaert 1998). The ME sector represents the bulk of informal businesses in the region. Larger SMEs operate from discrete premises, and are also mainly involved in the retail or trading sector. The owner, who is often a salaried government employee, often employs a family member to manage the business (Matsaert

1998). In contrast, in sectors such as services and manufacturing, owners often possess specific skills and are usually self-employed within the business (Nesongano 1997).

Constraints highlighted by businesses were lack of access to finance for expansion or working capital, lack of training, and high levels of cash withdrawals from the enterprises (Devereux et al. 1996). A recent study of Namibia's financial system concluded that:

> The main weakness of the formal financial system is the contrast between its increasing sophistication and its limited outreach. The system reflects the economy's general dualism. Large parts of the society and economy, including most SMEs, are as yet basically unserved by the formal financial system (NEPRU 1998, 5).

It was the constraint of poor access to capital that the LCS was set up to address in 1994.

The LCS—Objectives and Products

LCS is the only provider of financial services to the MEs and SMEs in the region. Other informal institutions, such as rotating savings and credit associations (ROSCAs), are very limited. The history of credit extension in the region has been troubled, with many loans offered by government and nongovernmental organizations (NGOs) being more akin to welfare grants, resulting in low levels of repayment (Devereux et al. 1996). Similarly, the concept of group lending is a new one in the region (KFSRE 1998b).

LCS was formulated in 1993 in response to the low levels of existing enterprise development, as well as high levels of poverty and food insecurity in the region (CARE Austria 1993). The main goals of the project until 1996 surrounded the dual purpose of "consolidation and formation of small scale enterprises mainly in the informal sector through improved access to capital" and "creation of an independent, private, cost effective and sustainable credit scheme" (CARE Austria 1993, 3). Institutional sustainability was measured by having in place an independent management structure and achieving full cost recovery within two years with less than 5 percent arrears. Over the case study period, LCS offered two distinct financial products: a group and individual loan product.

Early Stages of Project Development: Individual Loan Product

Failure to assess accurately the potential ME sector   LCS began its operations in April 1994, after a short period of initial research in 1993. The program was based on a CARE project in Maradi, Niger, using an individual loan methodology targeting SMEs rather than MEs.[1] The focus on individual loans was based on the donor's perception of the SME market as potentially large, with promising employment prospects. During the initial project design, the donor did not investigate the ME sector because MEs were not perceived as high-potential entrepreneurs (Strauss 1996). These perceptions, and the agents consulted during the design phase, focused LCS on the SME segment of the market.

Loan analysis was carried out entirely by an LCS manager who lacked experience of SME lending and had no permanent CARE backup in Namibia. Most training support was provided by short-term expatriate inputs. Loan approvals were influenced by LCS board members, who mainly belonged to the local chamber of commerce. As a result, LCS's loan portfolio was dominated by a few large and risky loans to local chamber members. At the end of 1995, the manager resigned, and LCS ceased to disburse loans until new management was brought in to improve the portfolio quality.

Initial Loan Approval and Governance Structures

Problematic partnerships created moral hazards in loan approvals   At the beginning of the project, a partnership agreement was formed between the local Kavango Regional Chamber of Commerce and Industry (KRCCI), LCS, and the Pahuka Training Program (PTP)—a program set up to develop SME training initiatives through building the capacity of the chamber. Both programs were funded by the same donor and sought to be complementary by offering coordinated access to training and finance.

Loan approvals were devolved to a newly created executive body—the Lisikamena Loan Board—composed of prominent KRCCI members and other community organizations. These agreements "vested considerable authority in bodies that had not effectively existed prior to the advent of the project and in individuals who had no experience running credit schemes" (Strauss 1996, 16–17). LCS's donor believed that by doing this, it would create a participative and community-driven approach. By devolving processes of loan approval to peers of applicants, LCS structures created prospects for moral hazard, as board members' interests began to run counter to the organization's objectives. KRCCI members agreed to large loans for themselves, resulting in high levels of nonperforming loans by the end of 1995 (ECI 1998).

Reassessment and Restructuring of LCS

LCS responded by tackling key areas of project design   LCS responded to these issues in a number of ways. In the governance arena, LCS prohibited members of a new approval body, the loan committee, from accessing loans in 1995. Second, it ensured that committee members were qualified to assess credit risks. Third, in 1996, the partnership with the KRCCI was terminated and the Lisikamena Board abolished. By the end of 1996, the original organizational structure was terminated and LCS became a locally implemented donor project, with the loan committee acting as the main advisory body.

To reduce nonperforming loans, the new LCS management halted loan disbursements at the start of 1996. Repayment rates improved after several court cases against KRCCI members and portfolio restructuring. Smaller individual loan disbursements began again in August 1996 using an improved methodology, focusing on smaller businesses.

LCS recognized that prospects for self-sufficiency with its individual product were limited, given limited SME demand, and that LCS should begin to target MEs. A group lending product, similar to the Grameen methodology, was introduced in late 1995. It was designed and drafted in Europe by the donor, with high levels of compulsory savings, which made it an expensive product for entrepreneurs. By June 1996, LCS had adapted it to local needs, which resulted in loan volumes rising. The group product was more pro-poor—with an average loan size of just N$800 (or US $170)—and yielded a high repayment (greater than 95 percent). Since 1996, LCS has successfully adapted its group product to become the main focus of its strategy (ECI 1998).[2]

Amid LCS's restructuring, in June 1996, an evaluation highlighted design and governance frailties (Strauss 1996). This report represented a landmark by changing the sponsoring institution's view of the project, realigning it with that of local LCS staff. After the report, improved donor support meant that systems and staff capacity were upgraded to address key areas, such as product formulation, governance structures, and repayment rates.

In summary, LCS's development was mixed because of the project's design, institutional structure, and donor power relations. LCS responded by reassessing its products and governance structures and its access to resources. We believe that these processes could have been helped by the use of an ALM analysis, and that some of these issues would have been raised during the project's design phase. In the next section, we use the actor-oriented approach to analyze retrospectively the socioeconomic context and linkages formed by LCS over the period discussed.

Figure 18.2
Actor Linkage Matrix: Lisikamena Credit Scheme, Namibia 1996

		1 LCS staff	2 Part-time MEs	3 Full-time MEs	4 Retail SMEs	5 Other SMEs	6 Large/formal enterprises	7 Suppliers/wholesalers	8 Kavango chamber
A	LCS staff	■			■				
B	Part-time MEs								
C	Full-time MEs								
D	Retail SMEs	■							■
E	Other SMEs								
F	Large/formal enterprises							■	
G	Suppliers/wholesalers				■		■		
H	Kavango chamber	■			■				■
I	Other business associations								
J	Cooperatives								
K	Training program	■							■
L	Donor	■							
M	NGOs								
N	Parastatals								
O	Other lenders/insurers						■	■	
P	Local government						■		
Q	SME fora								
R	National business associations								■
S	Businesses outside region								
T	Central government								

9	10	11	12	13	14	15	16	17	18	19	20			
Other business associations	Cooperatives	Training program	Donor	NGOs	Parastatals	Other lenders/insurers	Local government	SME fora	National business associations	Businesses outside region	Central government			
		■		■				■						A
														B
■				■										C
		■	■				■							D
														E
			■		■	■			■	■				F
						■	■		■					G
		■	■				■							H
														I
				■										J
				■										K
		■		■										L
	■						■							M
										■				N
									■					O
														P
														Q
			■	■				■						R
									■	■				S
	■				■					■				T

Using the ALM

Figure 18.2 shows the ALM for LCS in 1996 when the project decided to terminate its agreement with the KRCCI. The shaded cells indicate intense communication between actors running from horizontal (rows A to T) to vertical (columns 1 to 20).

This analysis looks at key project issues, such as target group, organizational structure, and project management (Strauss 1996). All of these issues are explored using the matrix, representing the flow of information and intensity of the project's information networks. Although these networks changed over time, certain features are common with the beginning of the project.

Disaggregation of the Target Group

The project target group remained largely SMEs during the initial two years. This is reflected in the focus on an individual loan product geared toward larger businesses. Looking at the matrix, we can see that the project failed to communicate fully with the poorer and more numerous ME grouping (see cells A2 and A3 and B1 and C1) until 1996. This effectively excluded them from access to loans because they did not have representation within the local chamber of commerce (cells B8 and C8), the main influencing set of actors. Part-time MEs were the most marginalized group of entrepreneurs (row B), as their full-time peers were more involved in the running of the local market boards and cooperatives (cells C9 and C13).

Use of the matrix could have increased awareness of the wider enterprise sector by showing that the majority of informal businesses were not being targeted as clients. The analysis could also have added a deeper understanding of clients' different needs and poverty levels. This could have avoided inappropriately designed products, lowered portfolio risk, and improved repayment rates. The perception of limitations of the potential borrower market by project designers and staff was based on the narrow focus of the project on the small SME market (cells A4, and less so A5), which ignored a large ME sector (Strauss 1996). Gradual evolution of the group product might have been accelerated by more focused ME research, the need for which could have been derived from the matrix (column 1) during the design phase.

Significant Networks and Partnerships

Much influence on the project design was exerted by a small group of entrepreneurs, which is observable from the ALM. Cell D8 shows that these retail businesses had the greatest influence on the KRCCI, which in turn approved LCS loans (H1). This group of retail SMEs made up the bulk of KRCCI's members and had strong communication with the project's donor, NGOs, PTP, and government (row D). In contrast, the chamber of commerce lacked links with formal businesses (H6), other enterprise sectors (H2, H3, H5 to H7), or business associations (H9). The matrix shows that the chamber served a restricted group of members concentrated in the retail sector (H4) (ECI 1998). Use of the matrix could have alerted the donor to connected and concentrated interests of the KRCCI and retail SMEs (columns 4 and 8).

Retail businesses had an effective network for influencing the design of LCS and other key actors. These businesses were therefore able to grant themselves easy access to credit, with little intention of repayment (Strauss 1996). The ALM could have alerted the project to the fact that large loans were being directed to a small group of interested parties (A4). Although it might have been hard to judge these behavioral traits at the start of the project, the matrix would have provided a warning two years earlier to divorce loan approvals from potential borrower groups.

Project Management Issues

The ALM can also be used to help understand internal project dynamics. On one level, the interactions of credit officers (Goetz 1998) can be examined using the technique by studying linkages with different groups (row A).

Internal analysis of interactions with the project donor gives a meaningful message: Communication from LCS to the donor was relatively weak (cell A12), although it was very strong in the opposite direction (L1). Implications of such an analysis suggest that LCS could not influence external donor decisions on project design without some external input. The 1996 evaluation provided that impetus and changed the power relations significantly within the project (Matsaert 1998).

The Determinants Diagram

Figure 18.3 shows a determinants diagram for the poor information flows between MEs and LCS and its donors. The cells affected are shown in the central shaded box, and influences are depicted by their strengthening or weakening characteristics.

Clearly microentrepreneurs had limited ability to communicate with the project actors or with representative bodies. The communication channels between the project and MEs were poor despite the creation of the initial

Figure 18.3
Determinants Diagram Analyzing Communication from
Microenterprises to Lisikamena Credit Scheme

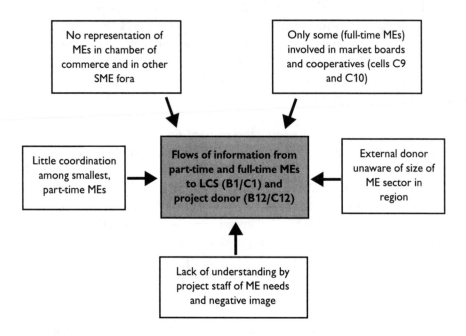

group loan product. However, there was a preconception among staff at this time (based on a lack of understanding of these businesses, and happily short-lived) that MEs were too small and risky to lend to.

All of these factors suggest that LCS could have carried out more baseline research into the ME sector and should have aimed to involve MEs in main-line representational bodies in which their views could be heard.

Using the Actor-Oriented Approach

In applying this approach, some valuable lessons have been learned—that might help others adopt the basic principles put forward, which are:

- Different stakeholders' views at different periods should be sought in drawing up the matrix.

- Assessing communication flows could require specific indicators to suit a specific context, objective, and time period.

- Gauging the full range of actor interactions might not be possible because of lack of transparency and access to all information flows; this emphasizes the need to prioritize a given set of interactions for a given objective.

- Categorizing actor groups, and thereby generalizing different actor actions, should be linked to stakeholder analysis and the objectives of the analysis.

The use of the ALM and determinants diagram in looking at the case study raises several important lessons for NGOs working in microfinance. The first is the importance of differentiating poorer groups of entrepreneurs (Mead and Liedholm 1998) and networks in project planning and design. The second is the significance of the delivery agency's structure and its interactions, and the third is the motives and expectations of different actor groups and the history of their involvement in the sector (Lyon 1998). Fourth, there is a set of issues raised concerning project planning and management and their need to incorporate contextual interactions. A fifth area of importance is the power structures between implementing agencies and donor institutions. Finally, lending methodologies need to be adapted to the local context (Johnson and Rogaly 1997).

Conclusions

This chapter took as a starting point some key issues that have become important recently in the micro- and small-enterprise literature. These included the importance of social networks and information linkages between different actors in analyzing motives, and the expectations and needs of clients and actors in service organizations. We believe there is a need to develop suitable planning approaches and tools in this area.

The chapter concentrated on the presentation of a planning approach that would address some of these issues. This "actor-oriented approach" (Biggs and Matsaert 1998) can be used to investigate linkages and information flows between key actors involved in enterprise development. The approach used two tools: an actor linkage matrix and a determinants diagram.

The approach was illustrated using a case study of the LCS in the Kavango region of Namibia during the period of 1994 to 1996. The scheme went through some difficult periods in the early part of its history. As a result of "learning by doing," it made significant changes to the definition and characterization of its client group, the products it provided, the way it interacted with clients, and the way it promoted institutional development. The case study uses an actor-oriented approach to analyze the socioeconomic context and linkages of key actors involved in the project. The resulting analysis suggests that some of the issues encountered would have been avoided by using the approach at an early stage in the project life.

The case study clearly underlines the need for NGOs to avoid a top-down blueprint approach to enterprise development. NGOs need to understand the influence that existing institutions and networks have on project design and outcomes, which goes beyond the replication of microfinance models (Lyon 1998). NGOs should also look inward to fully understand power relations within their organizations in order to optimize innovation and change. The NGO studied found it difficult, for a variety of reasons, to innovate its structure and management to the reality of entrepreneurs' needs on the ground.

We hope that this chapter has provided enough information for NGOs and others to assess whether the actor-oriented approach might be a useful addition to other planning frameworks in this area.

Notes

1. Average loan size was N$15,000 (US $3,200), but reached as much as N$80,000 (US $17,000).
2. All U.S. dollar amounts are translated from Namibian dollars using an exchange rate of N$4.7.

19

"Implementation by Proxy":
The Next Step in Power Relationships
between Northern and Southern NGOs?

Margaret Simbi and Graham Thom

> *We are not funders, we are capacity builders.*
> —Male northern NGO field representative,
> personal communication, November 1999

This chapter is about the working relationships between northern and African nongovernmental organizations (NGOs) and the impact these relationships have on fighting poverty. It looks at the threat to achieving development goals of a new type of relationship, implementation by proxy, and aims to hold up a mirror and ask whether this applies to your work.[1] It is written primarily for an audience of northern NGOs.

We have noticed an interesting development since 1998. There has been the increased take-up of organization assessment and organizational development techniques by some northern NGOs. When these techniques are combined with already comprehensive reporting and evaluation regimes, they can add up to what we term implementation by proxy. Under such a model, a northern NGO sets its own strategic objectives, effectively "tenders" for work by defining its funding areas, assesses the competence of African NGOs by using organizational assessment techniques, and then manages performance through frequent reports and visits. Such a process starts to look suspiciously like running one's own field office or engaging a subcontractor. This new approach is being carried out disingenuously under the label of capacity building and partnership rather than openly under the language of subcontracting.

Implementation by proxy might be seen as a new stage in a trend of four stages of development relationships. There was once a time when many northern NGOs ran development projects themselves, employing staff in country, or using expatriates to oversee work. A second stage emerged when a number of northern NGOs that had implemented projects or played a funder role moved to a "partnership model," in which local organizations applied to northern NGOs to carry out development projects and northern NGOs "responded to local needs." Since the mid-1990s, this model has evolved into a third stage in which northern NGOs no longer simply provide funds, but must now also seek to add value and build capacity. This imperative is now strongly reinforced by Department for International Development (DfID) guidelines. Implementation by proxy appears to be emerging as the fourth stage in this progression. This fourth stage is not the logical progression for all northern NGOs, and some are seeking alternative futures, although we argue on the basis of experience that it is the dominant approach currently shaping relations with southern NGOs.[2]

The chapter starts by exploring the nature of implementation by proxy. It then shows how implementation by proxy is a complex product of pressures on northern NGOs, unequal power relationships, and the practice of partnership and capacity building. It introduces new management tools, such as organization assessments, that are making implementation by proxy possible. The chapter does not seek to offer solutions, although this is the subject of an ongoing research program for Transform.[3] The chapter draws on Transform's six years experience of working with NGOs on management and organization change programs in nine countries in southern and East Africa. It also draws on recent interviews with northern NGO managers and with African NGO managers in Kenya, Uganda, and Zimbabwe.

What Do We Mean by "Implementation by Proxy?"

In July 1999, a fifty-year-old male manager of an African NGO stood up at a workshop on "winning resources" attended by nine other African NGOs and described the reporting regime he had to go through for one funder. This regime included quarterly financial reports, biannual audits, annual evaluations, and quarterly monitoring visits. The facilitator asked the rest of the workshop whether they experienced the same level of supervision. Several people said "yes, but it is getting worse." One female manager then described how her organization was required to undergo an organizational assessment process before receiving funding. The funder ran a workshop with the staff looking at vision, mission, structures, and other attributes. The managers at the workshop expressed concern that the organizational process was another nail in the coffin of their ability to respond positively to the needs of their communities and be able to manage their own organizations.

This example illustrates a move to implementation by proxy, a situation in which an African NGO becomes a de facto subcontractor of the northern NGO under the mask of partnership. The northern NGO defines the parameters of the relationship, assesses the African NGO, and has comprehensive management structures in place to ensure compliance—yet at the same time persists in calling the relationship a "partnership," giving the impression that the African NGO is setting the agenda. Although one might argue cynically that this is a feature of many management systems today, we would argue that the operation is fundamentally unconstructive and disempowering (see Kaplan, Chapter 3). The language of partnership leads us to believe that the African organization is setting the agenda, or is at least doing it jointly. What is critical is that African organizations are being required to carry the responsibility for the potential failure of the project without the power to take this responsibility properly. The African NGO is placed in an ambiguous and compromising position. On the one hand, it is not enjoying the benefits implied by the language of partnership, whereas on the other hand, it is not enjoying possible benefits that "above the board" subcontracting might bring (such as role clarity, clear contracts, disbursement conditions, and clearly devolved authority). We would argue that this arrangement does not work for either side and ultimately does not work for the beneficiaries concerned.

What Is Driving This Shift?

We identify three things that appear to be spawning implementation by proxy. First, there is pressure from donors on northern NGOs to be capacity builders. They are being asked to add value beyond simply funding. This requirement is linked in part to a concern that development is failing and shows a desire for new solutions—solutions in which northern NGOs are seen to have skills and capacities lacking in southern organizations and are therefore to share with the southern NGOs. Second, this "solution" becomes possible and even obvious to donors and northern NGOs because of the power relationships embedded in these relationships. Dominant northern understandings of partnership and capacity building allow many to move to an implementation by proxy in an unquestioning fashion, assuming it to be the case that northern NGOs have skills and experience lacking in the South. Third, there has been the increasing development and adoption of new management tools, ideas, and practices—many drawn from the business sector—that provide the tools for the implementation and control of this approach.

Each of these is considered in turn in the following three sections.

Pressure on Northern NGOs

Southern NGOs need to understand the environment within which Northern NGOs are working is a very competitive one, which is increasingly demanding accountability to a number of different stake holders: our own trustees, our constituency, legal accountability to the charity commissioners and so on. But most importantly people in the North are beginning to ask—after so many years of funding aid and development projects—are they really making a difference? Are some more successful than others? Are there better ways or worse ways in which we can spend our money? I think those are legitimate questions and Southern NGOs have to work with their Northern counterparts to respond to them. (Senior male regional representative in Northern NGO, interview January 2000.)

Many U.K. NGOs have been having a challenging time in the past few years, operating in an uncertain environment. There has been concern on the part of donors, trustees, and some staff, especially senior management, about the perceived lack of impact of development work. At the same time, the funding has remained static, and in some cases declined, while the numbers of NGOs has proliferated, leading to increasing competition between agencies. So NGOs have been willing to conform to new donor requirements, often unquestioningly. Donors have also sought to exert greater control and find greater impact, and they (especially DfID, which has been redefining the joint funding scheme and block grants) have been playing a key role in defining reporting practices in the sector.

Restructuring has added to the uncertainty occurring within a number of agencies, a result partly of the need to keep up with changing concepts and approaches to development, especially the increasing pressure to advocate globally as project work falls increasingly out of fashion. The constantly changing context, a lack of confidence in past ways of working, and the mimicking of management approaches taken from outside the NGO sector have all added to a general sense of confusion in parts of the sector.

In response to these pressures, many northern NGOs are pursuing a number of strategic shifts, including shifts from projects to programs; measuring and demonstrating impact; ensuring quality; achieving global change; and restructuring. These demands can become the dominant calls for action within an agency, overriding quieter calls for finding ways of developing better relationships with partners. Striking a balance between these external demands and responding to calls for new relationships is not an easy task.

Power Relationships, Capacity Building, and Partnership

The pressures on northern NGOs and their responses occur in an environment characterized by complex relationships with many different actors. A key feature of this environment is that northern NGO-southern NGO relationships are often seen by African NGOs as parent-child relationships. These relationships have an impact on the operational relationships with communities and beneficiaries, and hence have a critical impact on the quality of development work. Ann Hudock (1995) reached this conclusion in her work with NGOs in Ghana, arguing that the key determinant in capacity building was the number and quality of external funding relationships. Sarah Lister (2000) extended this work in an interesting way by looking at a model to explain how power can operate, based on work in Central America. Biggs and Neame (1995) also explored the "room for maneuver" in development relationships, arguing that we are part of a chain of accountability, but there are options for change. In short, there is increasing support from research that power relationships are a key feature of the development landscape.

Capacity building and partnership have risen to become core operating concepts within the sector. At one level, they are simple ideas: "Partnership" says something about the nature of the relationship between a northern NGO and an African NGO; "capacity building" says something about processes that enable an African NGO to improve, or carry out, the work (although it has many wider interpretations). The aims of capacity building and partnership are lofty and good. However, in our experience, there are a number of problems with both the theoretical base and the practice of capacity building and partnership, partly because they are taking place in the context of unequal relationships. These problems contribute to the emergence of implementation by proxy.

On a theoretical level, capacity building is often defined as something done to African NGOs. This was captured in a definition by James (1994, 5) who said that capacity building was "*an explicit outside intervention to improve an organization's performance in relation to its mission, context, resources, and sustainability*" [emphasis added]. Implicit in this definition is a deficit on the part of the African NGO and a solution in the hands of an external agent. We take serious issue with this model, which runs against established management and development models that consider an organization or individual responsible for their own self-development.

On a practical level, African NGOs have reported serious problems with partnership, capacity building, and development relationships in general. In 1997, twenty African NGOs met in Harare, along with representatives from three northern NGOs at a conference facilitated by Transform. Following prior action research with NGOs in Zimbabwe by Margaret Simbi and Kudzai Chatiza, contributions from a range of participants, and three days of debate, the conference came up with a two-page declaration that called for change on both sides of the relationship.

Among other things, the declaration called for southern NGOs to become:

- Clear and confident about their social mandate, vision, mission, and values

- More than implementing agencies of northern NGOs

- More questioning and critical of themselves and more accountable to their stakeholders (Transform 1997)

It also stated, among other things, that northern NGOs:

- Should not masquerade as southern NGOs and should be clear about the roles of their field offices

- Be open about their policies, structures, functions, and funding

- Include southern partners in the development of their policies, structures, and procedures (Transform 1997).

The declaration was an assertive vision of a future beyond unequal relationships. The declaration has been circulated and presented at forums in both Africa and the United Kingdom and has elicited a mixed response. Some northern NGOs have actively engaged with it, discussed it at board level, or sought to adapt it for their own use. Other northern NGOs have found the declaration threatening or unhelpful and have made comments such as: "What about the African NGOs? They don't deliver to communities" (personal communication, 1999).

We have conducted further research to see whether the issues raised by the declaration are still current. We have recently conducted interviews with managers of NGOs in Kenya, Uganda, and Zimbabwe, as well as interviews with northern NGO managers. These discussions provide a fascinating glimpse into the operational reality of life in current relationships.

A "chain" and its effects are well described by a Kenyan manager:

. . . for instance DfID funds the Northern NGOs in the UK and the Northern NGOs fund the Southern NGOs who in turn work with the beneficiaries at that level. So we have four levels here. Everybody is telling the other what they think the other wants to hear, in order to derive whatever benefit they think they have. For instance, the community tells us, Southern NGOs, what they think we want them to tell us. The same thing the Southern NGOs tell the Northern NGOs. Probably the Northern NGOs tell their funders the same thing, so that, you know, in a way we are all cheating each other at different levels and not coming out and communicating to eradicate the poverty that we are out to do so (female NGO manager in Kenya, January 2000).

The above extract highlights the fact we are all part of a complex chain of accountability (for a more detailed exploration of the chain, see Thom 1998). A key link in this chain is "partnership." The majority of the African NGO partners we have interviewed expressed problems with "partnership," although this was not exclusively the case.

An area of concern is that of partnership. I'm not sure whether it is partnership, but we call it partnership. This is a very contentious area, in that your supporter or your donor gives you financial support, gives you ideas, ideologies, name it, here is a situation where there is a flow of goods or things in one direction and hardly is there a flow of the same in the other direction (male director of Kenyan NGO, January 2000).

These comments on partnership and the chain can be taken as abstract comments. However if we look at development practice, there are operational problems that can all be linked to chain-like behavior. For example, in relation to the selection of projects:

The Southern NGOs tend to follow the agenda of the Northern NGOs, for example, I'm doing a project on girl child labor and the Northern NGOs say they are funding a program on HIV/AIDS, then I veer to the other side and start doing a program on HIV/AIDS. What would be desirable is that if there was a proper dialogue, really more or less equal relationship without fear of the Northern NGOs withdrawing their funding, then we could really try to meet the needs of our beneficiaries (female NGO manager in Kenya, January 2000).

Another very contentious area is that of reporting, something over which there are universal complaints:

If a Northern NGO partner would like to get a three-month report, without which no funds are forthcoming, is that partnership? It is not. In fact it should cease from being partnership, . . . we work in the field, we are field workers, we work with semi-literate people, people with no tables, no computers, no telephones, you wait for a report for three to four weeks and the partner in the North wants it within one month, how do I get it? You get tension, even high blood pressure, because you want to finish it. Why should that happen? It should not happen (A male director of a Kenyan NGO, January 2000).

The above extracts may present a bleak picture. They are not designed to; rather, we are trying to make the point that power relationships are the sea in which we all swim, whether we realize it or not. The case studies can often be countered by other stories that justify or defend the northern NGO actions, often presenting powerful arguments. We believe we need to go beyond both sets of stories and move forward to alternatives. We argue that the consequence of the unequal power relationships is that African NGOs are less empowered, will be less effective in implementation, and have less impact on poverty.

This leads us to the final ingredient in the push for implementation by proxy.

The Arrival of New Tools

The emergence and increased use of a range of new management tools and language are facilitating the shift to implementation by proxy. We would highlight three trends. First, the traditional approaches that focused exclusively on the design and delivery of a project are being developed and codified into formal management information systems. Second, new techniques are emerging for assessing the capacity of the organization delivering the project and its performance; these are now being given prominence alongside basic project management.

Third, a new language of quality management is emerging, with talk of standards, benchmarks, and quality audits.

We would argue that none of these new approaches is by itself a problem, and some might be welcomed. However, the issues of why these tools are adopted, where they come from, what purposes they really serve, and how such tools and approaches are used and by whom are critical, as demonstrated in the research undertaken by Wallace et al. (1997).

Take organizational assessment: This is an area of work in which Transform has considerable experience, having facilitated organizational assessment processes with more than fifty different organizations in Africa.[4] These processes are political, delicate, and seem to work well when individuals feel free to talk openly about problems and solutions. The Transform process includes interviews with donors, but donors are never directly part of the assessment process. The data from the assessment is not presented to donors, although conclusions might be, if the African NGO chooses to do this.

Some northern NGOs are now seizing on these processes and training their own staff in how to use them, rather than having them done independently. They are then applying these processes directly as a part of their project cycle management. Such moves are entirely consistent with the shift in northern NGOs from being "funders" to being "capacity builders," but there are a number of problems with this new role for northern NGOs. Combined with unequal relationships and the existing reporting requirements, African NGOs feel managed and supervised. The problem is obviously multiplied when more than one northern NGO starts to do the same thing.

Organizational assessments form one new tool in the new armory of organizational development. We welcome the adoption of new ideas, but often come across examples of northern NGOs struggling, but not succeeding, in letting go of the process and allowing the NGOs they fund to get on with things by themselves. This is illustrated by the following case study by a consultant, in which a local NGO has been given its own budget to resource its own organizational development, but the sponsoring northern NGO cannot avoid getting involved:

This is quite a classic example of everyday occurrence with regards to capacity-building. Two months ago an NGO approached us to help them with skills needs assessment. Since most of the staff were new the intervention seemed very appropriate. The other reason for asking for a needs assessment was that they had also ventured into new areas of work and the capacities of the staff also need to be identified/assessed. We then asked for basic Terms of Reference (TORs) for the three days so that the time would be effectively used. The Northern NGO became aware that we were going to do the intervention. The Northern NGO demanded the Terms of Reference from the NGO and became part and parcel of the TORs processing. For two weeks the TORs moved backwards and forwards between the Northern NGO and the NGO. The Northern NGO during the process had managed to smuggle in some of their agenda i.e. focus on their new favored project area in addition to mainstreaming gender. We asked the NGO to send us the TORs and could not believe our eyes; the TORs were those fit for a major organizational evaluation and could not be done in less than three weeks – the NGO's hands were tied and they did not know how to proceed. (A case study told by a consultant)

What is interesting about this case is that the Northern NGO probably started to intervene because it thought it could "add value." Once in the loop it started to interfere, perhaps unconsciously. The net effect was confusion and disempowerment. The Northern NGO had not learnt to let go.

Conclusion

We have not sought to offer solutions in this chapter, but have highlighted what we see as a worrying trend. We have argued that three ingredients—pressures on northern NGOs, unequal relationships, and new management tools—can lead to a new form of relationship that is disempowering and ineffective. In this sense, we believe there is a strategic imperative to find ways of doing things differently and to resist the slide to implementation by proxy. We are not seeking to wind back the clock to year zero. The new tools of organizational strengthening and measurement can be used to enable rather than control, but it depends how they are used and who owns them.

We also feel there are grounds for optimism. The debates are still open, and there are futures other than implementation by proxy. We are encouraged that there is a willingness on the side of a number of northern NGOs to tackle these issues and that there is increasing experimentation with new forms of dialogue and practice, beyond the "truth and love" sessions that have been in vogue. In debates on partnership, we have reached a point at which we can take as a given that we would like shared values, shared visions, and better communication; let us now get down to business and look at concrete improvements in practice.

Notes

1. We are indebted to Kalombwa Chikoti, John Mwendwa, Rakani Naidoo, and John De Coninck for comments on the draft.
2. Some of the case studies exploring these North-South relationships and new ways of working with these realities were written up and presented at the Birmingham conference, *NGOs in a Global Future*, 1999: see, for example, Chatiza; Kasaizi; Negassa; Simbi.
3. Transform is a network of organizations in six African countries with a partner in the United Kingdom. It has been working with NGOs in nine African countries, offering management and organizational advice. The research work in this paper is based primarily on work in Uganda, Kenya, and Zimbabwe. Further information is available from Transformuk@aol.com.
4. The process that Transform offers lasts two weeks: a week to orient managers and a week of in-house consultancy. It looks widely across organizations and their work, including impact and internal issues that contribute to impact, such as leadership.

Abbreviations

AIDS	Acquired Immunodeficiency Syndrome
AKRSP	Aga Khan Rural Support Program
AL	Awami League, Bangladesh
ALM	Actor linkage matrix
APPEND	Alliance of Philippine Partners in Enterprise Development
BAIF	Bharatiya Agro Industries Foundation, India
BFHI	Baby Friendly Hospital Initiative, United Nations Children Fund
BNP	Bangladesh Nationalist Party
BP	British Petroleum
BRAC	Bangladesh Rural Advancement Committee
CBDA	Community-based development associations
CREDA	Centre for Rural Education and Development Action, India
CSO	Civil society organization
DfID	Department for International Development, United Kingdom
DRC	Democratic Republic of Congo
ECI	Ebony Consulting International
EP	European Parliament
EU	European Union
Fad'H	*Forces Armées d'Haiti* (the Haitian Armed Forces)
GINAN	Ghanaian Infant Nutrition Action Network
GLR	Great Lakes Region, Africa
HIV	Human Immunodeficiency Virus
IDB	Inter-American Development Bank
IEC	Information, education, and communication
IGC	Intergovernmental conference
JOICFP	Japanese Organization for International Cooperation in Family Planning

KFSRE	Kavango Farming Systems Research and Extension Project
KRCCI	Kavango Regional Chamber of Commerce and Industry, Namibia
LC	Liaison Committee of Development NGOs to the European Union
LCS	Lisikamena Credit Scheme, Namibia
LRO	Linking relief and development
ME	Microenterprise
MFO	Microfinance organizations
MNC	Multinational corporation
MOH	Ministry of Health
MSE	Micro- and small enterprise
MUST	Mbarara University of Science and Technology, Uganda
NGO	Nongovernmental organization
NIE	New institutional economics
ORW	Oral rehydration therapy
OTI	Office of Transition Initiatives, United States Agency for International Development
PPAG	Planned Parenthood Association of Ghana
QIP	Quick Impact Project, United Nations High Commission for Refugees
SME	Small to medium enterprise
TORs	Terms of reference
UNDP	United Nations Development Programme
UNHCR	United Nations High Commission for Refugees
USAID	United States Agency for International Development
WEETU	Women's Employment Enterprise and Training Unit, United Kingdom

Bibliography

Amin, S. 1974. *Accumulation on a World Scale: A Critique of the theory of Underdevelopment.* New York: Monthly Review Press.

Amin, S. 1976. *Unequal Development: An Essay on the Formations of Peripheral Capital.* Hassocks, England: Harvester Press.

Anderson, M. 1999. *Do No Harm: How Aid Can Support Peace—Or War.* Boulder, Colo.: Lynne Rienner.

Anderson, S. and J. Cavanagh. 1996. *The Top 200: The Rise of Corporate Global Power.* Washington, D.C.: Institute of Policy Studies.

Apthorpe, R. and D. Gasper, eds. 1996. *Arguing Development Policy: Frames and Discourse.* London: Frank Cass.

Argyris, C. 1990. *Overcoming Organizational Defences: Facilitating Organizational Learning.* London: Allyn and Bacon.

Aspinwall, M. 1998. "Collective Attraction: The New Political Game in Brussels." In J. Greenwood and M. Aspinwall, eds. *Collective Action in the European Union,* London: Routledge, pp. 196–213.

Attwood, D. W. 1992. *Raising Cane: The Political Economy of Sugar in Western India.* Boulder, Colo.: Westview Press.

Bagadion, B. U. and F. Korten, 1991. "Developing Irrigators' Organizations: A Learning Process Approach." In M. Cernea, ed. *Putting People First: Sociological Variables in Rural Development,* 2nd ed. New York: Oxford University Press, pp. 73–112.

Bangladesh Institute of Development Studies. 1996. *1987–1994: Dynamics of Rural Poverty in Bangladesh.* Dhaka: BIDS. Unpublished.

Baranyi S., S. Kibble, A. Kohen, and K. O'Neill. 1997. *Making Solidarity Effective: Northern Voluntary Organisations Policy Advocacy and the Promotion of Peace in Angola and East Timor.* London: Catholic Institute for International Relations.

Bebbington, A. J. 1996. "Organizations and Intensifications: Campesino Federations, Rural Livelihoods and Agricultural Technology in the Andes and Amazonia." *World Development* 24 (7): 1161–77.

———. 1999. "Capitals and Capabilities: A Framework for Analyzing Peasant Viability, Rural Livelihoods and Poverty." *World Development* 27 (12): 2021–44.

Beer, M., B. Spector, and P. Lawrence. 1984. *Managing Human Assets.* New York: Free Press.

Ben & Jerry's, 1996. *Social Report 1995.* Ben & Jerry's Homemade, Vermont. Report.

Biggs, S. and H. Matsaert. 1998. "An Actor-Oriented Approach for Strengthening Research and Development Capabilities in Natural Resources Systems." Paper prepared for the Mini Monitoring and Evaluation conference, Overseas Development Group, School of Development Studies, University of East Anglia, Norwich, United Kingdom, 25–26 August 1998.

Biggs, S. and A. Neame. 1995. "Negotiating Room for Maneuver: Reflections Concerning NGO Autonomy and Accountability within the New Policy Agenda." In M. Edwards and D. Hulme, eds. *Non-Governmental Organizations : Performance and Accountability*, London: Earthscan, pp. 31–40.

Blair, H. W. 1982. *The Political Economy of Participation in Local Development Programs: Short-term Impasse and Long-term Change in South Asia and the United States from the 1950s to the 1970s*. Monograph Series No. 4. Ithaca, N.Y.: Cornell University, Rural Development Committee.

———. 1984. "Agricultural Credit, Political Economy and Patronage." In D. W. Adams, D. H. Graham, and J. D. von Pischke, eds. *Undermining Rural Development with Cheap Credit*, Boulder, Colo.: Westview Press, pp. 183–93.

———. 1997. Civil Society, Democratic Development and International Donors in Bangladesh. Lewisburg, Pa.: Bucknell University. Unpublished academic paper.

———. 1998. *Spreading Power to the Periphery: An Assessment of Democratic Local Governance*, USAID Program and Operations Assessment Report No. 21. Washington, D.C.: USAID, Center for Development Information and Evaluation.

———. 2000. "Participation, Empowerment and Accountability at the Periphery: A Study of Democratic Local Governance in Six Countries." *World Development* 28 (1): 21–39.

Boas, M., M. Marchand, and T. M. Shaw, eds. 1999. "Special Issue: New Regionalisms." *Third World Quarterly* 20 (5), 987–1070.

The Body Shop. 1998. "Values Report." Littlehampton, U.K.: The Body Shop plc.

Bonifacio, A. 1992. *A Primer on Quick Impact Projects*. Managua, Nicaragua: United Nations High Commission for Refugees.

Borchardt, K. 1995. *European Integration: The Origins and Growth of the European Union*. Luxembourg: Office for Official Publications of the European Community.

Bossuyt, J. and E. De Belder. 1996. "Evaluation Report of the NGDO-EU Liaison Committee." Report prepared for 22nd General Assembly of European Non-Governmental Development Organizations, Brussels, April.

Brett, E. A. 1993. "Voluntary Agencies as Development Organizations: Theorizing the Problem of Efficiency and Accountability." *Development and Change* 24 (2): 269–303.

Brillantes, A. B. 1997. "State-Civil Society Relations in Policy Making: Focus on the Executive." In M. A. Wui and M. G. S. Lopez , eds. *State-Civil Society Relations in Policy Making*, vol. 2. Manila, Philippines: Third World Studies Center, Philippine Democracy Agency, pp. 21–32.

British Petroleum. 1998. *What We Stand For: Our Business Policies*. London: BP.

Britton, B. 1998. The Learning NGO. Occasional Papers Series No. 17. Oxford: International NGO Research and Training Centre.

Bruton, H. J. 1985. "The Search for a Development Economics." *World Development* 13 (10/11): 1099–1124.

Buckley, G. 1997. "Microfinance in Africa: Is It Either the Problem or the Solution?"

World Development 25 (7): 1081–95.

Cameron, J. 1992. "Monitoring the International Planned Parenthood Federation (IPPF) through the Planned Parenthood Association of Ghana (PPAG)." Consultancy report. London: Marie Stopes Consultancy.

Care Austria. 1993. "Micro-credit Scheme Kavango, Namibia–Project Plan Phase 1." English translation of Project Memorandum approved by Government of Austria. Vienna: Care Austria.

Chapman, J. 1999a. *Effective NGO Campaigning: Full Research Report.* London: New Economics Foundation.

——— 1999b. *The Response of Civil Society in Ghana to the Globalization of the Marketing of Breastmilk Substitutes. http://www.sidint.org.*

Chapman, J. and T. Fisher. 1999. *Effective NGO Campaigning: A New Economics Foundation Briefing.* London: New Economics Foundation.

———. 2000. "The Effectiveness of NGO Campaigning: Lessons from Practice." *Development in Practice* 10 (2): 151–6.

Charlier, L. M. G. 1998. "Review of the Impact and Effectiveness of Donor-Financed Emergency Poverty Alleviation Projects in Haiti." In *Haiti: the Challenges of Poverty Reduction,* vol. II. Washington, D.C.: World Bank.

Chatiza, K. M. 1999. "Seizing the Space: A Perspective from a Zimbabwean NGO." Paper presented at "NGOs in a Global Future," conference at Birmingham University, United Kingdom, 11–13 January.

Child, J. 1984. *Organization.* London: Harper Row.

Clark, A. M. 1995. "Non-Governmental Organizations and Their Influence on International Society." *Journal of International Affairs* 48: 507–25.

Clark, J. 1991. *Democratizing Development: The Role of Voluntary Organizations.* London: Earthscan, and West Hartford, Conn.: Kumarian Press.

———. 1992. "Policy Influence, Lobbying and Advocacy." In M. Edwards and D. Hulme, eds. *Making a Difference: NGOs and Development in a Changing World.* London: Earthscan, pp. 191–202.

Clay, E. J. and B. Schaffer, eds. 1984. *Room for Maneuver: An Exploration of Public Policy in Agricultural and Rural Development.* London: Heinemann.

Cleary, S. 1995. "In Whose Interest? NGO Advocacy Campaigns and the Poorest: An Exploration of Two Indonesian Examples." *International Relations* 12: 9–35.

Cliffe, L., ed. 1999. "Special Issue: Complex Political Emergencies" *Third World Quarterly* 20 (1): 1–256.

Clifton, R. and E. Maughan. 1999. *The Future of Brands: Twenty-Five Visions.* London: Macmillan Business.

Cohen, M., S. Fenn, and J. Naimon. 1995. *Environmental and Financial Performance: Are They Related?* New York: Investor Responsibility Research Center.

Conaty, P. and T. Fisher. 1999. *Microcredit for Microentrepreneurs.* London: New Economics Foundation.

Connolly, P. 1989. "The Politics of the Informal Sector: A Critique." In E. Mingione and N. Radclift , eds. *Beyond Employment: Household, Gender and Subsistence.* Oxford: Blackwell, pp.59–91.

Cornia, G. A. R. Jolly, and F. Stewart. 1987. *Adjustment with a Human Face.* New York: United Nations Children's Fund.

Coutsoudis, A., K. Pillay, E. Spooner, L. Kuhn, and H. M. Coovadia. 1999. "Influence of Infant Feeding Patterns on Early Mother-to-Child Transmission of HIV-1 in Durban, South Africa: A Prospective Cohort Study." *The Lancet* 354 (9177): 471–76.

Covey, J. 1992. "A Note on NGOs and Policy Influence." *IDR Reports*, vol. 9, no. 2. Boston: Institute for Development Research.

———. 1996. "Accountability and Effectiveness in NGO Policy Alliances." In M. Edwards and D. Hulme, eds. *Beyond the Magic Bullet: NGO—Performance and Accountability in the Post-Cold War World*. London: Earthscan and West Hartford, Conn.: Kumarian Press, pp. 167–82.

Crook, R. and J. Manor. 1998. *Democracy and Decentralization in South Asia and West Africa: Participation, Accountability and Performance*. Cambridge: Cambridge University Press.

Curtis, D. 1991. *Beyond Government: Organizations for Common Benefit*. London: Macmillan.

De Oliveira, M. D. and R. Tandon. 1994. "An Emerging Global Civil Society". In *CITIZENS Strengthening Global Civil Society*. Washington, D.C.: CIVICUS, pp 1–17.

Department for International Development. 1998. *Banking on the Poor: DfID and Microfinance*. DfID Enterprise Development Group Issues Paper. London: DfID.

Development Assistance Committee. 1998. *European Community: Development Co-operation Review Series Nº 30*. Paris: Organisation for Economic Cooperation and Development.

Devereux, S., F. Matsaert, and G. Van Rooy. 1996. "Credit and Savings in Kavango and Caprivi." Report to Government of Namibia and Commission of European Communities. Aylesbury, U.K.: Agrisystems.

Dicklitch, S. 1998. *The Elusive Promise of NGOs in Africa: Lessons from Uganda*. London: Macmillan.

Dignard, L. and J. Havet. 1995. *Women in Micro and Small Scale Enterprise Development*. London: Intermediate Technology Publications.

Drucker, P. 1999. *Management Challenges for the Twenty-first Century*. Oxford: Butterworth Heinemann.

Duffield, M. 1994. "Complex Emergencies and the Crisis of Developmentalism." *IDS Bulletin* 25 (4): 37–45.

Duffield, M. 1999a. "Globalization and War Economies: Promoting Order or the Return of History?" *Fletcher Forum of World Affairs* 23 (2): 21–36.

Duffield, M. 1999b. "Reading Development as Security: Post Nation-State Conflict and the Creation of Community." Paper presented "NGOs in a Global Future," conference at the University of Birmingham, United Kingdom, 11–13 January.

Dworkin, J., J. Moore, and A. Siegel. 1997. *Haiti Demobilization and Reintegration Program: An Evaluation Prepared for USAID*. Alexandria, Va.: CNA Corporation.

Ebony Consulting International. 1998. "Lisikamena Credit Fund for Small Business: Five Year Strategic Plan—Final Report." Johannesburg, South Africa: ECI.

The Economist. 1998. "The Other Government in Bangladesh." London. 25 July, p. 30.

Edwards, M. 1993. "Does the Doormat Influence the Boot?: Critical Thoughts on UK NGOs and International Advocacy." *Development in Practice* 3: 163–75.

———. 1996. "International Development NGOs: Legitimacy, Accountability, Regulation and Roles." A discussion paper for the Commission on the Future of the

Voluntary Sector and the British Overseas Aid Group. London: BOAG.

———. 1997. "Organizational Learning in NGOs." *Public Administration and Development* 17 (2): 223–34.

———. 1999a. *Future Positive: International Co-operation in the 21st Century.* London: Earthscan and Sterling, Va.: Stylus.

———. 1999b. "Legitimacy and Values in NGOs and Voluntary Organizations: Some Skeptical Thoughts." In D. Lewis, ed. *International Perspectives on Voluntary Action: Reshaping the Third Sector.* London: Earthscan, pp. 258–67.

Edwards, M. and D. Hulme, eds. 1992a. *Making a Difference: NGOs and Development in a Changing World.* London: Earthscan.

Edwards, M. and D. Hulme. 1992b. "Scaling-Up the Developmental Impact of NGOs: Concepts and Experiences." In M. Edwards, M. and D. Hulme, eds. *Making a Difference: NGOs and Development in a Changing World.* London: Earthscan, pp. 13–27.

Edwards, M. and D. Hulme, eds. 1996. *Beyond the Magic Bullet: NGO Performance and Accountability in the Post-Cold War World.* West Hartford, Conn.: Kumarian Press.

Edwards, M., D. Hulme, and T. Wallace. "NGOs in a Global Future: Marrying Local Delivery to Worldwide Leverage." *Public Administration* 19: 117–36.

Elkington, J. 1998. *Cannibals with Forks: The Triple Bottom Line of the Twenty-first Century.* Oxford: Capstone.

Esman, M. J. and N. T. Uphoff. 1984. *Local Organizations: Intermediaries in Rural Development.* London: Cornell University Press.

Fall, A. 1991. *Cereal Banks: At Your Service? The Story of Toundev-Patar, a Village Somewhere in the Sahel.* Translated by Olivia Graham. Oxford: Oxfam Publications.

Fals-Borda, O. and M. A. Rahman, eds. 1992. *Action and Knowledge: Breaking the Monopoly with Participatory Action Research.* London: Intermediate Technology Publications.

Farrington, J. and Bebbington, A. J. 1993. *Reluctant Partners? NGOs, the State and Sustainable Agricultural Development.* London: Routledge.

Fernandes, R. C. 1994. "Threads of Planetary Citizenship." In *CITIZENS Strengthening Global Civil Society.* Washington D.C.: CIVICUS, pp. 319–46.

Fisher, T. 1999. "Microfinancial Services in Britain" In B. Rogaly, T. Fisher, and E. Mayo, eds. *Poverty Social Exclusion and Microfinance in Britain.* Oxford: Oxfam UK/I, in association with the New Economics Foundation, pp. 92–130.

Fowler, A. 1995. *Participatory Self-Assessment of NGO Capacity.* INTRAC Occasional Papers No. 10. Oxford: International NGO Training and Research Centre.

———.1996. "Demonstrating NGO Performance: Problems and Possibilities." *Development in Practice* 6: 58–65.

———.1997. *Striking a Balance: A Guide to Enhancing the Effectiveness of Non-Governmental Organizations in International Development.* London: Earthscan.

———. 1998. "Authentic NGDO Partnerships: Dead End or Light Ahead?" *Development and Change* 29 (1): 137–59.

———. 1999. "Advocacy and Third Sector Organizations: A Composite Perspective." In *International Perspectives on Voluntary Action: Reshaping the Third Sector,* ed. D. Lewis. London: Earthscan, pp. 242–57.

Fox, J. and D. Brown. 1998. *The Struggle for Accountability: The World Bank, NGOs, and Grassroots Movements.* London: MIT Press.

Furlong, A. and F. Cartmel. 1997. *Young People and Social Change: Individualization and Risk in Late Modernity*. Milton Keynes: Open University Press.

Fyvie, C. and A. Ager. 1999. "NGOs and Innovation: Organizational Characteristics and Constraints in Development Assistance Work in The Gambia." *World Development* 27 (8): 1383–95.

Gaiha, R., P. D. Kaushik and V. Kulkarni. 1998. "Jawahlal Rozgar Yojana, Panchayats, and the Rural Poor in India." *Asian Survey* 38 (10): 928–49.

Gass, G., S. Biggs and A. Kelly. 1997. "Stakeholders, Science and Decision-Making for Poverty Focused Rural Mechanization Research and Development." *World Development* 25 (1): 115–26.

Gates, J. 1998. *The Ownership Solution*. London: Allen Lane.

Gavin, T. 1997. "The Nature and Role of Microfinance in Development." Unpublished master's thesis, Business School, University of Durham, United Kingdom.

Gellner, E. 1994. *Conditions of Liberty: Civil Society and Its Rivals*. Harmondsworth, U.K.: Penguin.

Gibb, A. A. 1993. "*Enterprise Agencies and Their Potential: Lessons from UK Experience*." Working paper, Business School, University of Durham, U.K.

Gibb, A. A. and G. Manu. 1990. "The Design of Extension and Related Support Services for Small Scale Enterprise Development." *International Small Business Journal* 8 (3): 10–26.

Giddens, A. 1998. *The Third Way: The Renewal of Social Democracy*. Cambridge: Polity Press.

———. 1999. *Runaway World: How Globalisation is Reshaping our Lives*. London: Profile Books.

Goetz, A. M. 1998. "Local Heroes: Patterns of Field Worker Discretion in Implementing GAD Policy in Bangladesh." In I. Matin and S. Sinha with P. Alexander, eds. *Proceedings of a Workshop on Recent Research on Micro-Finance: Implications for Policy*. Rural Research Unit at Sussex Working Papers No. 3. Brighton, U.K.: Institute of Development Studies, pp. 143–58.

Goetz, A. M. and R. Sen Gupta. 1996. "Who Takes the Credit? Gender, Power and Control over Loan Use in Rural Credit Programmes in Bangladesh." *World Development* 24 (1): 45–63.

Goldstein-Gelb, M., M. Owens, and P. Penrose. 1998. "Peer and Individual Microlending: Reflections from Organisations that Do Both." Paper presented at the Eighth Annual Conference of the Association for Enterprise Opportunity, Washington, D.C., April.

Gonella, A., M. Pilling, and S. Zadek. 1998. *Making Values Work: Contemporary Experiences in Social and Ethical Accounting, Auditing and Reporting*. London: New Economics Foundation in association with the Institute of Social and Ethical AccountAbility, Association of Certified and Chartered Accountants.

Goodhand, J. and D. Hulme. 1998. *The Role of NGOs in Complex Political Emergencies: Background Report to the Steering Committee*. Manchester, U.K.: Institute for Development Policy and Management.

———. 1999: "From Wars to Complex Political Emergencies: Understanding Conflict and Peace-building in the New World Disorder." *Third World Quarterly* 20 (1): 13–26.

Gore, C. 2000. "The Rise and Fall of the Washington Consensus as a Paradigm for Developing Countries." *World Development* 28 (5): 789–804.

Gourevitch, P. 1999. *We Wish to Inform You That Tomorrow We Will Be Killed with our Families: Stories from Rwanda.* New York: Farrar Straus and Giroux.

Gourlay, C. and E. Remacle. 1998. "The 1998 IGC: The Actors and their Interaction." In K. Eliassen, ed. *Foreign and Security Policy in the European Union,* London: Sage, pp. 59–63.

Government of the Republic of Namibia. 1996. *Living Conditions in Namibia: The 1993/1994 Namibia Household Income and Expenditure Survey.* Central Statistics Office. Windhoek, Namibia: National Planning Commission.

Goyder, G. 1961. *The Responsible Company.* Oxford: Basil Blackwell.

Greenwood, J. 1997. *Representing Interests in the European Union.* London: Macmillan.

Greenwood, J. and M. Aspinwall. 1998. "Conceptualizing Collective Action in the European Union." In J. Greenwood and M. Aspinwall, ed. *Collective Action in the European Union.* London: Routledge, pp. 1–30.

Grimble, R. and K. Wellard. 1997. "Stakeholder Methodologies in Natural Resource Management: A Review of Principles, Contexts, Experiences and Opportunities." *Agricultural Systems* 55 (2): 173–93.

Gutiérrez, Edgar. 1997. "Derechos Humanos y Sociedad Civil en la Difícil Transición Guatemalteca." In F. Birk, ed. *Guatemala: Oprimida, Pobre o Princesa Embrujada?* Guatemala: Friedrich Ebert Stiftung, pp. 19–89.

Hadenius, A. and F. Uggla. 1996. "Making Civil Society Work, Promoting Democratic Development: What Can States and Donors Do?" *World Development* 24 (10): 1612–39

Hann, C. and E. Dunn. 1996. *Civil Society: Challenging Western Models.* London: Routledge.

Hansen, Gary. 1996. *Constituencies for Reform: Strategic Approaches for Donor-Coordinated Civic Advocacy Programs.* USAID Programs and Operations Assessment Report No. 12. Washington, D.C.: USAID.

Hansohm, D., L. Blaauw, and A. Erastus-Sacharia. 1998. "The Promotion of SME in Southern Africa: Some Observations Relevant for Co-operation among SME Service Providers and the Use of Information Technology." Windhoek, Namibia: Namibia Economic Policy and Research Unit.

Haq, M. 1997. *Human Development in South Asia.* Dhaka: University Press.

Harper, M. 1998. *Profit for the Poor: Cases in Microfinance.* London: Intermediate Technology Publications.

Harriss, J., J. Hunter and C. Lewis, eds. 1997. *The New International Economics and the Third World.* London: Routledge.

Havers, M. 1996. "Financial Sustainability in Savings and Credit Programs." *Development and Practice* 6 (2): 144–50.

Hirschman, A. O. 1970. *Exit, Voice and Loyalty: Responses to Decline in Firms, Organizations and States.* Cambridge: Harvard University Press.

Hobart, M., ed. 1993. *An Anthropological Critique of Development: The Growth of Ignorance.* London: Routledge.

Hobsbawm, E. 1994. *The Age of Extremes.* London: Abacus.

Holloway, R. 1994. "Organizations of Civil Society: Bangladesh." In I. R. Serrano, ed. *Civil Society in the Asia-Pacific Region.* Washington, D.C.: CIVICUS, pp. 137–43.

Hossain, M. 1997. "Recent Trends in the Rural Economy of Bangladesh: Points to Be Considered in Formulating Policies and Strategies for Poverty Alleviation." In R. Rahman, ed. *Poverty and Development.* Dhaka: Bangladesh Institute for Development Studies, pp. 216–36.

Howell, J. 1997. "Post-Beijing Reflections: Creating Ripples, But Not Waves in China." *Women's Studies International Forum.* 20 (2): 235–52.

Hudock, A. 1995. "Sustaining Southern NGO Partners in Resource-Dependent Environments." *Journal of International Development.* 7(4): 653–67.

Hulme, D. and M. Edwards, eds. 1996. *NGOs, States and Donors: Too Close for Comfort?* London: Macmillan and St. Martin's Press.

Hutchcroft, P. 1991. "Oligarchs and Cronies in the Philippine State: The Politics of Patrimonial Plunder." *World Politics* 43 (3): 415–44.

Hyman, E. L. and K. Dearden. 1998. "Comprehensive Impact Assessment Systems for NGO Micro-enterprise Development Programs." *World Development* (26) 2: 261–76.

ICEA/DPPC (consultancy company). 1999. "Development and Humanitarian Assistance of the European Union: An Evaluation of Instruments and Programs Managed by the European Commission Final Synthesis Report." Brussels. Unpublished report.

Institute of Social and Ethical AccountAbility. 1999. *AA1000: Standards, Guidelines, and Tools.* London: Institute of Social and Ethical AccountAbility.

International Labor Office. 1972. *Employment, Incomes and Equality: A Strategy for Increasing Production Employment in Kenya.* Geneva: International Labor Organization.

James, R. 1994. *Strengthening the Capacity of Southern NGO Partners: A Survey of Current NNGO Approaches.* Occasional Paper Series No 5. Oxford: INTRAC.

Johnson, S. and B. Rogaly. 1997. *Microfinance and Poverty Alleviation.* Oxfam Development Guidelines. Oxford: Oxfam UK/I.

Kabeer, N. 1998. *Money Can't Buy Me Love: Re-evaluation of Gender, Credit, and Empowerment in Rural Bangladesh.* Discussion Paper No. 363. Brighton, U.K.: Institute of Development Studies.

Kasaizi, O. E. 1999. "Karadea: The Case of a Self Determining NGO." Paper presented at "NGOs in a Global Future." Conference at University of Birmingham, U.K. January 11–13.

Kavango Farming Systems Research and Extension Project. 1998a. "Case Study Monitoring Reports of the Kavango Farming Systems Research and Extension Project." Rundu, Namibia: KFSRE.

Kavango Farming Systems Research and Extension Project. 1998b. "Managing Land Together: Social Networks in Kavango Farming Systems." Rundu, Namibia: KFSRE.

Keane, J. 1988. *Democracy and Civil Society: On the Predicaments of European Socialism, the Prospects for Democracy and the Problem of Controlling Social and Political Power.* London: Verso.

Keck, M. and K. Sikkink. 1998. *Activists Beyond Borders: Advocacy Networks in International Politics.* London: Cornell University Press.

Keen, D. 1994. *The Benefits of Famine: A Political Economy of Relief in North-West Sudan.* Princeton University Press.

Kidder, T. 1997. "Macro Debates at the Micro Credit Summit." *Development in Practice* 7 (4): 432–35.

Korten, D. 1980. "Community Organization and Rural Development: A Learning Process Approach." *Public Administration Review* 40 (3): 480–511.

———. 1984: "Strategic Organization for People-centered Development." *Public Administration Review.* July/August: 341–52.

———. 1987. "Third Generation NGO Strategies: A Key to People-Centered Development." *World Development* 15 (supplement): 145–59.

———. 1990. *Getting to the Twenty-first Century: Voluntary Action and the Global Agenda.* West Hartford, Conn.: Kumarian Press.

———. 1997. *When Corporations Rule the World.* Hartford, Conn.: Kumarian Press.

Korten, D. C. and A. B. Quizon. 1991. *Toward Common Ground Among Governments, NGOs and International Assistance Agencies.* Delhi: The People-Centred Development Forum and the Asian NGO Coalition.

Kothari, R. 1984. "The Non-Party Political Process." *Economic and Political Weekly.* February, p. 219.

Lal, D. 1983. *The Poverty of Development Economics.* London: Institute of Economic Affairs.

Langdon, K. 1999. "Sustainable Livelihoods: In Search of Meaning." Unpublished master's thesis, Critical Management, University of Lancaster, United Kingdom.

Law, A. 1995. *A Hollow Success: Repatriation and Reintegration of Cambodian Refugees.* Melbourne, Australia: World Vision.

Leftwich, A. 1995. "Bringing Politics Back In: Towards a Model of the Developmental State." *Journal of Development Studies* 31 (3): 400–27.

———, ed. 1996. *Democracy and Development.* Cambridge: Polity Press.

Levitt, T. 1975. *The Third Sector: New Tactics for a Responsive Society.* New York: AMACOM, American Management Associations.

Lewis, D., ed. 1999. *International Perspectives on Voluntary Action: Reshaping the Third Sector.* London: Earthscan.

Lipton, M. 1977. *Why Poor People Stay Poor: Urban Bias in World Development.* London: Temple Smith.

Lisikamena Credit Scheme. 1998. "An Appraisal of the Financial Needs of Market Women in Rundu: Implications for Micro Lending Scheme Products." Draft report, September. Rundu, Namibia: LCS.

Lister, M., ed. 1998. *European Union Development Policy.* London: Macmillan.

Lister, S. 2000. "Power in Partnership? An Analysis of an NGO's Relationships with Its Partners." *Journal of International Development* 12 (March): 227–39.

Long, N. and A. Long, eds. 1992. *Battlefields of Knowledge: The Interlocking of Theory and Practice in Social Research and Development.* London: Routledge.

Lubkemann, S. 1998. *Humanitarianism and War Fieldwork Case Study on the Effects of Innovative Practices: The Manica Province Integrated Health Project in Mozambique, 1990–97.* Providence, R.I.: Brown University. Unpublished paper.

Lyon, F. 1998. "Trust, Networks and Norms: The Creation of Social Capital in Agricultural Economies in Ghana." Draft Paper for Department for International Development, Department of Geography, University of Durham, United Kingdom.

MacKewan, A. 1999. *Neo-liberalism or Democracy: Economic Strategy, Markets, and Alternatives for the Twenty-first Century.* London: Zed Books.

Maguire, R., E. Balutansky, J. Formerand, L. Minear, W. G. O'Neill, T. Weiss, and S. Zaidi. 1996. *Haiti Held Hostage: International Responses to the Quest for Nationhood, 1986–1996.* Occasional Paper No. 23. Providence, R.I., Thomas J. Watson Institute for International Studies.

Malena, C. 1995. "Relations between Northern and Southern NGOs." *Canadian Journal of Development Studies* 16: 7–30.

Malkki, L. H. 1995. *Purity and Exile: Violence, Mercy and National Cosmology Among Hutu Refugees in Tanzania.* Chicago: University of Chicago Press.

Manor, J. 1999. *The Political Economy of Democratic Decentralization.* Washington, D.C.: World Bank.

Matsaert, F. 1998. "Compulsory Savings and Credit:A Joint Liability?" Unpubished master's dissertation. University of East Anglia, Norwich, United Kingdom.

Maxwell, S. 1998. "Comparisons, Convergence and Connections: Development Studies in North and South." *IDS Bulletin* 29 (1): 20–31.

Mayoux, L. 1997. "Women's Empowerment and Micro-Finance Programs: Approaches, Evidence and ways Forward." Draft overview paper for Pilot Project: Microfinance and Women's Empowerment: Strategies for Increasing Impact. Milton Keynes, U.K.: Open University.

McGuire, P. B. and J. D. Conroy. 1997. "Bank-NGO Linkages and the Transaction Costs of Lending to the Poor through Groups." *Small Enterprise Development* 8 (1): 4–15.

Mead, D. C. and C. Liedholm. 1998. "The Dynamics of Micro and Small Enterprises in Developing Countries." *World Development* 26 (1): 61–74.

Ministry of Agriculture, Water and Rural Development, Namibia. 1997. "Farm Management Report of the Kavango Region, Namibia—November 1995 to June 1996: Analysis Report 1." Windhoek, Namibia: Directorate of Planning, MAWRD.

Montinola, G. P. 1999. "Parties and Accountability in the Philippines," *Journal of Democracy* 10 (1): 126–40.

Morduch, J. 2000. "The Microfinance Schism." *World Development* 28 (4): 617–69.

Mosse, D. 1998. "The Making and Marketing of Participatory Development—A Skeptical Note." Draft paper for Conference, Participation: The New Tyranny?, International Department of Public Management, University of Manchester, United Kingdom. 3 November.

Murphy, C., ed. 2000. *Egalitarian Social Movements in Response to Globalization.* London: Macmillan Press.

Mushtaque A., R. Chowdhury and R. Cash. 1996. *A Simple Solution: Teaching Millions to Treat Diarrhoea at Home.* Dhaka: University Press.

Myrdal, G. 1968. *Asian Drama: An Inquiry into the Poverty of Nations.* New York: Pantheon.

Najam, A. 1999. "Citizen Organization as Policy Entrepreneurs." In D. Lewis, ed. *International Perspectives on Voluntary Action.* London: Earthscan, pp. 142–81.

Namibia Economic Policy and Research Unit. 1998. "Finance Policy on Small and Medium Enterprises: Draft Study for Discussion." Version 4, April. Windhoek, Namibia: NEPRU.

Negassa, Y. 1999. "The Experience of Disengagement from the FAO: Action for Development Setting Out on Its Own. Paper presented at "NGOs in a Global Future," conference at University of Birmingham, United Kingdom. 11–13 January.

Nelson, P. 1997. "Conflict, Legitimacy and Effectiveness: Who Speaks for Whom in Transnational NGO Networks Lobbying the World Bank?" *Non-Profit and Voluntary Sector Quarterly* 26: 421–41.

Nerfin, M. 1987. "Neither Prince nor Merchant: Citizen—An Introduction to the Third System." *Development Dialogue* 1: 170–95.

Nesongano, M. 1997. "Kavango Small Business Survey." Windhoek, Namibia.

North, D. C. 1989. "Institutions and Economic Growth: An Historical Introduction." *World Development* Special Issue 17 (9): 1319–32.

———. 1990. *Institutions, Institutional Change and Economic Performance.* Cambridge: Cambridge University Press.

Nuitjen, M. 1992. "Local Organization as Organizing Practices—Rethinking Rural Institutions." In N. Long and A. Long, eds. *Battlefields of Knowledge: The Interlocking of Theory and Practice in Social Research and Development.* London and New York: Routledge, pp. xx.

Nyamugasira, W. 1998. "NGOs and Advocacy: How Well Are the Poor Represented?" *Development in Practice* 8: 297–308.

O'Brien, R., A. M. Goetz, J. A. Scholte and M. Williams. 1998. *Complex Multilateralism: Global Economic Institutions and Global Social Movements.* London: Economic and Social Research Council.

Olson, M. 1971. *The Logic of Collective Action: Public Goods and the Theory of Groups,* 2nd ed. Cambridge: Harvard University Press.

Organization for Economic Cooperation and Development. 1997. "Final Report of the DAC Ad Hoc Working Group on Participatory Development and Good Governance, Parts I and II." Paris: OECD.

Otero, M. and E. Rhyne. 1994. *The New World of Micro Enterprise Finance: Building Healthy Financial Institutions for the Poor.* London: Intermediate Technology Publications.

Overseas Development Administration. 1995. "Guidance Note on How to Do Stakeholder Analysis of Aid Projects and Programs." London: Social Development Department, ODA (now Department for International Development [DfID]).

Overseas Development Institute. 1998. *The State of the International Humanitarian System.* ODI Briefing Paper No. 1. London: ODI.

Oxfam. 1996. *Policy Department Strategic Plan, 1996–2001.* Oxford, U.K.: Oxfam UK and Ireland.

Patterson, S. 1996. *A Report on a Survey of the Former Fad'H in Haiti.* Washington, D.C.: Winner, Wagner and Francis.

Pearce, J. 1998. "Building Civil Society from the Outside: The Problematic Democratization of Central America." *Global Society* 12 (2): 177–196.

Pearson, R. 1997. "Credit for Micro-Entrepreneurs: Issues Relating to Policies on Welfare to Work and Local Economic Development." School of Development Studies, University of Norwich, United Kingdom. Unpublished paper.

———. 1998a. "Microcredit Meets Social Exclusion: Learning with Difficulty from International Experience." *Journal of International Development* 10 (6): 811–22.

———. 1998b. "On Our Terms: Developing Financial Services for Women in a Globalizing World." Plenary paper for 15th anniversary conference of Mama Cash, Amsterdam, November.

————. 2000 (forthcoming). "All Change? Women, Men and Reproductive Work in the Global Economy." *European Journal of Development Research.*

Pearson, R. and E. Watson. 1997. "Giving Women the Credit: The Norwich Full Circle Project." *Gender and Development* 5 (3): 52–57.

Planned Parenthood Association of Ghana. 1992. "Three Year Plan 1993–1995." Accra: PPAG.

Pottier, J., ed. 1993. *Practising Development: Social Science Perspectives.* London and New York: Routledge.

Prendergast, J. 1997. *Crisis Response: Humanitarian Band-Aids in Sudan and Somalia.* London: Pluto Press.

Price Waterhouse Cooper. 1998. *A Strange Affair? The Emerging Relationship Between NGOs and Transnational Companies.* London: Price Waterhouse Cooper and the University of Notre Dame.

Putnam, R. 1995. "Bowling Alone: America's Declining Social Capital." *Journal of Democracy* 6 (1): 65–78

Quiggin, J. 1993. "Common Property, Equality, and Development." *World Development* 21 (7): 1123–38.

Quigley, K. F. E. 1997. *For Democracy's Sake: Foundations and Democracy Assistance in Central Europe.* Washington, D.C.: The Woodrow Wilson Center Press.

Revens, R. 1983. *The ABC of Action Learning.* Manchester, U.K.: International Foundation for Action Learning.

Reyes, S. L. 1997. "Legislative Advocacy for a New Anti-Rape Law: A Case Study." In M. A. Wui and M. G. S. Lopez, eds. *State-Civil Society Relations in Policy Making*, vol. 2. Manila: Third World Studies Center, Philippine Democracy Agency.

Richardson, P. A. and K. J. Langdon. 1998. *Synthesis of Evaluations of Assistance to the Enterprise Development Sector.* London: Department for International Development.

Richter, J. 1998. *Engineering of Consent: Uncovering Corporate PR.* Dorset, U.K.: The Corner House.

Robinson, M. and G. White. 1997. *The Role of Civic Organizations in the Provision of Social Services: Towards Synergy.* Helsinki: United Nations University/World Institute for Development Economics.

Roche, C. 1999. *Impact Assessment for Development Agencies: Learning to Value Change.* Oxford: Oxfam Publications.

Roche, C. and A. Bush. 1997. "Assessing the Impact of Advocacy Work." *Appropriate Technology* 24 (2): 9–15.

Rondinelli D. A., J. R. Nellis, and G. S. Cheema. 1983. *Decentralization in Developing Countries: A Review of Recent Experience.* World Bank Staff Working paper No. 581. Washington, D.C.: The World Bank.

Rudolph, L. I. and S. Hoeber Rudolph. 1987. *In Pursuit of Lakshmi: The Political Economy of the Indian State.* Chicago: University of Chicago Press.

Rye O. G. 1998. "Bureaucratic Interests and European Aid to Sub-Saharan Africa." In M. Lister, ed. *European Union Development Policy.* London: Macmillan, pp. 64–96.

Sahley, C. 1995. *Strengthening the Capacity of NGOs: Cases of Small Enterprise Development Agencies in Africa.* Oxford: International NGO Research and Training Centre.

Salamon, L. and H. K. Anheier. 1992. "In Search of the Nonprofit Sector, Parts I and II" *Voluntas* 3(2): 125–52, 3(3): 267–309.

Schechter, M. G., ed. 1999. *The Revival of Civil Society: Global and Comparative Perspectives*. London: Macmillan.

Scholte, J. A. 2000. *Globalization: A Critical Introduction*. London: Macmillan Press.

Schumpeter, J. A. 1934. *The Theory of Economic Development*. New York: Oxford Press.

Scott, M. 1999. "Supper with the Devil? Canadian NGO-Diplomatic Collaboration Pre- and Post 'Ottawa Process.'" Paper delivered at "NGOs in a Global Future," conference at the University of Birmingham, United Kingdom (11–13 January).

Sen, A. 1987. *Food Economics and Entitlements*. Helsinki, Finland: World Institute for Development Economics Research, United Nations University.

———. 1989. *Hunger and Public Action*. Clarendon Press and Oxford University Press.

Senge, P. 1990. *The Fifth Discipline: The Art and Practice of the Learning Organization*. London: Century Business.

Serrano, I. R. 1994. "Civil Society in the Asia-Pacific Region." In *CITIZENS Strengthening Global Civil Society*. Washington: CIVICUS, pp. 271–317.

Shah, G. 1988. "Grass-Roots Mobilization in Indian Politics." In A. Kohli, ed. *India's Democracy: An Analysis of Changing State-Society Relations*. Princeton, N.J.: Princeton University Press, pp. 262–304.

Shaw, T. M. 1997. "Beyond Post-Conflict Peacebuilding: What Links to Sustainable Development and Human Security?" In J. Ginifer, ed. *Beyond the Emergency: Development within UN Peace Missions*, London: Frank Cass, pp. 36–48.

———. 1998. "African Renaissance/African Alliance: Towards New Regionalisms and New Realism in the Great Lakes at the Start of the Twenty-first Century." *Politeia* 17 (3): 60–74.

Shaw, T. M. and S. J. Maclean. 1999. "The Emergency of Civil Society: Contributions to a New Human Security Agenda." In Ho-Won Jeong, ed. *The New Agenda for Peace Research*. Aldershot, U.K.: Ashgate Publishing.

Shaw, T., S. J. Maclean, and K. Orr. 1998. "Peace-Building and African Organizations: Towards Subcontracting or a New and Sustainable Division of Labor?" In K. van Walraven, ed. *Early Warning and Conflict Prevention*, The Hague: Kluwer, pp. 149–61.

Shaw, T. M. and J. Nyang'oro. 1999. "Conclusion: African Foreign Policies in the New Millennium: Alternative Perspectives and Practices." In S. Wright, ed. *African Foreign Policies*, Boulder, Colo.: Westview Press, pp. 237–48.

———. 2000. "African Renaissance in the New Millennium? From Anarchy to Emerging Markets?" In R. Stubbs and G. R. D. Underhill, eds. *Political Economy and the Changing Global Order*. Toronto: Oxford University Press, pp. 275–84.

Simbi, M. 1999. "Harare Declaration." Paper presented at "NGOs in a Global Future," conference at the University of Birmingham, United Kingdom. 11–13 January.

Singh, H. 1994. "Constitutional Base for Panchayati Raj in India: The Seventy-third Amendment Act," *Asian Survey* 34 (9): 818–27.

Smillie, I. 1995. *The Alms Bazaar: Altruism under Fire—Non-profit Organizations and International Development*. London: Intermediate Technology Publications.

———. 1999. "Relief and Development: The Struggle for Synergy." Providence, R.I.: Thomas J. Watson Institute. Unpublished paper.

Smillie, I. and J. Hailey. 2000. *Managing for Change: Leadership, Strategy and Management in Asian NGOs*. London: Earthscan.

Sobhan. S. 1997. "Internal and External Perceptions of Cultural Identity." In W. van

Schendel and K. Westergaard, eds. *Bangladesh in the 1990s: Selected Studies*, Dhaka: University Press, pp. 33–42.

Sogge, D., ed. 1996. *Compassion and Calculation: The Business of Private Foreign Aid.* London: Pluto Press.

Strauss, R. 1996. "Lisikamena Credit Program, Rundu, Namibia: Final Evaluation Report." San Francisco. Unpublished report.

Stuart, L. and P. Collinson. 1999. "Fashioning the Phoenix Factor." *The Guardian*, January 9, pp. 2–3.

Thin, N. 1995. "Mud at the Grassroots: Participatory Development in the Joint Funding Scheme." Discussion paper for the ODA-NGO workshop on Participation, Edinburgh, 10–12 July.

Thom, G. 1998. *Challenging the Chain.* Transform Occasional Paper No. 3. London: Transform.

Timberman, D. G. 1990. *A Changeless Land: Continuity and Change in Philippine Politics.* Singapore: Institute of Southeast Asian Studies.

Transform. 1997. "Harare Declaration." Transform Occasional Paper No. 2. London: Transform.

Treasury. 1999. "H M Treasury Policy Action Team 3: National Strategy for Neighbourhood Renewal Enterprise and Social Exclusion." London.

United Nations Commission for Trade and Development. 1998. *World Investment Report.* Geneva: UNCTAD.

United Nations Department for Development Support and Management Services/ United Nations Industrial Development Organizations. 1995. "Post Conflict Recovery: UNHCR's Capacities and Perspectives." In *Post Conflict Reconstruction Strategies.* Proceedings from a colloquium at Stadtschlaining, Austria, 23–24 June.

United Nations Development Programme. 1996. "Namibia: Human Development Report 1996." Windhoek, Namibia: UNDP.

———. 1997a. "Background to the Global Research Framework of Decentralized Governance Programme." New York: UNDP.

———. 1997b. "Decentralized Governance Program: Strengthening Capacity for People-Centered Development." Draft. Management Development and Governance Division, Bureau for Policy and Program Support. New York: UNDP.

———. 1997c. "Governance for Sustainable Human Development: A UNDP Policy Document." New York: UNDP.

———. 1998a. *Human Development Report.* New York: UNDP.

———. 1998b. *Human Development Report on Uganda.* New York: UNDP.

———. 1998c. *Linking Relief to Development.* Kigali, Rwanda: UNDP.

———. 1999a. *Bangladesh Assessment.* Dhaka: UNDP.

———. 1999b. *Human Development Report 1999.* New York: UNDP.

United Nations High Commission for Refugees. 1993. *Quick Impact Projects.* PTTS Discussion Paper No. 8. Geneva: UNHCR.

———. 1994. *Preliminary Guidelines, Preparation and Design of Quick Impact Projects.* PTSS Discussion Paper No. 10. Geneva: UNHCR.

———. 1997. *Reintegration in the Transition from War to Peace.* Geneva:UNHCR.

United States Agency for International Development. 1994. "Strategies for Sustainable Development." Washington, D.C.: USAID.

————. 1996. "Constituencies for Reform: Strategic Approaches for Donor-Supported Civic Advocacy Programs." Program and Operations Assessment Report 12. Washington, D.C.: USAID.

————. Undated. USAID. Office of Transition Initiatives. Report on establishing OTI.

Uphoff, N. 1995. "Why NGOs Are Not a Third Sector: A Sectoral Analysis with Some Thoughts on Accountability, Sustainability and Evaluation." In M. Edwards and D. Hulme, eds. *Beyond the Magic Bullet: NGO Performance and Accountability in the Post-Cold WarWorld.* London: Earthscan, pp. 17–30.

Uvin, P. 1998. *Aiding Violence: The Development Enterprise in Rwanda.* West Hartford, Conn.: Kumarian Press.

Uvin, P. and D. Miller. 1996. "Paths to Scaling Up: Alternative Strategies for Local Nongovernmental Organizations." *Human Organization* 55 (3): 344–54.

Vakil, A. C. 1997. "Confronting the Classification Problem: Toward a Taxonomy of NGOs." *World Development* 25 (12): 2057–70.

Van Rooy, A. 1999. "Civil Society As Idea: An Analytical Hatstand?" In A. Van Rooy, ed. *Civil Society and the Aid Industry.* London: Earthscan, pp. 6–29.

VanCity. 1998. "VanCity Social Report 1998." Vancouver: VanCity.

Von Pischke, J. D. and D. W. Adams. 1992. "Microenterprise Credit Programs: Déjà Vu." *World Development* 20 (10): 1463–71.

Waddock, S. and S. Graves. 1997. "The Corporate Social Performance-Financial Performance Link." *Strategic Management Journal* 18: (4): 303–19.

Wade, R. 1998. "The Asian Debt-and-Development Crisis of 1997–?: Causes and Consequences." *World Development* 26 (8): 1535–53.

————. 1990. *Governing the Market: Economic Theory and the Role of Government in East Asian Industrialization.* Princeton, N.J.: Princeton University Press.

Wallace, T., C. Crowther, and A. Shepherd. 1997. *Standardizing Development: Influences on UK NGOs' Policies and Procedures.* Oxford: Worldview Press.

Wheeler, D. and M. Sillanpää. 1997. *The Stakeholder Corporation: A Blueprint for Maximizing Stakeholder Value.* London: Pitman.

Wheeler, N. 1997. "Humanitarian Intervention and World Politics." In J. Baylis and S. Smith, eds. *The Globalization of World Politics: An Introduction to International Relations.* Oxford: Oxford University Press, pp. 391–408.

White, G. W. 1988. *Developmental States in East Asia.* London: Macmillan.

Whitman, J. and D. Pocock, eds. 1996. *After Rwanda: The Coordination of UN Humanitarian Assistance.* New York: St. Martin's Press.

Wilson, W. J. 1987. *The Truly Disadvantaged: The Inner City, the Underclass, and Public Policy.* Chicago: University of Chicago Press.

————. 1996. *When Work Disappears: The World of the New Urban Poor.* New York: Alfred Knopf.

Wood, E. M. 1990. "The Uses and Abuses of Civil Society." *Socialist Register 1990.* 60–84.

Wood, G. D. 1994. *Bangladesh: Whose Ideas, Whose Interests?* Dhaka: University Press.

Wood, G. D. and R. Palmer-Jones, with Q. S. Ahmed, M. A. Manal and S. C. Dutta. 1991. *The Water Sellers: A Co-operative Venture by the Rural Poor.* London: Intermediate Technology Publications.

World Bank. 1997a. "Namibia: Rising to the Challenge of Poverty Reduction." Technical Paper for Preparation of Poverty Reduction Strategy for Namibia. Washington, D.C. and Windhoek, Namibia: World Bank.

World Bank. 1997b. *World Development Report 1997: The State in a Changing World.* Washington D.C.: World Bank.

World Business Council for Sustainable Development. 1997. *Exploring Sustainable Development: WBCSD Scenarios, 2000–2050.* Geneva: WBCSD.

World Development Movement. 1998. "Making Investment Work for People: An International Framework for Investment." Consultation Paper. London: WDM.

Wrong, D. H. 1979. *Power: Its Forms, Bases and Uses.* Oxford: Blackwell.

Young, D., B. Koenig, A. Najam, and J. Fisher. 1999. "Strategy and Structure in Managing Global Associations." *Voluntas: International Journal of Voluntary and Non-Profit Organizations* 10: 323–43.

Yunus, M., with A. Jolis. 1998. *Banker to the Poor.* London: Atrum Press.

Zadek, S. 1998. "Balancing Performance, Ethics, and Accountability." *Journal of Business Ethics* 17 (13): 1421–41.

——— 1999. "Values, Ethics and Accountability." Paper prepared for the Committee of Inquiry on a New Vision for Business: A New Vision for Business. London.

Zadek, S., and F. Amalric. 1998. "Consumer Works!" *Development* 41 (1): 7–15.

Zadek, S. and J. Chapman. 1998. "Revealing the Emperor's Clothes: Does Social Responsibility Count?" Paper prepared for the Conference Board, New Economics Foundation, London.

Zadek, S., S. Lingayah, and S. Murphy. 1998. *Purchasing Power: Civil Action for Sustainable Consumption.* London: New Economics Foundation.

About the Contributors

STEPHEN BIGGS is a senior lecturer in the School of Development Studies, University of East Anglia, Norwich, United Kingdom.

HARRY BLAIR is presently on leave from Bucknell University, United States (where he works as professor of political science), working as senior democracy specialist at the United States Agency for International Development.

JOHN CAMERON teaches at the University of East Anglia, United Kingdom, and has worked directly with NGOs and NGO support projects in Ethiopia, Ghana, Nepal, Pakistan, Palestine, and the United Kingdom.

JENNIFER CHAPMAN has worked freelance in the development field with the private sector, government, NGOs, and academia for more than fifteen years.

SARAH CROWTHER works as short course coordinator at the Centre for Development Studies at the University of Swansea.

KAREN DOYLE is the associate director at the Aspen Institute's Economic Opportunities Program in the United States.

MICHAEL EDWARDS is director of the Governance and Civil Society program at the Ford Foundation, New York.

CHRISTIAN L. FRERES is research coordinator at Asociación de Investigación y Especialización sobre Temas Iberoamericanos in Madrid, Spain.

JOHN HAILEY is director of research at Oxford Brookes University Business School, United Kingdom, and a founder of the Oxford-based International NGO Training and Research Centre.

M. EMRUL HASAN is coordinator of training and advocacy at the South Asian Network of Microfinance Initiatives in Bangladesh.

JUDE HOWELL is a fellow of the Institute of Development Studies, Brighton, United Kingdom.

ALAN HUDSON is a research fellow in International Political Economy at the Open University working on issues of globalization, sovereignty, and global governance.

DAVID HULME is professor of Development Studies in the International Department of Public Management at the University of Manchester.

EDUARDO JIMENEZ is a freelance microfinance specialist currently assigned to the National Credit Council in the Philippines under the United States Agency for International Development Credit Policy Improvement Project.

SUSAN JOHNSON is an economist who worked for six years for ActionAid before becoming a lecturer in Development Studies at the University of Bath, United Kingdom.

ALLAN KAPLAN is a director of the Community Development Resource Association in South Africa, which promotes organizational development in organizations working for social transformation.

MAHBUBUL KARIM is senior vice-president of Proshika, one of the most influential NGOs in Bangladesh.

THALIA G. KIDDER is the global adviser on microeconomics for Oxfam GB, based in the regional office for Central America in Managua, Nicaragua.

KAREN LANGDON works at the Foundation for SME Development, formerly the Small Business Centre, at Durham University Business School, United Kingdom.

DAVID LEWIS is a lecturer at the Centre for Civil Society, Department of Social Policy, London School of Economics and Political Science.

FRANK R. MATSAERT is enterprise development adviser for the United Kingdom Department for International Development (DFID) based in the Central Africa office in Zimbabwe.

PAMELA MBABAZI is a lecturer in rural development and acting dean of the Faculty of Development Studies at Mbarara University in Uganda.

JENNY PEARCE is a professor in the Department of Peace Studies at Bradford University, United Kingdom.

RUTH PEARSON is professor at the Centre for Development Studies, University of Leeds, United Kingdom.

PAT RICHARDSON is director of network development at the Foundation for SME Development, United Kingdom, formerly the Small Business Centre, at Durham University Business School, United Kingdom.

TIMOTHY M. SHAW is director, Centre for Foreign Policy Studies, and professor of political science and international development studies at Dalhousie University, Halifax, Canada.

MARGARET SIMBI works for CAC Consulting, Zimbabwe, which is a partner in the Transform Network.

IAN SMILLIE is a freelance writer and consultant based in Ottawa, Canada.

GRAHAM THOM is the London-based director of Transform Africa, which forms part of the Transform Network.

TINA WALLACE works part-time as a senior lecturer/researcher in the Business School at Oxford Brookes University, United Kingdom, and as a consultant to the NGO sector.

SIMON ZADEK is visiting professor at the Copenhagen Business School and chair of the Institute of Social and Ethical Accountability.

Index

Books of related interest
from Kumarian Press

Civil Society at the Millennium
CIVICUS, edited by Kumi Naidoo

This publication documents how far civil society has come and provides insight into what its future role will be. The thematic underpinnings examined include globalization, governance, youth participation, women and leadership, sustainable development, government, religion, poverty, indigenous people, volunteering, and technology. *Civil Society at the Millennium* is key to developing a clearer understanding of the role of civil society as a legitimate actor in public life.

US $18.95 / Paper: 1-56549-101-7

Knowledge Shared:
Participatory Evaluation in
Development Cooperation
Edward T. Jackson and
Yusuf Kassam, editors

This book examines an approach to evaluation that enables citizens and professionals alike to jointly assess the extent to which the benefits of development are shared—and by whom. It presents leading-edge analysis on the theory and practice of participatory evaluation around the world.

US $25.95 / Paper: 1-56549-085-1

Nongovernments:
NGOs and the Political
Development of the Third World
Julie Fisher

This definitive work on nongovernmental organizations provides a complete overview of the composition and the types of NGOs that have emerged in recent years. Julie Fisher describes in detail the influence these organizations have had on political systems throughout the world and the hope their existence holds for the realization of sustainable development.

US $24.95 Paper: 1-56549-074-6
US $45.00 Cloth: 1-56549-075-4

Beyond the Magic Bullet:
NGO Performance and
Accountability in the
Post-Cold War World
Michael Edwards, David Hulme

In the volume, experts review the issues of NGO performance and accountability in international development assistance and provide guidance with respect to the process of assessment. Case studies from Central America, Asia, South America, East Africa and North Africa.

US $18.95 / Paper: 1-56549-051-7
US $38.00 / Cloth: 1-56549-052-5